The Alaska Highway in World War II

The Alaska Highway in World War II

The U.S. Army of Occupation in Canada's Northwest

K. S. Coates
and
W. R. Morrison

University of Oklahoma Press : Norman and London

Other Books by K. S. Coates and W. R. Morrison

Land of the Midnight Sun: A History of the Yukon (Edmonton, 1988)
Interpreting Canada's North: Selected Readings (eds.) (Toronto, 1989)
For Purposes of Dominion: Essays in Honour of Morris Zaslow (eds.) (Toronto, 1989)
Taking the North down with Her: The Sinking of the Princess Sophia (Toronto, 1990)
My Dear Maggie: Letters from a Western Manitoba Pioneer (eds.) (Regina, 1991)

Library of Congress Cataloging-in-Publication Data

Coates, Kenneth, 1956–
    The Alaska Highway in World War II : the U.S. Army of occupation
in Canada's Northwest / K.S. Coates and W.R. Morrison.—1st ed.
        p.   cm.
    Includes bibliographical references and index.
    ISBN 0-8061-2425-3
    1. Alaska Highway—History.   2. World War, 1939–1945—Northwest,
Canadian.   3. United States. Army—History—World War, 1939–1945.
4. Northwest, Canadian—History.   I. Morrison, William R. (William
Robert), 1942–   . II. Title.
D768.15.C62   1992
940.53'7191—dc20   91-50861
                                                                    CIP

The paper in this book meets the guidelines for permanence and durability of the Committee on Production Guidelines for Book Longevity of the Council on Library Resources, Inc. ∞

To Catherine Anne Coates
and
Linda Clair Morrison

with love and many thanks
for their unstinting support,
patience, and encouragement

Contents

Illustrations		ix
Maps		xi
Tables		xiii
Preface		xv
Introduction		3
1.	Prelude to Occupation	13
2.	Invasion of the Bulldozers	38
3.	The Native People and the Environment	70
4.	Law and Order in the Occupied Northwest	102
5.	Men, Women, and the Northwest Defense Projects	124
6.	The Transformation of Northern Communities	158
7.	Whitehorse: Creation of a City	181
8.	Saying Goodbye to the Yankees	200
9.	The North at War's End	218
	Conclusion: Historiographical Reflections on the Army of Occupation	235
	Notes	243
	Bibliography	291
	Index	303

Illustrations

Signing the Agreement to Build the Highway, 1942   *Page*   25

General William M. Hoge of the U.S. Corps of Engineers   32

Card Players Aboard a Transport Ship   42

Building a Bridge over Edith Creek, Yukon, 1942   48

A Truck and Bulldozer Engulfed by Mud   51

Welding the Canol Pipeline   56

Lunchtime along the Canol Route   59

Building the Beatton River Bridge, 1944   62

"Suicide Hill" on the Pioneer Road, 1942   65

Tent Camp of the 18th Engineers Headquarters, 1942   74

A Family Camped at the Beatton River   78

Inspecting the Canol Pipeline   82

Moose and Hunters   88

Young Native Men   93

Black Soldiers and White Civilian Workers on the Canol
Project   98

Line Outside the Liquor Store, Whitehorse   109

Black Troops Building a Bridge over Goose Creek near
Teslin, Yukon   115

Rescue of a Truck Carrying Fourth of July Celebration
Beer   121

Halloween Dance, U.S. Army Air Force   138

Truckload of Women Visiting an Army Hospital   148

Loading Barges at Dawson City   162

Fire after Dawson Creek Explosion, 1943   169

Fourth of July Concert by the 18th Engineers Band   177

Winter View of Whitehorse   185

U.S. Army Camp at Whitehorse   190

Breakfast Line at Whitehorse   195

The Peace River Bridge, 1944   208

Maps

Global Distribution of U.S. Army Forces, April 1945   5

The North before World War II   15

Northern Development during World War II   39

Tables

1. U.S. Expenditures on Airfields as of
   April 24, 1944   *Pages* 44–45

2. U.S. Troops Engaged on Alaska Highway
   Construction, 1942–43   47

3. Progress of Pioneer Road Construction, 1942.   49

4. Operating Military Personnel, Northwest Service
   Command, December 31, 1943   54

5. Highway Maintenance Camps Between Dawson Creek
   and the Canada-Alaska Boundary   63

6. Total Civilian Workforce, Canol Project Construction,
   1942–44   68–69

7. Native Alcohol-related Convictions and Police
   Manpower, Southern Yukon, 1940–49   83

8. Strength of the RCMP in the Northwest, 1940–44   103

9. Charges by B.C. Provincial Police in Peace River
   Subdivision, 1940–45   104

10. Sex Ratios in the Canadian Northwest, 1941   130

11. Sexual Contacts Resulting in Venereal Disease,
    Dawson Creek, B.C., March–June 1943   144

12. U.S. Land Leases and Assignments, January 31, 1945   173

13. School-age Children, Alaska Highway Maintenance
    Employees, December 1944   175

14. School-age Children, Alaska Highway Maintenance
    Employees, August 1945   176

15. Disposition of Construction Equipment Used in the
    Northwest   209

16. Manpower, Department of National Defence,
    Northwest Highway System, September 1946   217

17. Alaska Highway Permits Granted, 1947   224

Preface

OUR GOOD FRIEND the Alaskan historian Claus-M. Naske always laughs a little uneasily when we use the phrase "American army of occupation" in speaking of the Canadian Northwest during World War II, because the concept of occupation is usually associated with violence, confrontation, and civilian hardship. In fact, the American "invasion" of this part of Canada witnessed none of those miseries; instead, American soldiers and civilians came there peacefully by the tens of thousands, with the permission and encouragement of the Canadian government, and to the relief and joy of many residents of the region. This was not an occupation of conquest, but one of development and transformation, matched only by the similarly dramatic events of the Klondike gold rush, forty years earlier.

Canadians tend to be rather prickly where Americans are concerned; the standard images of American-Canadian relations—the elephant and the mouse, the eagle and the beaver—suggest something of Canadian uneasiness and ambivalence towards their great neighbor. A Canadian politician a generation ago put the feeling nicely: "The Americans are our best friends," he said, "whether we like it or not." We must confess that we began this project with two preconceptions in the same tradition: that the American invasion of the Canadian Northwest was one of the most important episodes in the history of the two countries' relations, and that a study of this episode would reveal the heavy hand of American "manifest destiny," attached to the archetypal ugly American.

As we learned more about the subject, however, we discovered that only the first of our assumptions was valid. The complex relationship between Canadians and Americans during this period was indeed most revealing of the two countries. But our second assumption, born perhaps of typical Canadian self-righteousness about the United States, was not supported by our archival research and interviews. This does not mean that there was no friction between the two unequal partners in the Canadian Northwest, only that its scale and nature were different from what we had expected.

This book, like most works of scholarship, has had a lengthy gestation. Ken Coates first began working on the history of the Northwest Defense projects in 1982, when he contributed to the fortieth-anniversary symposium on the building of the Alaska Highway. This meeting, held in Fort St. John, British Columbia, in 1982, rekindled a deep interest in the history of the region during the Second World War. Coates was raised along the Alaska Highway, living in Whitehorse from 1964 to 1974, and had studied Yukon history at the University of British Columbia. Bill Morrison, from Hamilton, Ontario, had written a study of the Royal Canadian Mounted Police in the North, and had taught northern history at Brandon University. Our partnership dates from 1983, when Coates accepted a teaching position at Brandon. We discovered a shared interest in the Canadian North—though we approach the region and the discipline from somewhat different directions—and a talent for working on joint projects, thus beginning a partnership which is now in its tenth year.

This is not our first book on the region. We have published a survey history of the Yukon Territory and a monograph on the sinking of the *Princess Sophia,* have coedited three volumes of academic essays on the North, and have written academic papers on different aspects of the subject. In the present case we have cooperated on everything from the initial planning, finding financial support, and carrying out archival research and interviews with former defense project workers and regional residents, to the writing and rewriting necessary to a project of this sort. Like our other work, this is in every sense a joint undertaking.

That this project has reached completion is due in substantial measure to the support and encouragement of others. We are thankful for the financial support received from the Social Science and Humanities Research Council of Canada, Brandon University's Research Committee, the President's Research Committee at the University of Victoria, and the Senate Research Committee and the Centre for Northern Studies at Lakehead University. Crucial help was provided by Judith Powell and Barbara Kelcey, our research assistants, and by Brenda Clark and Jacob Marshall, who carried out the bulk of the interviews. We owe a tremendous debt to a number of archivists (always the life-support system for historians), particularly Terry Cook and Doug Whyte at the National Archives of Canada, the staff of the National Archives of the United States, the Office of the Chief Historian of the United States Army Corps of Engineers (particularly Dr. John Greenwood and Martin Gordon), the Edmonton Municipal Archives, and the friendly and helpful staff of the Yukon Territorial Archives. We have benefitted tremendously from the counsel and insight of our friends and colleagues, especially Peter Baskerville, Ian MacPherson, Eric Sager, Claus-M. Naske, Shelagh Grant, Richard Diubaldo, and Heath Twitchell. They bear no responsibility for any errors contained in this book, but must share in whatever merits it may have.

This book draws heavily on the memories and reminiscences of hundreds of people who participated in the events it describes. We approached them through veterans' organizations, reunion mailing lists, and personal contacts. Their response to our requests for interviews, photographs, and other memorabilia was unfailingly generous, and made us aware of our responsibility to the history of their experiences. We hope that we have done justice to them. It is noteworthy that none of the respondents put any restrictions on the information they provided. We have nonetheless attempted to deal responsibly with this information, some of which is quite sensitive, and in some cases we have concealed the identity of the informant or the subject. We would like in particular to thank the following people, who so kindly responded to our questionnaire and

provided data for this project: Norman Allison, Donald Amos, C.
E. "Red" Anderson, Marvin and Mabel Armitage, Thelma Ashby,
A. G. Askew, Kaare Aspol, C. Bafford, Duncan Bath, Chuck Bax-
ter, J. E. Bedford, Bill Bennett, Charles Biller, Robert and Dell
Black, H. M. Blackwood, Homer Blackwood, Bob and Lil Brant,
Agnes Brewster, Barbara Brocklehurst, Vera Brown, A. Brutto,
Howard Burrel, D. K. Campbell, Phyllis Church, Ruth Clemo,
Aleatha and Marshall Close, Dick and Marge Coates, Muriel Coats,
Gileen Colcleugh, Murel Gwen Collip, J. D. Cooper, C. T. Cotton,
Crawford Cowieson, Sylvia Cranston, G. B. Criteser, W. H. Croft,
Louis Cyr, Bob and Barb Dempster, Hugh Devitt, Evelyn Dobbin,
G. C. Drake, Tom Dunbar, George Ford, Alex Forgie, R. Fowler,
Lorne Frizzell, Merle and Audrey Gaddy, Stacia Gallop, Raymond
Ganser, J. Garbus, Harry George, Gordon and Lorna Gibbs, M.
E. Golata, W. A. Gorham, Willis Grafe, Rex Graham, Kitty Grant,
P. and M. Greenan, Nancy Greenwood, Harold Griffin, Cyril Grif-
fith, L. G. Grimble, Clarence Haakenstad, Selmer Hafso, Fred
Hammond, Harvey Hayduck, J. D. Hazen, Chuck Hemphill, Ed
Herzog, Richard Hislop, M. Hope, John Hudson, Daniel Johnson,
Gunnar Johnson, Mary Johnson, Vernon Kennedy, Charles Knott,
Con and Dot Lattin, Phyllis Lee, Brig. Gen. H. W. Love, Laura
MacKinnon, Mickey and Effie McCaw, A. C. McEachern, R. C.
McFarland, Helen McLean, Donald Miller, Adam Milne, Bruce
Milne, Roy Minter, J. Mitchell, T. E. Molyneux, John Mueller,
Claus-M. Naske, Walter Nelson, E. O'Neill, Bob Oliphant, R. A.
Panter, Ben and Addie Parker, Ena Parsons, Joan Patterson, Gerry
Pelletier, Frank and Ester Peters, Walter Polvi, Hampton Pri-
meaux, A. J. S. Protherow, William T. Pryor, Jim Quong, Peggy
Read, Cale Roberts, K. L. Rudhardt, Donald Saunders, Ray Savela,
L. H. Schnurstein, Carl Schubert, Rudy Schubert, June Scully,
Bernice Sillemo, Bud and Doris Simpson, Earl and Barbara Smith,
Earle Smith, Lake Southwick, Frank and Agatha Speer, Mildred
Spencer, Frank Steele, Cliff and Colette Stringer, John and Ruth
Stringer, Jolyne Sulz, Jim and Iris Sutton, Norman Swabb, Duane
Swenson, Ray Talbot, Charlie Taylor, Jim Tedlie, Joan Thomas,
Jean Waldon, E. R. Walker, H. Walker, Paul E. Warren, Harvey
Weber, Bub and Barb Webster, Olga Whitley, E. J. Wiggans, J.

Williams, Wendell Williamson, L. E. Willis, L. Williscroft, Bruce F. Willson, Vern and Alice Wilson, Henry Wright, and Peggy Wudel.

A project of this duration requires sacrifice on the part of our families. They have, with good grace and for the most part without complaint, tolerated our lengthy research trips and our seemingly endless hours in front of our word processors. To our children—Laura, Mark, and Bradley Coates, and Ruth, Claire, John, and Catherine Morrison—we offer our thanks for their cheerfulness and energy. We hope that our love of history and the Canadian North will rub off on them, and that they will capture through this book a sense of the importance of history in understanding the contemporary world. We owe the most thanks to our wives—Cathy Coates and Linda Morrison—whose commitment to our work is a perennial source of inspiration.

WILLIAM R. MORRISON

Thunder Bay, Ontario

KENNETH S. COATES

Victoria, British Columbia

The Alaska Highway in World War II

Introduction

Edmonton is a town where fantastic things can happen, like the American telephone operator at U.S. Army headquarters who may have plugged in and greeted a Canadian major-general with the salutation, "U.S. Army of Occupation"!
—J. J. Honigman, "On the Alaska Highway," January 1944

MILITARY CONQUEST and occupation are familiar historical themes. Waves of invaders, sweeping across continents, have often left occupying armies behind them to divide the spoils of war and impose their culture, their religion, or their ideology on the vanquished. In many countries the pain of occupation has helped form a national identity. In French Canada, for example, the conquest of 1759–60, likened by one historian to rape, still lingers in the national psyche.[1] A similar situation occurred in the southern United States, where for generations the losers in the Civil War resented the Reconstruction occupation by northern "carpetbaggers," and the damage they caused. The same is true in Germany and Japan, though there the damage was soon repaired by economic triumph. It is particularly true of the Eastern European countries, which found themselves after 1945 behind an iron curtain which has only recently rusted and collapsed. Even the stationing of troops in a colony peopled by those of the same culture can be viewed as a form of unfriendly occupation, as the British in America found to their sorrow in 1775.

But occupation need not be linked to conquest. There are many examples, particularly in this century, of friendly or allied powers sending troops and civilian personnel to another country. In such cases, though, it is useful to distinguish between armies of liberation, which are involved in combat, and armies of occupation, which are not. During both wars, Canada maintained a substantial force in Great Britain, and Britain in turn had large numbers of troops in Iceland and in other countries.[2] More recently, the United States and the Soviet Union have had hundreds of thousands of troops stationed around the world, defending the superpowers' strategic interests and propping up some friendly and not so friendly regimes. These forces—particularly in Asia and Latin America—have played an important role in the efforts of the great powers to expand their economic and social dominance.

Some of these armies of occupation are welcomed by their host countries, some are resented, and some are in a process of change from one condition to the other. Many play a crucial domestic role in the country they occupy. The establishment of a foreign military base brings millions of dollars into the local economy, sometimes pushes a region into the front line of international rivalries, and often has a dramatic effect on the social equilibrium of the occupied country. The effect of the presence of the American military on South Vietnam is a case in point, though the Americans regarded themselves as liberators rather than occupiers. And the effects can last years after the occupiers have left, as the sorry tale of the children fathered by American soldiers in Vietnam bears witness. The same has been true to a greater or lesser degree of the Philippines, Korea, postwar Europe, and a number of Latin American countries. It is also the experience of those countries until recently under occupation by the Soviet Union and its client states.[3]

Even in the case of the friendliest occupations, such as the one that is the subject of this book, there is always a certain amount of tension between host and occupier, some of it traceable to the nature of the military itself. Trained in the military arts, inspired by patriotism tending to chauvinism, totally certain of the importance of their presence and the absolute value of their cultural baggage,

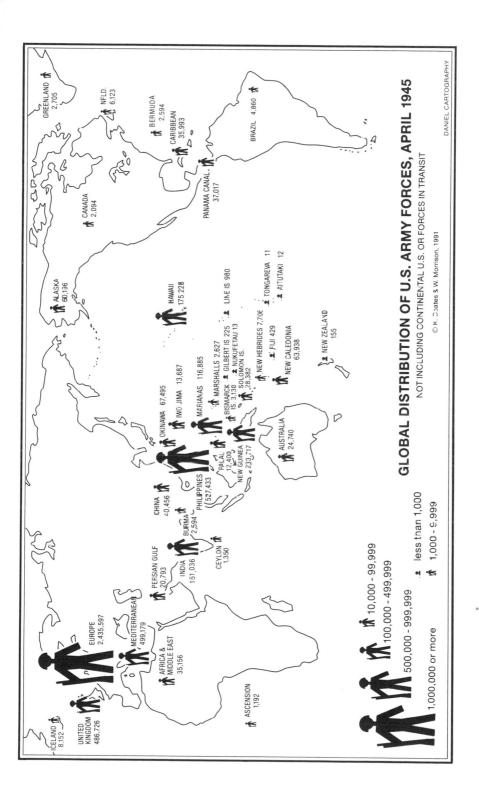

GLOBAL DISTRIBUTION OF U.S. ARMY FORCES, APRIL 1945

NOT INCLUDING CONTINENTAL U.S. OR FORCES IN TRANSIT

© K. Dates & W. Morrison, 1991

DANIEL CARTOGRAPHY

the armed forces approach the duties of occupation with a swagger and lack of subtlety that even the most receptive country is likely to find offensive.

The scale of the American peaceful occupation of Allied territory during World War II was truly vast. Fighting a two-ocean war, and having the twin goal of protecting both the Allies and itself, the United States in 1941 began a huge international expansion. Tens of thousands of troops and support personnel were sent to dozens of countries. These men, and a small number of women, provided military garrisons; built airfields, roads, and other military projects; advised local armed forces; and assisted America's allies in many other ways to prepare for a possible invasion, and later, for an attack on the Axis powers.[4]

While some of these occupations took place near combat zones, others occurred far from the front lines. The occupiers provided support services—warehouses, equipment repair, recreational facilities, training, and administration—for the men in the field. In many locations, including the Canadian Northwest, the bases never came under attack, nor was there even the serious possibility of it; cynics armed with hindsight would later marvel at the military mind that could funnel millions of dollars and thousands of men into places like Surinam, Tonga, and Norman Wells. But in the fearful and chaotic days of early 1942, as the Axis powers advanced across Europe and the Pacific, any horror seemed possible, and no region could consider itself safe against invasion. As the leading Allied power and one that, unlike Britain, did not require a major share of its military resources for home defense, the United States bore the expense and (according to its own priorities) the responsibility for defending the entire free world.

This is not to suggest that the Americans were so pure in motive as to ignore their own immediate and postwar interests. Many American leaders, from President Roosevelt through the ranks of the military, viewed the war as a result of the unwillingness of the democracies to shoulder their global duties. Once the United States had committed itself to the war,[5] therefore, its leaders began to plan for the country's postwar responsibilities and to determine the best way of using the billions of dollars of wartime investment to America's long-term advantage.

There was nothing particularly Machiavellian or inherently wrong about this expansion of American power and influence, though the country's critics would later read U.S. motives and intentions in the worst possible light. No doubt there were expansionists in the United States who rejoiced that the war was about to place the country in its rightful place in world affairs—as jingos like Teddy Roosevelt had welcomed the Spanish-American War and World War I. But in the main it was a case of Americans discovering, under very difficult conditions, a new international responsibility, while at the same time having little knowledge of the areas they were required to occupy and few plans for the coming expansion. Once unleashed on the Allied world, the American military tackled its assignments with vigor and singlemindedness, often with less tact and attention to local sensibilities than officials in Washington would have wished. In the process of building facilities—ranging from airfields, roads, communications systems, and military bases to Coca-Cola bottling plants—in isolated locations around the world, the American armed forces became internationalized. They were exposed to new countries and cultures, and brought to a realization of their country's role in the postwar world.

The event covered in this book—the American occupation of the Canadian Northwest—is but one example of a worldwide process that took place on a vast scale. By January 1943, the U.S. Army had over 1 million troops engaged in foreign service; two years later the figure had increased to 5.3 million, of whom some 3 million were in the European theater. Hundreds of thousands, however, filled noncombat roles in countries from Iceland to the South Pacific.

At the height of the war, in January 1943, the U.S. Army had large concentrations of military personnel in such places as the Canadian Northwest (almost 15,000), Panama (65,000), Iceland (37,000), Fiji (23,000), New Caledonia (30,300), Solomon Islands, (33,073), and Australia and New Guinea (116,000). In April 1945, as the war was winding down, the army still had almost 500,000 men in England, over 20,000 in Australia, 161,000 in India, over 8,000 in Iceland, 6,000 in Newfoundland, 36,000 in Panama, and 5,000 in Brazil.[6]

Most of these establishments were temporary. Typically, engineering troops would come to an area, build a road, airfield, or

military base, and move on. Their place would be taken by combat
troops in training, or by other branches of the armed services who
would operate the new facilities. Usually there was a rapid influx of
troops, followed by the departure of most of the initial force and
the establishment of semipermanent operating units, which often
remained on site for the duration of the war.

There was also a racial aspect to the U.S. occupation of allied
territories.[7] Black soldiers made up nearly 10 percent of U.S.
service personnel during the war.[8] They were, however, generally
barred from combat service, and were often assigned to construction units. As such, they played an important part in the many
branches of the American army of occupation. Black soldiers saw
service in all theaters, but there were clear priorities in their
distribution.[9] American officials feared that the presence of large
numbers of black troops in England would cause difficulties with
the local population.[10] Only 8 percent of the American troops in
Great Britain in January 1943 were black; in contrast, in the Northwest Service Command, black soldiers made up 25 percent of the
total—this in spite of the alleged intolerance of black troops for
cold-weather service. Proportionately large numbers of black
troops were sent to Alaska, northwest Africa, and isolated Pacific
islands. A small percentage were sent to the Caribbean and Australia; in the latter country, they were generally sent to the rural
areas.[11] As a historian of the American occupation of Trinidad
commented,

It was the belief in the racial inferiority of the black soldier which dictated
American military policy that black soldiers should stay in Trinidad. . . .
No foreign country welcomed [them]. . . . To satisfy domestic agitation
that black troops serve overseas, American military authorities decided
that, because of their inferiority, these troops were to serve only in inactive
theatres.[12]

The American occupation, whether brief or prolonged, whether
carried out by black or white troops, almost always had a dramatic
impact on the host country. The Americans changed the landscape
wherever they went, with new roads, airfields, pipelines, military
bases, and new communications and other services. Regions once
largely isolated, like Greenland, northern Queensland in Australia,

and the Canadian Northwest, were showered with new facilities— if they were lucky, the ones they had been demanding from regional and national governments for years.[13] Third World countries from Surinam to Tonga were engulfed by a wave of modernization that disrupted their cultures and their economies.

A major difficulty was the question of sex. The American forces, of course, were overwhelmingly made up of young men, so that their arrival created an instant sexual imbalance in the local population. Women living in the occupied regions found themselves much in demand; prostitution expanded rapidly, venereal disease became a problem, and drinking, violence, and petty crime all escalated.[14]

The U.S. government was scrupulous in negotiating formal agreements with the host countries covering the control of its personnel, but these diplomatic arrangements did not always solve the social, sexual, and racial problems that accompanied the occupying forces. The cliché "oversexed, overpaid, and over here," coined in Britain during the war summarized the response of other countries to the presence of the exuberant, aggressive, and comparatively wealthy American troops.[15]

The Americans in almost every case went out of their way to accommodate themselves to local conditions and national feelings; pamphlets and indoctrination lectures warned the troops with varying degrees of success against being what were later called "ugly Americans." Particular efforts were made to avoid even the suggestion that local sovereignty was in danger. Again, these efforts were not always successful. It was an article of faith with most Americans that their system of government was the best in the world, and that other countries would be doing themselves a favor in imitating it; it was only natural that many soldiers in foreign countries would give voice to this feeling. The host countries often tolerated excesses on the part of the occupying forces, excusing them as the inevitable result of the presence of youthful, often ignorant and naïve young men, and a small price to pay for the military security they represented. The large number of war brides, especially from Australia and Britain, suggests that relations between American men and local women were not always exploitative.[16]

The widespread adoption of certain aspects of U.S. social and material culture has a more ambivalent resonance. American movies were already popular everywhere; now baseball became a craze in many occupied areas, as did music, cigarettes, beer, Coca-Cola, candy bars, American mannerisms, and American slang. Commentators then and since have had difficulty assessing the short- and long-term effect of manifestations of American culture, but most agree that it was palpable.[17]

The occupied regions generally had little warning of the American invasion, and most were ill prepared for it, for the exigencies of war did not permit long negotiations or a careful consideration of its possible negative effects. With little planning, and with military considerations taking first priority, it is not surprising that the wartime defense projects carried out by the occupying troops frequently did not reflect the wishes and concerns of the occupied populations. Facilities were generally built in the right place for military purposes, but often in the wrong place for local needs. At the end of the war, responsibility for these facilities was passed back to regional and national governments, which often abandoned them as white elephants.

In occupied regions where there was an aboriginal population, the needs of these people were often totally ignored in the wartime rush. Indigenous societies were to bear a disproportionate share of the social and cultural cost of these friendly invasions. Social structures, particularly in indigenous areas, suffered severe dislocation as a result of the reorientation of power and command systems around American military personnel. And in an era when few people worried about the human impact on the environment, little thought was given to the effect of these projects on natural resources. Some areas recovered quickly, as the jungle swallowed airfields and other construction projects; in other places the scars lasted for decades. The economies of host regions also suffered in competition for workers and supplies with an insatiable and inexhaustibly wealthy U.S. military machine. In some places the local economy rebounded quickly after the war, using the wartime facilities as a springboard to renewed prosperity. In other places the disruptions were more severe and proved difficult to repair; in some, the entire structure of society was changed, as was the case of the cargo cults of the South Pacific Islands.[18]

Critics of American postwar foreign policy have examined wartime activities for signs of a plan for imperial expansion. But there was no such plan. American expansion between 1941 and 1945 had no master scheme of world domination; rather, it was an ill-coordinated series of projects conceived in haste and panic, with little attention to fiscal sanity, local conditions, or even America's long-term needs. U.S. industry and the country's military, starved and reined in during the 1930s, became, once unleashed, a juggernaut. The result was a massive and rather incoherent expansion of U.S. military presence around the globe, taking Americans into some of the most isolated corners of the world.[19] The exception among the Allies was the Soviet Union, a nation that more than any other feared the results of a friendly occupation, and thus did not permit any significant numbers of American troops or support personnel on its soil.

Once at war, and armed with a mighty industrial machine and the willingness to spend undreamed-of sums, the United States thrust itself onto the world stage with the enthusiasm, recklessness, and can-do spirit that had characterized the nation's internal expansion in the past. Much of the Allied world, and later many of the Axis powers, were profoundly changed by the American advance.[20] The study of Americans in contact with local populations and government sheds a unique light on regional development and the wartime history of occupied regions, as well as on American attitudes and culture. Studies have been made of the American impact on Britain, Australia, the South Pacific, and other regions.[21] There has not yet, however, been a systematic study of the effect of the American occupation of the Canadian Northwest during World War II.

Canada has experienced occupying forces of varying degrees of friendliness over long periods of its history. Colonial forces of occupation were a permanent feature of Canadian life for more than two hundred years, beginning in the 1660s.[22] The last garrison of British infantry did not leave Canada until 1871, and small imperial naval establishments were maintained at Halifax and Esquimault until the early years of the twentieth century. American forces attacked and held parts of Canada in 1775 and during the War of 1812. But the most substantial occupation of Canadian territory came during World War II, when tens of thousands of foreign soldiers and civilians descended on the country.[23] Many came to train at air bases under the Commonwealth Air Training Plan. The majority, however, came to the Canadian Northwest to work on major military construction projects—the Northwest Staging Route, the Alaska Highway, Canol Pipeline, the Haines Lateral, and dozens of subsidiary projects.

This was a peaceful army of occupation; the main weapons were the shovel, not the rifle, and the bulldozer, not the tank. But such a force—more than 40,000 soldiers and civilian workers—could not help but recast the sparsely populated and undeveloped Northwest. Inhabited by nomadic Indian bands and a small non-Native population which depended mostly on an equally small mining industry, the region had long stood outside the mainstream of North American development. The arrival of the Americans changed that situation overnight, bringing home the strategic, social, and economic realities of the world conflict.

This is a study of the American occupation of the Canadian Northwest during World War II. It does not examine the political and diplomatic aspects of this occupation, except as they illuminate the realities and problems of life in the region.[24] Instead, this is an attempt to explain the social, economic, environmental, and cultural aspects of the American invasion of the Northwest between 1942 and 1946. This also presents an opportunity to consider a case study of the much broader phenomenon of the U.S. international advance during World War II—a phenomenon that had sweeping economic and social effects, many of which are still in evidence.

1. Prelude to Occupation

IN THE SPRING of 1942 the Canadian Northwest was asleep, as it had been since the end of the great Klondike gold rush, forty years earlier. At the turn of the century, dreams of a northern resource empire had aroused brief but intense interest in Canada's northwestern frontier, an interest that revived in 1920 when oil was discovered at the midpoint of the Mackenzie valley. After that episode, however, the region, like other resource frontiers—the Australian outback, Greenland, and Alaska—faded into the background of national economics and politics. Yet it never quite disappeared from the public consciousness, for it remained a land of adventure and mystery, a land more of legend than reality.

In 1942 the Northwest, a huge region taking in the Yukon Territory, the Mackenzie River valley, northern British Columbia, and northern Alberta, was a sparsely populated land with an uneven economic base. Now and then Canada was seized by a burst of enthusiasm for northern development, typically sparked by prophets like the scientist-promoter Vilhjalmur Stefansson in the United States, who vigorously thumped the tub in the 1920s for his vision of a northern empire. But southern dreams and the piteous cries for committed interest and support from those few non-Natives who chose to spend their lives in the region had no real impact on Canada or its government, whose blueprint for the country's development pointed in every direction but north. The Northwest remained a region caught in its past, like a fly in amber, unable to escape the legend of the Klondike gold rush, yet unable to integrate itself into the national economy.

The region had no real metropolitan center, though Edmonton had long fancied itself in that role. The Alberta capital, once a small fur-trading post, had promoted itself during the gold rush as the gateway to the Klondike, enticing several thousand would-be prospectors to attempt the all-Canadian route to the Klondike by way of the Mackenzie valley. This example of small-town boosterism gone mad was at best foolish and at worst almost criminal, since the route was the most difficult rather than the easiest route to the goldfields, and a number of stampeders died trying to follow it.[1] Yet Edmonton did not soon outgrow the gilded visions of urban greatness based on northern development—a vision that is commemorated in its annual summer festival, called "Klondike Days."

After 1900 the label of "gateway to the Klondike" no longer brought in business, so Edmonton began to promote itself more generally as the gateway to the north, a role it took quite seriously. Unlike the claims of the Klondike era, which were cruel lies from start to finish, there was substance in the town's new assertion of dominance over a northern hinterland. As mineral exploration expanded in the region, and as the agricultural frontier reached into the northern sections of Alberta and British Columbia, Edmonton began to acquire new status and economic power. The Peace River country, an anomalous stretch of prairie land running northwest of Edmonton into British Columbia, held considerable economic promise. In the 1930s, many farmers fled the drought on the Palliser Triangle, loaded their goods into trucks or "Bennett buggies," and headed to the more northerly parkland or the Peace River country.[2] Along with the migrants came the infrastructure of a new country— wagon roads, towns, post offices, land offices, government services, and the beginning of a railway network. It was not much at first, and fell short of the prosperity promised by those desperate for an alternative to dryland farming, but it did bring settlement to the northern limits of market agriculture in Canada.[3]

But this advance of settlement did not reach as far as the North-

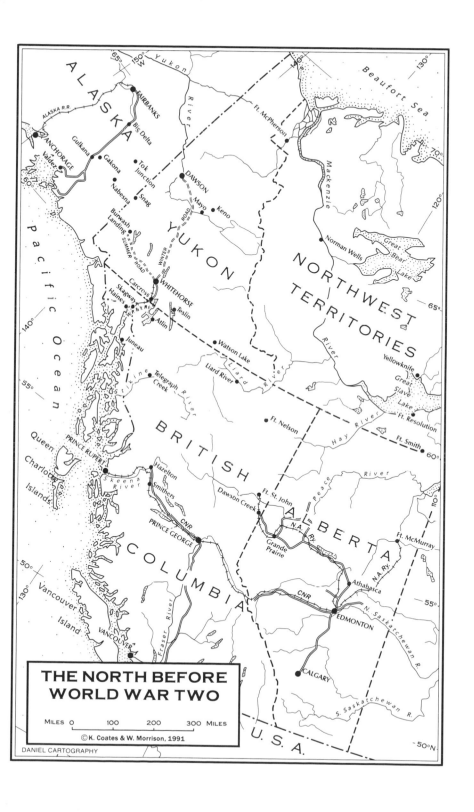

THE NORTH BEFORE
WORLD WAR TWO

MILES 0   100   200   300 MILES

© K. Coates & W. Morrison, 1991

DANIEL CARTOGRAPHY

west Territories. The Northwest Territories continued to be dominated by the fur trade, still profitable, though stripped of the glamor
that had surrounded it in the early days. Here the Hudson's Bay
Company was in control, using its virtual monopoly of the transportation system and southern markets to defeat competition and
dictate the nature of the regional economy.[4] The company was
strong enough to weather the depression, and by the end had
managed to buy out most of its important competitors. Its Native
workforce had few options. Overhunting had reduced their returns,
increasing their dependence on the company, which used its control
of the welfare system to keep the Natives on their traplines.[5]

Before 1940 the watchword of the federal government in the
Northwest was parsimony. It had limited expectations for the region, gave little to it, and asked little in return. On occasion, when
bonanzas beckoned, the government bestirred itself, but when
these proved chimerical or transitory, it soon lost interest. The
discovery of oil at Norman Wells in 1920, for instance, raised
expectations and moved the government to impose Treaty 11 on
the Dene of the Mackenzie valley as preparation for a new day of
prosperity. But when the promise of the initial discovery faded, the
government lost interest, failing to fulfill many of the promises
contained in the treaty.[6] The government funded several Roman
Catholic and Anglican residential and day schools (which released
it from any obligation to provide for the Natives' education), offered
medical care in a few centers, and provided a small police force in
the region.[7] But the government's priority was to leave the Indians
as hunters and trappers, a solution popular with most of them and
one that reduced demands on the federal treasury.[8]

Throughout the 1920s and 1930s, a number of non-Natives did
seek out opportunities in the region, particularly when high fur
prices brought non-Native trappers to the North. Their arrival, as
an employee of the Northern Trading Company at Fort Resolution
noted, upset the traditional economic patterns:

Last year the influx of trappers was so great that in some sections, there
is a very grave danger that the animals will become extinct in a very short
time. Between Resolution and Smith we have no less than fifty-five white
trappers (a trapper for every three miles) so you can get some idea how
devoid of game this district will be after this winter. Heretofore this

territory has been supporting ten to fifteen families from year to year, but this winter they have all been forced to abandon their homes and seek other trapping grounds. The inevitable outcome of this influx will be that the country will soon be trapped out, the Indian destitute, with no means of supporting himself. The Government will be compelled to feed and clothe the whole population. . . . Another very objectionable feature is the class of trappers this year; with few exceptions, they are a collection of the riff raff from outside, without capital or means.[9]

To stave off widespread destitution in the region, which would have led to unwelcome calls for financial assistance, the federal government, without consulting any of the local inhabitants, in 1923 established several large game preserves, to be used exclusively by treaty Indians: Yellowknife, 70,000 square miles; Slave, 2,152; and Peel, 3,300. While the creation of these preserves did curb hunting by non-Natives, it also led to hardship among the nonstatus Indians (those not included in the treaty) and Métis (people of mixed blood), who were denied access to the preserve.[10]

Southern promoters tended to ignore the fur trade in favor of the region's mineral resources. Ever since the Klondike gold rush, prospectors had been active in the Northwest, locating a number of small deposits that brought no immediate wealth but at least kept hopes alive.[11]

Two significant mineral discoveries were made in the prewar period. The discovery of pitchblende (radium ore) on the shores of Great Bear Lake in 1929 sparked considerable interest and led to the establishment of Eldorado Mines.[12] Near Great Slave Lake, prospectors uncovered deposits of hard-rock gold, a strike that resulted in the founding of the town of Yellowknife. They dug several mine shafts, and poured the first gold brick in 1938. The mines proved to be profitable, and a sizeable community, permanent by northern standards, developed.[13] Following the arrival of an officer of the Royal Canadian Mounted Police (RCMP), the town lost some of its rough edges; a government official observed that "as a direct result of the 'clean-up' a great many more decent women went into the community and the whole character of the place was changed for the better."[14] Many prospectors believed that this was just the beginning, that the region had many Yellow-knifes, yet to be found.

The Yukon, by contrast, was static or declining in this period; it was a land where the future seemed already to have happened. The Territory's heyday at the turn of the century had set expectations that could never again be matched, though prospectors kept looking, setting off echo booms in places like Atlin in British Columbia, Livingstone Creek, Silver City, and Conrad in the Yukon, and Tanana, Fairbanks, Ruby, and Iditarod in Alaska. The Yukon, shriveled and near death, passed into corporate hands, including the British and Yukon Navigation Company that held a virtual monopoly over regional transportation; Treadwell Yukon, operator of the Keno-Elsa silver/lead mines developed in the 1910s; and the Yukon Consolidated Gold Corporation, a union of the large dredging companies that owned much of the gold-bearing ground in the Klondike.[15]

By the 1930s most Canadians had half forgotten the north, though Robert Service's verses were still stock items for recitations at school concerts, and there was a perennial fascination with the exoticism of Eskimos.[16] The Yukon had had its day in the sun during the Klondike gold rush, when tens of thousands of prospectors, most of them American, had ventured northward. All found adventure, but only a handful found gold. The event—spectacular, mysterious, exotic, and heavily promoted—permanently fixed the Yukon and the Klondike in the vocabulary of the western world.

The gold rush cast a dark shadow over the Yukon's later years. Dawson atrophied, sustained mainly by ever diminishing government grants to an emaciated territorial administration. Whitehorse, once the transportation hub of the entire Northwest, shrank in importance and size. The population of the Yukon, which had reached 40,000 in 1898, had shrunk to just over 4,000 in 1921; by 1941 it was still only 4,900.

The territory's fur trade remained strong, although the Hudson's Bay Company, which had opened the district in the 1840s, remained out of the competitive business. A local firm, Taylor and Drury, dominated the industry through the 1920s and 1930s, and operated posts throughout the territory. There were other small signs of economic vitality. Big-game hunting found a certain niche among the hunting elite of North America; there was also a small fur-farming sector.[17] Tourism, fueled by continued fascination with the Klondike experience, remained strong through the era preceding

World War I, but provided only a brief seasonal boost to a sagging and seemingly terminally ill economy. The Yukon still had its optimists, including a small band of local businessmen who hoped for a return to the prosperity of the past, but few non-Natives stayed around for very long. The non-Native population in the Yukon, as in the Mackenzie River valley, remained extremely transient, locked into a southern orientation and a belief that they would have to move on.

There was little connection between the reality of life in the Canadian Northwest and the promoters' vision of a Canadian resource empire. By the 1930s, few Canadians put much stock in the visions of prosperity repeated unceasingly by such promoters of the North as Vilhjalmur Stefansson. People in the North had resigned themselves to economic stagnation, although most harbored some dreams of prosperity and the discovery of a new Eldorado. For the present, however, they remained locked into a resource-dependent economy, reliant on a few commodities whose prices were set in distant markets, and on the continued profitability of a small number of mineral properties.

The economic structure of the Northwest dictated the region's social structure. The agrarian areas—north-central Alberta and the Peace River country—mirrored the Canadian rural norm of widely dispersed farmhouses, carefully spaced villages with a small number of stores and services, and a few larger regional centers, such as Grande Prairie and Dawson Creek. Native people dominated much of the northern rim of the provinces and the Mackenzie and Yukon river basins. In these fur-trading districts with a small number of non-Natives (usually traders, missionaries, and police officers, along with a few non-Native trappers), Native people continued their mobile way of life and their reliance on trapping and hunting for most of their food and income. The major territorial settlements remained non-Native enclaves. Few Natives found their way into the mining camps, most of which were run by engineers from the South and staffed by workers imported from "outside."[18] There was greater interracial contact in the Northwest Territories, where non-Natives were a decided minority, than in the Yukon, which was still dominated by non-Natives.

The Northwest was not ready for a massive invasion in 1942. Its population was small and widely scattered. There were few towns of any size; Dawson City, with 1,043 residents, was the largest in the region. Smaller centers, like Whitehorse (population 754) and Keno (unorganized), were resource-based and largely seasonal towns, tied into the rhythms of the sub-Arctic climate. Farther south, in northern Alberta and the Peace River country, the situation was little different. Frontier communities like Athabasca and Fort McMurray survived on the basis of Native harvesting, prospecting, and transportation. The farming centers, like Grande Prairie and Dawson Creek, grew slowly in the uncertain years of the Depression. Not only was the Northwest not prepared for an influx of soldiers and construction workers, it was having some difficulty maintaining its population and making sure that the provincial governments did not reduce even further their support for these marginal areas.

Despite its isolation, the Northwest was aware of the world situation in 1940. When the war began in September 1939, Canadians throughout the Northwest quickly responded to the call to arms. Twenty-five years earlier, during World War I, the citizens of the region had made a tremendous effort to prove their loyalty to their country and their devotion to the war effort. Yukoners in particular enlisted in numbers far beyond their proportion to the general population, donated disproportionate sums to patriotic organizations, and oversubscribed the government's war bond drives.[19] The same thing happened in the fall of 1939:

Day by day planes are picking up prospectors from outlying areas and bringing them into the Yellowknife area, from where many are heading south. Practically all southbound aircraft is loaded to capacity. In some cases pilots leave their mechanics to squeeze in an additional passenger. Besides prospectors going south there are many young men who have been employed in local mines and prospect camps going out to enlist, showing an apparent preference for the air force.[20]

The government assisted the enlistment efforts where it could, sending recruiting officers to the main centers and exempting all prospectors and miners who enlisted from penalties and threats of cancellation of mineral licenses as a result of their absence.[21] As in World War I, northerners also made large donations to patriotic and national funds—evidence that isolation did not discourage patriotism.

For decades the lack of good transportation connections with the rest of the continent had been a problem for the residents of the far Northwest. Moreover, it was often as difficult to get around in the region as it was to get into it. Bush pilots, like the famous "Wop" May and Grant McConachie, had pioneered northern air routes for prospectors and small-scale developers, but regional air service remained rudimentary.[22] Access to the Mackenzie River valley was difficult, and the route was dominated by the Hudson's Bay Company, whose river barges delivered supplies to the trading posts, Native settlements, and small mining camps in the region.[23]

Transportation facilities were somewhat better in the Yukon Territory, which had an outlet to the Pacific by way of the White Pass and Yukon Railway, which connected Whitehorse, at the head of navigation of the Yukon River, with the Alaskan seaport of Skagway. The British and Yukon Navigation Company (BYNC), which owned the railway, also ran a fleet of sternwheelers that dominated river travel throughout the Yukon. Access to the outlying areas was more difficult. The Taylor and Drury Company ran small steamers on some of the Yukon River's tributaries, and the expansion of mining in the Keno-Elsa area had encouraged the BYNC to extend its riverboat service up the shallow and treacherous Stewart River to Mayo.[24]

The situation was slightly better in northern Alberta and British Columbia. The Northern Alberta Railway had reached Grande Prairie and Dawson Creek by 1931, but north of those towns transportation was primitive. For decades British Columbia politicians had promoted a north-south railway, the Pacific Great Eastern, but the project had stalled at Quesnel in the 1920s, and was not to reach the Peace River country until after World War II.

There were a few roads, hardly more than trails, throughout the northern part of the provinces. Dawson Creek was linked to Fort St. John by a passable road, complete with ferries across the rivers; a rough trail ran northwest from Fort St. John to Fort Nelson. A series of wagon roads, some dating from the Klondike gold rush, ran north from Edmonton into the Mackenzie watershed. The Yukon had a few roads, including a winter road that linked Whitehorse to the territorial capital at Dawson, a road from Whitehorse to the southern Yukon community of Carcross, and a wagon trail west from Whitehorse to Champagne and Kluane Lake. These were at best rudimentary, permitting pack trains or light wagons to reach distant trading posts and settlements. Once in a while an automobile would venture into the outlying areas—George Johnston, a Native leader from Teslin, had one delivered to him by barge—but the region's transportation system was suitable neither for mechanized travel nor for the movement of large numbers of people.[25]

The isolation of the Canadian Northwest was a serious hindrance to its economic development. Regional boosters found it hard to get southerners interested in the prospects for development when it was so difficult to bring southern goods to northern markets, or to send northern resources to southern factories and consumers. The Klondike gold rush spawned scores of proposals, some practical, most lunatic, for transportation networks reaching north to the Land of the Midnight Sun. Two of them—the railway from Skagway and the telegraph line to Whitehorse and Dawson City—were realized.[26] Another promising project, a rail link between the Stikine River in British Columbia and the Yukon, foundered on partisan federal politics and Canadian naïveté about American commercial intentions in the Northwest.[27] But when the gold rush faded, so did the dream of a land link between the Northwest and the rest of the continent.

During the forty-year period between the end of the gold rush and World War II, a few promoters continued to insist that the Northwest needed only a little encouragement to boom again. Both Alberta and British Columbia sought to annex the regions to the north of them. In 1937, T. "Duff" Pattullo, premier of British Columbia, who had cut his political and business teeth in the Yukon at the beginning of the century, proposed that his province should annex the Territory. The federal government sensed a chance to end four decades of incessant demands from the Northwest, and negotiations began between Ottawa and Victoria, despite the anguished protests from those Yukon residents who wished to preserve their frail autonomy. The Dawson City Board of Trade complained that "the miners, large and small, the trappers, the merchants, and the general body of the inhabitants of the Yukon are irreconcilably opposed to the annexation, which if carried out would convert the present contented and optimistic outlook of the people into one of discouragement, resentment and bitterness."[28] But the deal fell through, not through any concern for democracy on the part of federal or provincial governments, but because the question of the Yukon's denominational schools threatened to embarrass the politicians.[29]

This proposal led to others. A group in Alberta's Peace River country, wondering how British Columbia could consider absorbing the Yukon when it had not even fully included their district into the province's economy, suggested that the establishment of

a single administration to govern the Yukon Territory, the Mackenzie River Basin, and the northern portions of British Columbia and of Alberta as included in the area commonly known as the Peace River country would tend to encourage proper and necessary development of lines of communication by highway and water routes which have been denied or neglected by existing governments. It would tend to materially encourage any project for the establishment of an international highway extending into the Yukon Territory and Alaska.[30]

The proposal made a certain amount of sense, for northern Alberta and British Columbia had more in common with the Yukon and the Mackenzie valley than with the rest of their provinces, but the idea was ignored by Ottawa and the provincial capitals. The government of Alberta instead submitted its own proposal in 1941 for the annexation of the Mackenzie basin, but nothing came of it.[31]

Short of political annexation, the best way to integrate the Northwest into the provincial spheres of influence was the construction of a good transportation link; in a real sense, this was better than annexation, for political links might have no real effect, while a road had practical as well as symbolic value. In the late 1920s, a group of politicians from Alaska, the Yukon, and British Columbia had proposed the construction of a highway from British Columbia to Alaska. The Yukon gold commissioner of the day, G. I. MacLean, wrote that "such a road would be of inestimable value to the North country, not only from the tourist standpoint, but also in opening up the Territory and assisting in its development." But the federal government, as usual indifferent to the politically irrelevant far

Northwest, refused even to consider providing the necessary funding for such a project.[32]

The issue resurfaced ten years later, just before the war, this time sparked by Premier Pattullo, an aggressive booster of northern development. The idea gathered considerable support among politicians in Washington state and Alaska, and even found favor with President Roosevelt. But once again, Ottawa and the ever-hesitant Prime Minister King balked at such a major expenditure of public money. The fact that Pattullo seemed to have lined up some American private investment raised the possibility of U.S. control over the highway, and this, along with the suspicion that the American military had designs on it, dampened what little enthusiasm Ottawa had for the project. Once more, the plan began to fade away.

At last, however, there was sufficient regional support for the idea in Canada and the United States to keep it alive, and the leaders of both countries appointed commissions to study it further. President Roosevelt set up the Alaska International Highway Commission to work together with the American group in assessing the need for the highway and suggesting a possible route. King's lack of enthusiasm for the proposal was indicated by his naming Charles Stewart to head the Canadian commission: Stewart was sick in hospital and could not immediately assume his duties. Despite Canadian foot dragging, however, the commission eventually began its work.

The Canadian commission visited northern British Columbia and the Yukon Territory and discovered, to no one's surprise, that the project was popular there. At Whitehorse, everyone spoke in favor of it except for the president of the White Pass and Yukon Railway, who insisted that there would not be enough traffic to justify the project. He denied that he was speaking in the interests of his company, asserting that "the scheme was visionary and impractical and would serve no useful purpose."[33] At the same time there was a lively debate over the best route for the highway. Some argued for a coastal route, running east of the coast mountain range to the Yukon near Whitehorse, then to Dawson City and Fairbanks. Many Alaskans preferred this route, which held out the possibility of a feeder road to the territorial capital of Juneau. From the beginning,

Canadian Prime Minister W. L. M. King signing the agreement to build the highway, February 1942. Pierrepont Moffat, U.S. Ambassador to Canada, is on the left, and Colonel O. M. Biggar, chairman of the Canadian Section of the Permanent Joint Board on Defence, is on the right. (National Archives of Canada, PA-130488)

American officials were strongly in favor of using Whitehorse as the focal point of the route:

Both Mr. Magnusson and Governor Riggs stressed the importance of Whitehorse as a key point in any scheme. They talked about completing the Fairbanks-Whitehorse section as an interim measure. The Canadian delegation preferred the cheaper route straight to Dawson but readily admitted the force of the American arguments that logic required that the airline, the road, the railroad, and water transportation all coincide in one given point.[34]

Although some Canadian officials approved of the project, they realized that "the political situation here was such that the Government could not agree to any further projects of a public works nature unless their strategic need as war measures were previously admitted."[35]

A major impediment was that American military planners refused

to support a project that appeared to be of little strategic importance, and was primarily of economic benefit to civilians.[36] Henry
Stimson, U.S. secretary of war, wrote in August 1940, "It is the
opinion of the War Department that the value of the proposed
highway as a defense measure is negligible and that the legislation
proposed . . . should not be favorably considered."[37] Clearly, despite strong support in the Pacific Northwest and some interest in
the Yukon, the highway was not going to be built as a peacetime
project. Nor did the Americans seem in the summer of 1940 to be
unduly worried about a Japanese threat to Alaska.

The main competition to the coastal proposal was the proposed
interior route, which would start in Prince George and go north
through the mineral-rich Tintina Trench, bypassing Whitehorse on
the way to Dawson City and Fairbanks. But according to George
Jeckell, controller of the Yukon, northerners were indifferent to the
debate:

The residents of the Yukon Territory have never at any time become very
excited or enthusiastic over the project. The labouring class naturally are
in favour of the project from the spending standpoint. The mining operators
and business interests are not much concerned, for they do not see where
much benefit will accrue to the Territory after the construction period is
past, when possibly they will be saddled with the cost of a very large part
of the highway maintenance expense.[38]

In April 1940 the Alaska International Highway Commission made
public its report, which recommended the adoption of "Route A,"
the coastal route.[39] By this time, and long before the Canadian
commission had issued its report, Canada was at war, and Ottawa
had more important concerns than building a highway for the benefit
of Americans across what it considered a wasteland. Regional promoters assumed that the project would now be shelved, although
some northern residents believed that military priorities might soon
force a reconsideration of the concept. Three years earlier the
Yukon's former member of Parliament Martha Black had noted that

the United States, as all know, is keeping a watchful eye on Japan; she has
a huge fund for war preparedness; she wants the Pacific highway built
through from British Columbia and the Yukon to Fairbanks and other
Alaskan points. If the present plans, which have been tentatively approved
by the United States government, go through, the road in Yukon will cut

out both Whitehorse and Dawson. In case of war, the United States will commandeer the road whether we like it or not.[40]

The Canadian highway commission's report, which was released in July 1941, supported the interior route from Prince George to Dawson City.[41] This route, which would have bypassed Whitehorse, took a very different course than that proposed by the Americans. The report was greeted with some enthusiasm in Dawson, but with disapproval in Whitehorse.[42] Diplomatic negotiations continued over the highway project. From the American perspective, the low priority given it by the military hampered efforts to promote it and reduced Canadian enthusiasm for it.

This hesitancy about the project was due in part to the presence of a competing proposal. The promoters in British Columbia and Washington state were not the only ones trying to interest the authorities in a road to the far Northwest, for a similar group was being formed on the Canadian prairies and the American Great Plains. Developers and promoters in Edmonton had fond memories of the wealth that had flowed into the community as a result of their campaign during the Klondike gold rush to tout the town as the "all-Canadian route" to the goldfields; perhaps, they felt, the war might bring a similar bonanza. F. S. Wright, editor of the *Nor'West Miner* and a long-time civic booster, began pushing for an Edmonton-to-Alaska highway in response to the publicity surrounding the British Columbia proposals. "Cheap construction, better climate conditions, productive areas farming and mining and also scenic beauty all favor this [the Alberta] route," he claimed.[43]

Wright's enthusiasm was infectious, and the thought of a huge construction project based in Edmonton was alluring; as a result, local businessmen and politicians rallied to his support. J. A. Mackinnon, the local member of Parliament, was more cautious, warning that the premier of British Columbia and "those associated with him at the Coast would fight very hard to maintain it as originally planned."[44]

Wright was not easily discouraged, and his enthusiasm for the project grew when during a visit to Montana and North Dakota in the spring of 1941 he discovered that politicians in the northern Great Plains were also interested in a prairie route to the Northwest. A group called the Wahpeton Portal Highway Association

was especially keen and proposed to send Wright to speak before
a committee in Washington, D.C., that was studying the question
of the highway.[45] The reason why towns in North Dakota should
have supported the idea is at first not evident, but they believed
that a highway through Edmonton would draw traffic from the
eastern seaboard through the northern Great Plains towards Alberta; the states in its path would profit from money spent by
travelers, as well as from a massive road upgrading. The Americans
also proposed a conference of politicians and officials from the
prairie provinces and representatives from the municipal and state
governments of the northern plains states to draw up a joint proposal.[46] The result was the formation of the United States–Canada–
Alaska Prairie Highway Association, with wide representation from
the region on both sides of the international boundary.[47] The group's
morale rose in December 1941 when the U.S. Federal Planning
Commission announced that a highway through Edmonton was
under active consideration, the first public indication that the coastal
route, long the frontrunner, was being seriously questioned.[48]

The United States–Canada–Alaska Prairie Highway Association
met regularly through 1941 and attracted wide support for its
proposal. At a meeting called by the city of Regina in May 1941,
representatives were present from Alberta (Calgary, Edmonton,
Peace River), Saskatchewan (Estevan, Moose Jaw, Saskatoon,
Battleford, Regina, Weyburn), North Dakota (Minot, Kenmare,
Devils Lake, Bowbells, Bismarck, Fargo, Wahpeton, Velva, Portal,
Drake).[49] The fact that some of these places had populations of only
a few hundred echoed the railroad booms of the nineteenth century,
when even a hamlet could dream of the prosperity that a major
international route might bring.

The American chair of the association, H. L. Halvorson of Minot,
North Dakota, and his Canadian counterpart, J. A. Mackenzie of
Regina, pressed the case for the prairie route to the Canadian and
American authorities.[50] The association passed resolutions backing
the building of the highway "in order to adequately provide for the
defence of this vulnerable portion of the continent." It also stated
its belief that an open consideration of all options for the highway
would show that the prairie route "will be found shorter, cheaper,
easily constructed, easily maintained, and of a great commercial

value during and after the war in a territory least accessible to enemy attack, and accessible to the greatest number of junctions with the highway connection to all the neighbouring states and provinces."[51]

Endorsements came from municipal councils and from provincial and state politicians, along with financial contributions to support the association's lobbying efforts in Ottawa and Washington.[52] Reports supporting these efforts were circulated to government officials.[53] The group also secured support from the famous Arctic promoter and explorer Vilhjalmur Stefansson, who wrote articles in *Harpers* and *Foreign Affairs* supporting the project.

But the initial response to the project was far from positive. T. A. Crerar, the Canadian minister of mines and resources, responded to a resolution submitted by the Edmonton municipal council by writing, "I think it unlikely, therefore, that from the purely defence point of view, and this is one of the important considerations with the United States, that Government would be interested in a highway so remote from the Pacific Coast as would be one which passed through the City of Edmonton, especially since the United States Government will have to provide the bulk of the monies for such an undertaking." The organization was not put off by these discouraging words, and it continued to lobby by mail and in person with officials in both capitals.[54]

The highway to Alaska was not the only defense-linked transportation project under debate in the summer of 1941. Before the war, there had been much talk of developing "great circle" aviation routes from North America to the Orient. A string of airfields stretching from Edmonton through the Northwest to Alaska would have to be built before this idea could become reality. With the growing threat of Japanese militarism in the late 1930s, military authorities saw the military possibilities in the idea, and the Permanent Joint Board on Defence, established in 1940 to plan continental defense, urged the expansion of existing commercial facilities in the Canadian Northwest for future defence purposes.[55]

The Canadian government agreed with this idea, and in 1941 it began to expand existing airfields and build new landing strips between Edmonton and Fairbanks. This line, called the Northwest Staging Route, was funded by Ottawa and built by Canadian contractors, with major landing fields at Grande Prairie, Fort St. John, Fort Nelson, Watson Lake, Whitehorse, Prince George, and Smithers. The U.S. military was quick to make use of the route to ferry men and equipment to its expanding number of military bases in Alaska.[56]

Although the Japanese attack on Pearl Harbor of December 7, 1941, came as a surprise and shock to most Americans, the aggressive advance of Japanese power had already moved the U.S. government to take steps for the defense of Alaska, including building several large bases at Anchorage, Fairbanks, and on the Aleutian Islands. In 1940 an Alaskan Defense Force was established, and several thousand troops were sent north from the lower forty-eight states to reinforce the Territory's defense. The Japanese attack on Pearl Harbor, however, completely altered the pace and importance of the debates over the route of the proposed Alaska highway. Impelled by government propaganda, racism, and genuine fear of invasion, a wave of fear swept the continent, particularly along the West Coast. The threat posed by the "yellow peril," which in retrospect seems grossly overblown, was taken very seriously, particularly as the Japanese continued their seemingly unstoppable advance across southeast Asia and the Pacific Islands. The Germans too seemed invincible in 1941; under the circumstances, it was essential that immediate steps be taken to defend the far Northwest from invasion.

The North American economy, already running close to capacity, was geared up for a total war effort. Hundreds of thousands of Americans were drafted into the armed forces, providing the United States with the military power to defend its shores and to take the battle to the Axis powers in the Pacific and in Europe. But some saw a serious gap in these measures—the northwestern corner of the continent, a neglected frontier with no land connection to the rest of the continent. For half a century it had been supplied by ship, and to a small degree by airplane. No adequate means existed of provisioning in an emergency a region that at its farthest reach, the tip of the Aleutians, was closer to Tokyo than to Seattle.

Suddenly the spotlight of national attention was directed at the defense of Alaska, and particularly the need for a safe overland supply route from the south. The United States, now joined in a defense partnership with Canada, became more insistent in its dealings with Ottawa. Washington gave priority to plans for the Alaska highway and seriously considered a plan to connect the oil fields at Norman Wells with the Pacific coast. Although the U.S. War Plans Division did not see any immediate need for this project on military grounds, it argued that this was a good time for America to get its foot in Canada's northern door, to "take advantage of the present war to secure the necessary agreements from Canada to start work now and finish perhaps many years to come."[57] Washington accepted this advice, and expanded the request to include a military pioneer road to Alaska. Canadian officials were doubtful about the usefulness of the road and the oil project, calling the highway a "dubious egg," but could not see any way to oppose the American request, which soon was further revised to call for a full modern highway. Ottawa did insist that the road be built and paid for entirely by the United States, and that the sections running through Canada be turned over to the nation six months after the end of the war. Canada, for its part, provided the right-of-way, waived import duties and other taxes, offered special arrangements for incoming American workers, and permitted free use of timber and gravel as required.[58]

The main problem was the route. At the beginning of 1942 there were four choices. The first two were the coastal and interior routes north through British Columbia, recommended by the Alaska Highway Commission set up before the war and backed by strong political and commercial interests in British Columbia and Washington state. Third, Vilhjalmur Stefansson proposed a typically visionary and impractical integrated highway and pipeline route north from Edmonton to Norman Wells, then west to Fairbanks. Finally, the United States–Canada–Alaska Prairie Highway Association lobbied vigorously for its vision of the development of the Northwest by a road through North Dakota and Edmonton. The attack on Pearl Harbor only intensified the rivalry.

Discussions within the U.S. diplomatic corps and civil service did not echo the public interest in northwestern defense. Military strategists had always assigned low priority to the highway and could not, even with the increased threat to Alaska, bring themselves to consider it an urgent question. The public and political pressure was, however, forcing the decision makers to choose,

General William M. Hoge, who was in charge of building the Alaska Highway as first commander of the U.S. Corps of Engineers in the region. He is shown here as commander in chief of the U.S. Army in Europe, 1954. (U.S. Corps of Engineers)

and by January 1942, when a cabinet committee began meeting on the question, there were signs that a highway would be built, and that official attention was shifting away from the British Columbia routes towards the prairie route. This was not because planners were responsive to North Dakota's wish to funnel military traffic through the state, but because army representatives on the cabinet committee believed that the prairie route could be based on the existing Northwest Staging Route airfields and also because it was shorter than its competitors. As one official noted, "I know practically nothing about military strategy, but it seems to me that ultimately these airports will be connected by highways to facilitate delivery of gasoline and other supplies. The jump from the last of the airports to the Alaska border is short." He added that such a route would "break the hearts of the politicians in the Pacific Northwest."[59] It also aroused the fury of Alaska governor Gruening, who "bothered the Secretary of War and the Secretary of the Navy and others until [Secretary Ickes] felt called upon to send for him and admonish him that the Secretary of the Interior declared policy for the Department."[60]

Early in February 1942, the Committee of Public Roads met in Washington, D.C., to consider House Resolution 3095, sponsored by Delegate A. Dimond of Alaska, which called for the construction of a highway through British Columbia.[61] Alerted by telephone that the meeting was to take place, Halvor Halvorson, president of the prairie group, chartered a plane to Washington to present his case. He had to sit through the first two days while proponents of the British Columbia route, including Dimond, Governor Gruening, and former governor Riggs, made their case. Finally, on February 6, 1942, Halvorson was called to testify. As he later recounted, he found it "a little embarrassing to take issue" with those defending the rival route. Nonetheless he made a vigorous presentation, arguing that

the Mountain route was not feasible because there was no way to ascertain the cost of it, that surveying it alone would take more than would be needed to build across the prairie; that if it was built, it would be vulnerable to attack, if coast-wise shipping were blockaded by a foreign foe; that mountain highways could not be kept open the year around thru that territory, because of excessive snow in the winter and excessive rain in the summer at some points on the highway; that the prairie route could be kept open as an all-weather route the year round.[62]

To his delight, he found that the commission was of the same mind, having two days earlier decided to adopt the route he proposed. His victory was complete; even his suggestion that the project proceed by way of negotiation with Canada rather than by act of Congress had been adopted. Halvorson was taken aback by the violent attacks made on his proposal by its opponents. He discovered that "all the interests in Alaska were opposed," which he attributed to their business connections with Seattle. Halvorson could afford to be magnanimous, and he ended his triumphant report to his committee with the words, "Let us do everything we can to be ready to serve the public, when that time [peace] comes, by having available, usable, safe, modern highways. They have been the forerunners of civilization since the days of the Appian Way, built so many thousands of years ago by the Roman Empire and still in use."[63]

Although the public announcement was delayed, rumors of the decision quickly circulated throughout the Northwest. The cities and villages of the prairies were astonished and delighted by their victory. Visions of highways bearing thousands of trucks and cars full of soldiers and civilians pumping dollars into the local economies danced through their heads, and they quickly began to bombard officials with requests that connecting highways, or better still the main route to Edmonton, be routed through their towns.[64] On the West Coast there was mourning; the decision had destroyed the vision of a generation of Washington state, British Columbia, and Alaska politicians. Also left out in the cold was the old Yukon capital of Dawson City, which heard its death knell in the announcement; a decade after the road was finished it had to watch as the territorial administration was shifted to its rival, Whitehorse.

Negotiations between Canada and the United States as to the specific terms for the American use of Canadian soil for the construction of defense projects were concluded with a formal signing on March 18, 1942.[65] There were no celebrations; U.S. authorities had requested that Canada "soft-pedal news of all developments . . . which might tend to attract the attention of our enemies."[66]

The actual routing of the road through northern British Columbia and the Yukon was not decided at this stage, for none of the planners knew anything about the country. The general idea was to link the existing Northwest Staging Route airfields, and several more in the planning stages, thereby ensuring a land connection between these increasingly important military establishments. The actual route was left to the discretion of the first commander of the U.S. Army Corps of Engineers in the region, Brigadier General William Hoge.[67] In the early spring of 1942 he selected a route that generally followed existing wagon roads and trails: from Dawson Creek to Fort St. John and on to Fort Nelson, and from Whitehorse to Burwash Landing. For the areas in between, he relied on Les Cook, a well-known bush pilot, to locate suitable passes through the mountains and over uncharted ground.

Now that the decision was made, the U.S. Army rapidly swung into action. Immediate plans were made for building of a pioneer road, to be completed "at the earliest possible date to a standard sufficient only for the supply of the troops engaged on the work."[68] At the same time surveying and construction of a civilian-grade highway was to be undertaken under the supervision of the Public Roads Administration (PRA), to be ready for full use by 1943.[69]

Having the army and a civilian organization working simultaneously on different aspects of the same highway had the potential for trouble, and a clear delineation of responsibilities was required. An agreement of March 1942 set out the Public Roads Administration's tasks: reconnaissance surveys, preparation of plans and specifications, negotiations with and supervision of private contractors (who would work on a cost-plus basis), location of the civilian road as close as possible to the army's pioneer road, and maintenance of the road when it was finished. For its part, the Army Corps of Engineers was required to conduct all negotiations with the Canadian authorities (concerning duty-free entry of supples, right-of-way, policing of the highway, free use of raw materials such as timber and gravel, and free entry of American workers into Canada), to provide the PRA with the money required for its work, to construct a pioneer road, to expedite the transportation of men and material, and to provide proper clearances through the State Department and Canadian Customs. The agreement also defined the standard of the highway, which was to include a two-lane, gravel-surfaced road, timber bridges, and concrete or metal culverts.[70]

Two survey battalions were immediately sent to work south from Whitehorse and north from Fort St. John. They were to be followed by construction crews, which were to work north and south from Whitehorse; others would work north from Fort Nelson, and a general service regiment, drawn from the group headed for Fort Nelson, was to be based at the head of the existing road system south of that town, working north towards it.[71] All these decisions were made before the Canadian government had actually agreed to the construction of the highway. The troops were ready to move as soon as Ottawa agreed to the project; in fact, some were on the move even before Canada gave its assent.[72]

To complicate matters further, the U.S. government was at the same time contemplating the construction of a pipeline from Norman

Wells to supply the airfields, the highway, and the military bases in Alaska. Vilhjalmur Stefansson once more put his influence behind the plan, arguing that oil from Norman Wells could "relieve the United States of its fuel problem in Alaska." The project, he said, would cost less than the construction of a single battleship, which may have been true, but did not make it a good idea.[73] Nevertheless, the project now seemed feasible, given the urgent needs of Alaskan defense.

In the construction of what came to be called the Canol Project, the U.S. Army moved with remarkable speed, but with an equally remarkable lack of a sense of direction. There were few experts familiar with the Norman Wells field, and even fewer who had any idea of the difficulties involved in building a pipeline across the Richardson Mountains. Undeterred, the Americans pushed ahead and in April 1942 decided to proceed with the project. Ottawa was unenthusiastic about the idea, but could think of no defensible reason to oppose it, so on May 16, 1942, Canol was approved. As with the Alaska highway, the Canadian government granted rights-of-way and work sites, and waived oil royalties; additional arrangements for both the highway and pipeline projects established regulations for the importation of goods and purchase of Canadian supplies.[74] The United States agreed to pay for the project. At the end of the war, Canada had the option of purchasing the pipeline and refinery, or turning the entire facility over to the Permanent Joint Board on Defence for disposal.[75] Work crews arrived in northern Alberta early in June.

Few World War II military projects would match the Canol endeavor for pure folly and poor planning; one commentator called it a "junk-yard of military stupidity."[76] But the pipeline and refinery project was on the fast track, to be completed as quickly as U.S. Army personnel and civilian contractors could work. From the beginning, Canadians questioned the value of the Canol Project as a war-time venture and wondered, not without cause, if Americans had long-term designs on the resources of the far Northwest. J. K. Cornwall, an Edmonton businessman, remarked, "I visualize the U.S.A. controlling to a large extent the development of Canada's north land, due to their financial power and experience. Canada's finances are principally located in the eastern part of our country and they know comparatively very little about its possibilities."[77]

These were matters for the future, and 1942 was no time to be suspicious of the Yankees, once rivals but now valued neighbors and much-needed military allies; the challenge facing the U.S. Army, Public Roads Administration, dozens of civilian contractors hastily recruited to work on the highway and pipeline, Imperial Oil (owners of the Norman Wells field), and Standard Oil of New Jersey (responsible for the Whitehorse refinery) was to get the crews into the field and to keep the now-urgent military projects on schedule.

After decades of neglect and seemingly fruitless debate over various schemes for frontier development, the spotlight of history was shining again on the Canadian Northwest. Its residents had not been consulted or informed of any of the negotiations leading up to the decisions to build the Northwest Staging Route, Alaska highway, and Canol pipeline, but this was in the Canadian tradition of ignoring the people in frontier regions and reflected both governments' preoccupation with sudden military urgency. The roads, airfields, and pipelines were not, therefore, what northerners would have built had they had any measure of control over the decision. They were, however, a huge change from what the Northwest had received from the Canadian government before 1940. If the military projects were not the answers to the dreams of Northwest residents, they were certainly better than nothing. Under the circumstance, any suggestion of ingratitude seemed uncalled for, given the military concerns of a continent at war and the generosity of the U.S. government in agreeing to take on these massive and expensive projects with no financial contributions from the Canadian national, provincial, or territorial governments.

2. Invasion of the Bulldozers

ONCE THE DECISION was made to go ahead with the highway (originally called the Alcan and later the Alaska Highway) and the Canol project, the massive American military-industrial machine swung into action. The deadlines were tight, especially for the highway builders, for the U.S. Army had been ordered to have a pioneer road—that is, a rough road suitable for slow travel by heavy trucks—open by the fall of 1942. The upgraded highway and the pipeline-refinery complex would take longer, until 1943 and 1944 respectively, but it was clear that the Northwest defense projects had high priority; it was equally clear that the government did not expect the war to end soon.

The wartime projects represented a major advance over the existing transportation network in the Northwest. Where there had been few or no roads, a pioneer road more than 1,500 miles long would be built in less than a year, to be followed by an improved road built more or less to civilian standards (though not to the standard the Americans had promised in the initial agreement). A similar rough road was built from Norman Wells to Whitehorse, a distance of nearly 600 miles, with an oil pipeline running along its length. Improved navigation facilities were built along the Mackenzie River system, and other pipelines ran northwest from White-

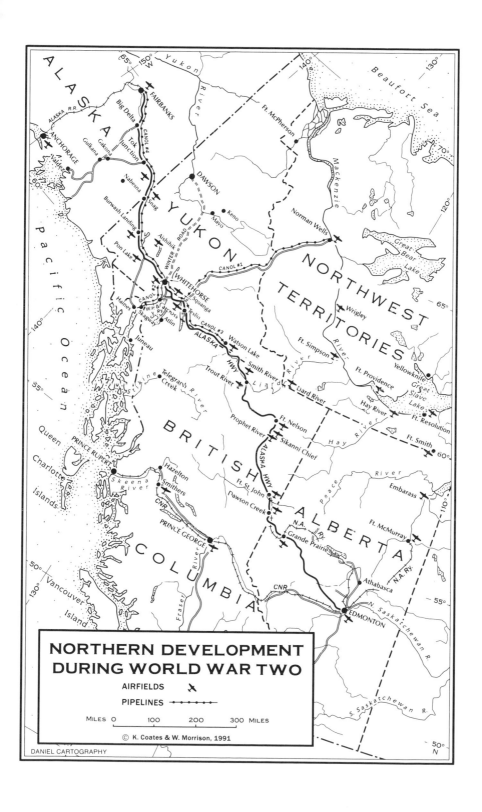

NORTHERN DEVELOPMENT
DURING WORLD WAR TWO

AIRFIELDS ✈

PIPELINES •───•───•

MILES 0   100   200   300 MILES

© K. Coates & W. Morrison, 1991

DANIEL CARTOGRAPHY

ALASKA

YUKON

NORTHWEST TERRITORIES

BRITISH COLUMBIA

ALBERTA

Pacific Ocean

Beaufort Sea

Queen Charlotte Islands

Vancouver Island

FAIRBANKS
Big Delta
Tok Junction
ANCHORAGE
Valdez
Gulkana
Gakona
Nabesna
Burwash Landing
Pon Lake
Aishihik
Snag
DAWSON
Keno
Mayo
Norman Wells
Ft. McPherson
WHITEHORSE
Squanga
Haines
Skagway
Atlin
Juneau
Teslin
Telegraph Creek
Watson Lake
Wrigley
Ft. Simpson
Ft. Providence
Yellowknife
Great Bear Lake
Great Slave Lake
Trout River
Smith River
Liard River
Hay River
Ft. Resolution
Ft. Smith
Prophet River
Ft. Nelson
Sikanni Chief
Hazelton
Smithers
Ft. St. John
Dawson Creek
Embarass
Ft. McMurray
Grande Prairie
Athabasca
EDMONTON
PRINCE RUPERT
PRINCE GEORGE
Skeena River
Stikine River
Fraser River
Peace River
Hay River
Liard River
Mackenzie River
Yukon River
N. Saskatchewan R.
S. Saskatchewan R.

ALASKA HWY
ALASKA HWY
CANOL #1
CANOL #2
CANOL #4
WINTER ROAD
CNR
N.A. Ry.
N.A. Ry.

150° W
140°
130°
120°
110°
130°
65°
70°
65°
60°
60°
55°
55°
50°
50° N

horse to Fairbanks, southeast to Watson Lake, and southwest to the Pacific Ocean at Skagway. A new road connected the Alaska Highway to salt water at Haines, Alaska. The existing Northwest Staging Route airfields were upgraded, and additional landing fields built. All sorts of ancillary facilities, such as a telephone network, were installed. Given the builders' initial ignorance about the country, the difficulties of its climate and terrain, the urgency with which the projects were built, and the logistical problems involved in their construction, these were remarkable accomplishments, though the Canol project soon became one of the war's leading symbols of bad military planning.

The Northwest was totally unprepared for the invasion. The Alaska Highway was to run through what was in many ways still a wilderness: The Canadian part of the route—a narrow corridor from Fort St. John through Whitehorse to the Alaska border—had a population of less than 5,000, many of whom were Native people living a seminomadic, harvesting way of life. The people of this corridor were simply overwhelmed by the civilian and military invasion. There were not enough hotels, restaurants, or other facilities even to begin to cope with the arrival of thousands of workers in a period of only a few weeks in the late winter of 1942. The same was even more true of the Mackenzie River valley, at the eastern end of the Canol pipeline.

The Americans began to arrive in the Northwest in March and April 1942. Those working on the southern part of the Alaska Highway came by train and airplane to Edmonton, then were shuttled, along with their machinery and equipment, to Dawson Creek, Fort St. John, and as far along the route as trucks could go. Others came to Whitehorse by plane or via the railway from Skagway to begin work on the middle section of the road. Still others were flown to more isolated camps, and to the Mackenzie valley. The highway was not built from one end to the other; work proceeded on several sections simultaneously. Thus the invasion was not a steady progress. Instead, the Americans appeared in many places at once and began working immediately in various directions. Those on the scene were struck by the rapidity of the change in the landscape, and were moved to note in their diaries and letters the dramatic contrast between millennia of silence and peace, and the noise and confusion of the highway construction.

Along with the troops and civilian workers came an armada of heavy equipment. The army, which kept meticulous records of this sort of thing, counted 11,107 pieces of heavy equipment used in the Northwest defense projects; specifically, 904 tractors, 2,790 dump trucks, 2,374 other trucks, 89 crushers, 374 blade graders, 370 scrapers, 174 steam shovels, and 4,032 pieces of other equipment—automobiles, bulldozers, snowplows, booms, boilers, cranes, derricks, draglines, compressors, generators.[1] In some ways, the residents were as much impressed by this invasion of bulldozers as by that of the workers—over 5,000 trucks had suddenly arrived in a region where there were hardly that many people. This demonstration of the power of the American industrial economy was awe-inspiring. Significantly, one of the aspects of the defense projects that caused the most resentment in the Northwest was the rumor, part truth and part exaggeration, that millions of dollars' worth of trucks, bulldozers, and other equipment was deliberately wrecked by the army after the projects were finished because it was not worthwhile taking them back to the United States, and the authorities did not want local residents to have them.

The Alaska Highway was not launched entirely into a vacuum. Its route had essentially been determined by the Northwest Staging Route (NWSR), much of which was already in place by 1942. The prairie route northwest from Edmonton had triumphed over its competitors largely because the planners sensibly decided that it would be easier to build a road if the construction could be supported by air through existing facilities. That this led to a route which virtually no one in the Pacific Northwest, Alaska, or the Yukon wanted was irrelevant, since the highway was not being built for the residents' benefit. One of the first jobs of the construction crews was therefore to strengthen and supplement the NWSR. Several new fields, including ones at Aishihik and Snag,[2] and a number of emergency strips were added to the Edmonton-Fairbanks corridor, and another string of fields was built north from Edmonton into the Mackenzie valley. The Canadians kept control of the original NWSR fields, which they had built (except for the

Civilian workers playing cards aboard a transport ship heading for the Northwest. Note the four-tiered bunks. (U.S. Army Corps of Engineers)

one at Edmonton, where the Canadians managed the air control only), while the Americans were responsible for all the new ones.

The NWSR gained new prominence late in 1942 after the United States extended the Lend-Lease program to the Soviet Union. The Americans supplied massive amounts of military material, including as many as 10,000 planes which, marked by the Soviet red star, were flown along the staging route to Fairbanks, where they were turned over to Soviet pilots.[3]

By the summer of 1942, a number of airfields were in operation. Along the route the Alaska Highway was to follow, fields had been built at Grand Prairie, Fort St. John, Fort Nelson, Watson Lake, and Whitehorse, in Canada; and at Northway and Big Delta, Alaska. Late in the summer, Major Linwood McCloud was ordered to investigate sites for more airfields; he recommended that eight be built, at the following locations: Dawson Creek, Mile 170 of the Alaska Highway, 75 miles north of Fort Nelson, the junction of the Trout and Liard rivers (209 miles north of Fort Nelson), Pine Lake (87 miles west of Watson Lake), the north end of Squanga Lake, Pine Creek (110 miles west of Whitehorse), and Burwash Landing.[4] Smaller fields were built for the Canol Project.

Over $41 million was spent on the construction, improvement, and maintenance of these airfields between 1942 and 1944. As the foundation on which all the Northwest defense construction rested, they were given a higher priority even than the highway and the pipeline, though they never achieved the publicity of the more glamorous projects (see table 1).

Even with this massive expenditure—and it must be remembered that $41 million was a far more impressive sum fifty years ago than today—facilities at these airfields were rudimentary. Few of them had hangars—only the ones at Edmonton, Whitehorse, and Fairbanks in 1943—making cold-weather operations difficult. Since it was impossible to shelter planes in the winter, engines froze, rubber hoses became brittle, and oil congealed. It was a major challenge to keep planes in the air under such circumstances, and just as difficult to repair them. Hangars were in the plans, but were slow to appear. The Americans blamed this on the Canadian Department of Transportation, which was responsible for their construction, accusing it of refusing to put up temporary shelters quickly, since it "definitely has in mind the development of post-war commercial airline activities, and as a result permanent construction is preferred."[5]

Despite these limitations, however, the airfields were impressive installations, especially when they suddenly appeared in the midst of the wilderness or tiny sub-Arctic communities. The fields at Whitehorse and Fort Nelson, for instance, were "Class III Sub-Depots." These involved the construction of 21 buildings, with a permanent detachment of 9 officers and 213 enlisted men to run the field.[6] A signal detachment of one officer and twenty enlisted men was also to be based at each Class III Sub-Depot (plus casuals estimated at fifty-five men and ten officers).[7] In the summer of 1943, when much construction was still under way in Whitehorse, the field had a large complement of men including 75 Royal Canadian Air Force (RCAF), 287 U.S. Army Air Force (USAAF), 168 Canadian Army, 146 American Army, 270 Canadian civilians, and an estimated 650 American civilians (taking over from the Canadian workers). Watson Lake, a much smaller field, had 40 RCAF, 10 USAAF, 61 U.S. Army, 175 Canadian civilians, and 30 American civilians. The small fields, like Teslin, had slightly more than 100 workers, most with temporary construction crews.

Initial work on the airfields was undertaken by Canadian workers, serving under the direction of the Department of Transportation and the RCAF. In the summer of 1943, construction was turned over to American civilian contractors; Canadians in the area were moved from the main airports in Whitehorse, Watson Lake, Fort

Table 1   U.S. Expenditures on Airfields as of April 24, 1944

Airfield	Expenditure (US $)
Northwest Staging Route	
Edmonton Air Base	5,248,822
Edmonton Satellite Field	6,853,683
Grande Prairie Air Base	1,968,015
Fort St. John Air Base	4,415,441
Fort Nelson Air Base	6,186,892
Watson Lake Air Base	4,156,695
Whitehorse Air Base	8,297,429
Calgary Air Base	28,517
Prince George Air Base	164,732
Subtotal	37,320,266
Alaska Highway Flight Strips	
Dawson Creek (Flight Strip #1)	428,220
Sikanni Chief (#2)	599,947
Prophet River (#3)	422,084
Liard Canyon (#4)	537,584
Pine Lake (#5)	287,162
Squanga Lake (#6)	297,101
Pon Lake (#7)	471,227
Burwash (#8)	219,362
Subtotal	3,262,687

Continued

Table 1 *Continued*

Airfield	Expenditure (US $)
Mackenzie-Athabasca Flight Strips	
Waterways	108,754
Embarras	59,112
Fort Smith	110,230
Resolution	65,803
Hay River	100,030
Providence	111,252
Mills Lake	43,075
Fort Simpson	162,701
Wrigley	93,372
Norman Wells	298,075
Canol Camp	111,746
Subtotal	1,264,150
Total Expenditure	41,847,063

SOURCE: NA, RG 338, box 25, Report of the Meetings of Representatives of the United States and Canadian Governments, 24–25 April 1944, U.S. Expenditures on Airfields, 24 April 1944, Schedule A.

NOTE: Schedule B, which calculated U.S. Expenditures on Airfields for items of permanent value, also dated 24 April 1944, and subtotals of $31,311,196, $3,262,687, and $1,264,150, and a total of $35,838,033. In addition, construction work undertaken by the Canadian government in 1944 at the request of the U.S. government totaled $5,161,000, with major resurfacing work at Edmonton, Grand Prairie, Fort Nelson and Watson Lake.

Nelson, Fort St. John, and Grande Prairie to "intermediate" fields at Snag, Aishihik, Teslin, Smith River, and Beatton River, where they were to upgrade the existing airfields and complete the required buildings.[8] By fall, a network stretching from Edmonton, Alberta, to Alaska (and beyond to Russia) was in working order.

Work was proceeding even faster on the construction of the Alaska Highway. The decision to build via the prairie route had been greeted with howls of protest from across the Northwest. British Columbians were understandably angered by the choice, which cut them off from their northern "empire." Yukoners were also angry, particularly the residents of Dawson City, who saw the road pass hundreds of miles from their town. Patriotic concerns and the need to support the war effort actually did little to dampen the protest, which boiled through the spring and summer of 1942. Proponents of the coastal or interior routes continued to press their case, arguing that one of these roads should be built as well.[9] The U.S. government ignored the protests, as did Canadian federal authorities. At the same time, agitation began for the construction of a railway from Prince George to Alaska, another long-touted project that died on the vine in 1942 after surveys and cost-accounting had been completed.[10]

The decisions had been taken, the army was in the field, and civilian contractors were being massed for summer work in the Northwest. The plan was to build a rough road as quickly as possible, to be followed by a road built more carefully to civilian standards. It was one of the largest construction projects ever undertaken in North America, and required thousands of military and civilian workers (see table 2). It also was carried out at unprecedented speed. The decision to build the road was made in February 1942, and the U.S. Army Corps of Engineers received orders late that month. In the first week of March the troops began to arrive by train in Dawson Creek, and soon survey and locating crews, some working for the army and some for the Public Roads Administration (PRA), were working with Native guides to lay out the road along the agreed route. Two main headquarters were established: one at Fort St. John for the southern part of the road, and the other in Whitehorse for the northern section.

The army had decided for the sake of speed to build the road in several sections at once, starting from the parts of the region most accessible to the outside—Dawson Creek and Delta, the end points of the road, and Whitehorse, near the middle. It also decided to send troops on a winter march from Fort St. John to Fort Nelson, a distance of over 250 miles, to establish another construction beachhead there. For this purpose the 35th Engineers regiment left the railhead on March 10 and reached Fort Nelson on April 5, enduring temperatures of $-35°F$ on the way. Despite this remarkable speed, however, the troops when they got to their destinations had to wait for two months to begin work, since spring thaws made construction work impossible. They began work on April 11, and by the end of September had finished 305 miles of road.

Table 2   U.S. Troops Engaged on Alaska Highway Construction,
1942–43

Unit	Arrival	Departure	Officers	Men
18th Engineers	Apr. 1942	Jan. 1943	55	1,459
Co. D, 29th Eng.	Apr. 1942	Feb. 1943	5	186
35th Engineers	Mar. 1942	Feb. 1943	46	1,230
Co. D, 58th Med.	Mar. 1942	Feb. 1943	5	54
73d Engineers	Apr. 1942	Feb. 1943	6	215
74th Engineers	Mar. 1942	June 1943	10	328
93d Engineers	Apr. 1942	Jan. 1943	46	1,250
95th Engineers	June 1942	Jan. 1943	48	1,228
97th Engineers	Apr. 1942	Jan. 1943	51	1,227
340th Engineers	Apr. 1942	May 1943	46	1,260
341st Engineers	May 1942	July 1943	43	1,146
438th Engineers	July 1942	Jan. 1943	4	118
Co. A., 648th Eng.	Mar. 1942	Nov. 1942	8	270
Signal Det. B	May 1942	Feb. 1943		16
Signal Det. H	Apr. 1942	Feb. 1943		4
Signal Det. D	May 1942	Feb. 1943		15
Signal Det. I	June 1942	Feb. 1943		16
Signal Det. I	Apr. 1942	Feb. 1943		16
Finance Dept.	Mar. 1942	—	1	10
Finance Dept.	Apr. 1942	—	1	10
Quartermaster	—	—	5	127
Quartermaster	Apr. 1942	—	2	86
Quartermaster	Apr. 1942	—	1	5
133d Quarter. Truck	Aug. 1942	May 1943	4	120
134th Quarter. Truck	July 1942	May 1943	4	120
140th Quarter. Truck	Apr. 1942	May 1943	3	126
141st Quarter Truck	July 1942	May 1943	3	114
Total			394	10,756

SOURCE: *The Alaska Highway: Interim Report from the Committee on Roads, House of Representatives* (Washington, D.C.: Government Printing Office, 1946), pp. 104–5).

The experience of the first regiments sent to Whitehorse—the 340th and 93rd Engineers (the latter was a black unit)—was typical of the way the army of occupation penetrated the Northwest. They had to cool their heels in Skagway from April until June waiting for

Building a timber bridge over Edith Creek, Yukon, 1942. (Yukon Territorial Archives, R. A. Carter Collection, 1485)

their heavy equipment to catch up with them. Once supplied, the 93rd moved to Carcross, the midpoint of the Yukon and White Pass Railway, which they used as a base to work their way westward towards Teslin, a distance of 99 miles. The 340th traveled across country to Teslin, then by boat to Morley Bay on the east shore of Teslin Lake, where they established base camp. Their equipment went by steamer and barge from Whitehorse to the Teslin River, then along Teslin Lake to the camp. The 340th then began to work in both directions, towards Nisutlin Bay and also southeastward. On September 24, having passed Watson Lake, the 340th met the 35th Engineers working toward them at Contact Creek.

The northern section of the highway, from Whitehorse to Fairbanks, was also built in several sections simultaneously. The 18th Engineers arrived in Whitehorse in early April and began building to the northwest; by October 25 they had completed 313 miles of pioneer road. The 97th Engineers (another black unit) landed in Valdez in May and, after working on the Richardson Highway and the Gulkana-Nebasna road, began building through the Metasta Pass and then pushed down the Tok River to the Tanana River. They then continued southward, linking up with the 18th Engineers just outside Beaver Creek, a month after the 35th and 340th had met at Contact Creek. It was the last week of October 1942, and the pioneer road was finished—just seven months and two weeks from the day the first troops arrived in Dawson Creek.[11] Most of it was built in a period of five months (see table 3).

Table 3   Progress of Pioneer Road Construction, 1942

Date	Mileage	Remarks
Apr. 30, 1942	8	By 35th Engineers
May 31, 1942	95	By 4 regiments
June 30, 1942	360	By 7 regiments
July 31, 1942	794	By 7 regiments
Aug. 31, 1942	1,186	Fort Nelson reached
Sept. 30, 1942	1,479	Whitehorse reached
Oct. 25, 1942	1,645	Completed

SOURCE: United States, House of Representatives, *The Alaska Highway: An Interim Report* (Washington, D.C.: Government Printing Office, 1946), p. 15.

A dry recitation of troop movements and construction statistics gives little indication of how tough the road was to build. The logistical problems were enormous, especially because everything from route location and surveying to bridge construction and right-of-way clearing was going on simultaneously. In his official summary of the highway project, Brigadier-General Sturdevant described the job:

In a typical operation of a regiment engaged in breaking new trail through the forest we find in the lead, of course, the locating party which indicated the centre line by blazes or pieces of cloth. The clearing crew with three shifts of tractor operators followed. One large bulldozer ran along the marked centre line clearing a narrow trail. Other large machines were then assigned tasks along this trail. Pushing the trees laterally to both sides they made a clearing from 60 to 90 feet wide. Having finished a task a bulldozer would leap-frog forward to its next similar task. On much of the route the forest growth was dense but the trees were usually not large nor deeply rooted. Where the ground was firm, ten or twelve bulldozers could clear two to three miles through solid forest each day. The smaller bulldozers were used to follow the large tree movers cleaning off moss, muck and lesser debris. The clearing crew was generally several miles beyond the reach of trucks and had to be supplied by pack train or tractor drawn sleds or Athey trailers. The men slept in pup tents and moved camp nearly every day.

A crew consisting generally of a company followed the clearing crew constructing log culverts and small bridges and was followed in turn by another crew engaged in ditching, corduroying if necessary, and rough grading sufficient to permit passage of truck traffic in weather not too wet.

The remainder of the regiment, perhaps two or three of the six companies, might be distributed along the road thirty to forty miles in rear of the clearing crew and be engaged in widening the narrow places, reducing the worst grades, gravelling soft spots and smoothing with motor patrols. This operation completed the pioneer road which was generally 18 to 24 feet wide. As means permitted later in the season, still further improvements in grade and alignment were undertaken both by Army and Public Roads Administration forces and the entire road has now [1943] received a light surfacing with gravel.

Two light ponton companies each equipped with 675 feet of floating bridge material were parcelled out to the regiments. The ponton detachments promptly put in floating bridges over streams that could not be forded, or ferries where available material was insufficient for bridges. Pile or trestle bridges were constructed as soon as possible to release the ponton equipage.[12]

This careful military prose played down the human difficulties of the job. Mosquitoes and black flies plagued the men, particularly those who were unlucky enough to be working near still water. The bulldozers routinely stripped the top layer of soil from the underlying permafrost, which thawed in the spring, turning much of the route into a quagmire. And the men were pushed relentlessly to finish the job as quickly as possible. The long sub-Arctic summer days meant the work could go on almost around the clock; men often worked until they dropped, falling asleep for a few hours at the work site, not even bothering to return to camp.

The logistical problems often delayed the work. The bulldozers advanced so quickly that they outran deliveries of oil, gasoline, and replacement parts. Mechanics kept their machines going by the time-tested technique of jerry-rigging and pilfering parts from equipment left unattended. Huge traffic bottlenecks built up at Dawson Creek, Skagway, and Whitehorse, closing supply pipelines. The road itself was a bottleneck; it was rough, slow, subject to

A truck and a bulldozer engulfed by mud at the southern end of the highway, summer 1942. (NAC, PA-171417)

regular bridge washouts, and often impassable even to heavy trucks. The workers coped as best they could; the 18th Engineers, for instance, had to start work on their section of the highway with pick and shovel while they waited for their trucks and bulldozers to arrive on the railway from Skagway.

Some military units had to resort to desperate expedients to get supplies. One construction unit went into the bush on a winter trail, then became isolated when the thaw came.

They were supplied entirely by air, but for some time when the lakes were breaking up neither ski nor ponton planes could land . . . Finally a desperate effort was made to relieve their plight by dropping stuff from a plane. Here are the results of the first try: First pass over, the plane dropped mail, so the boys rushed out to get their long-delayed letters. Next pass the plane dropped a sack of bridge spikes. The bag broke and the spikes rained down on the mail-reading soldiers like shrapnel. The third pass was to drop an axle and several bearings, tied to a parachute for safety. The parachute ripped apart on the way down—they're still digging in the muskeg [bogs] for the bearings. On the fourth pass over the camp a side of beef was

dropped; the pilot went back and reported he just missed the fuel dump—
what he really barely missed was the nitro-starch (explosive) dump. The
next time the plane came up a sack of mail was thrown overboard, but it
caught on the tail of the plane, and went all the way back to Whitehorse in
that position. So the pilot figured a few weights might help and loaded the
sack with small bearings—the weights worked all right, just enough to carry
the mail sack through the top of an oil drum into a diesel fuel bath.[13]

The White Pass and Yukon Route Railway was a problem
throughout the war. Built in the waning days of the gold rush, it
had made a profit even during the Yukon's bleakest days by virtue
of its monopoly over the regional transportation network.[14] The
line's managers, used to an easy-going routine, were overwhelmed
by the demands of the U.S. Army in the spring of 1942. Tons of
goods piled up on the Skagway docks, hampering the construction
efforts inland. U.S. officials believed they could do a better job
and leased the line from its owners, assigning the 770th Railway
Operating Battalion to run it.[15] The losers in this arrangement were
the Yukoners, who still depended on the railroad for their supplies,
and who now found that both passenger and civilian freight traffic
were given low priority by the Americans.[16] The army also neglected maintenance, leaving the line in sorry shape at the war's
end. Despite all these difficulties, however, the work went ahead,
and in late October 1942 a rough pioneer road had been completed
from Dawson Creek to Fairbanks.

On November 20, 1942, Canadian and U.S. officials gathered at
Soldier's Summit, an isolated spot near Burwash Lake, to celebrate
the completion of the Alaska Highway. It had cost $19.7 million, or
$17,221 per mile, a trivial sum by modern standards. The comple-
tion was only nominal, however, since much of the road fell apart
in the spring thaw of 1943, and most of it had to be rebuilt. Some
who worked on it claimed that it was essentially impassable even
as it was opened.[17] But from the beginning the highway had been
more than just a road: it was a reaffirmation of the United States'
commitment to the defense of North America, and a pledge that
the far Northwest would be defended against invasion. In November
1942, as the tide of war seemed at last to be turning in favor of the
Allies—in Churchill's phrase, it was not the beginning of the end

but the end of the beginning—the completion of the pioneer road was evidence that North America was secure.[18]

The opening ceremonies received wide publicity. Reporters from the Canadian Broadcasting Corporation (CBC) and the American networks, and from several magazines and newspapers were at Soldier's Summit, as were a number of politicians and dignitaries. The cold of late November did not shorten the speeches, as each speaker commented at length on the spirit of international cooperation that had marked the project. Some, after praising the military for its work, predicted that the highway would be the foundation of postwar prosperity throughout the Northwest. There was symbolism in the ceremony: the Royal Canadian Mounted Police (RCMP) supplied a guard of honor in scarlet tunics, and four U.S. enlisted men, two white and two black, held the ribbon. Nay-sayers were silent; even harsh critics of the route, like Governor Gruening, had nothing but praise for the completed project.[19]

The opening of the Alaska Highway and the subsequent publicity the route received left the North American public with the impression that the army had built a completed road, which would be open to civilian traffic as soon as the war ended. This belief was mistaken on two counts: the road was far from completed in November 1942, and the army had not built all of it. Yet these misconceptions persisted for years, and the contribution of the Public Roads Administration and civilian contractors was almost totally ignored by the public.[20] A great deal of work remained to be done after the official opening, and as late as the end of 1943 there were still nearly 11,000 military men in the region, working under the general direction of the PRA (see table 4). The work continued until the end of the war, though without the publicity and sense of urgency that surrounded the first construction phase.

The PRA's mission in building and rebuilding the highway differed from that of the army in that quality rather than speed was the priority. The original plan was that the PRA would use the army's road as an access route to build a final road; this was changed over time to have the PRA incorporate more of the original pioneer road into its construction. Initial specifications (later reduced) called for a 36-foot-wide road, hard-surfaced for 28 feet of its width. The

Table 4   Operating Military Personnel, Northwest Service Command, December 31, 1943

Units	Officers	Nurses	Warrant officers	Enlisted men	Total personnel
NW Div. Eng.	167				167
Whitehorse	163	17	6	1,901	2,087
Dawson Creek	91	14		1,500	1,605
Skagway	78	12	5	1,793	1,888
Prince Rupert	13			170	183
Edmonton	75	21	2	626	724
QM Truck Regt.	94		3	3,534	3,631
Misc.	18			774	792
Total	699	64	16	10,298	10,910

SOURCE: NA, RG 319, Army Center of Military History, manuscript file ACMH 3-1.1/AA/v.5, "The Canol Project," p. 436.

bridges were to be timber-trestle, to be replaced eventually by 24-foot-wide steel bridges capable of bearing 40 tons gross weight. Grades were not to exceed 7 percent—a steep grade, but many hills on the army's pioneer road were much steeper than that—and curves were to be kept within acceptable limits.

The PRA had been working on the highway since the first tree was bulldozed, but it was in 1943 that its major contribution to the project began. The agency sent crews to the camps of the Civilian Conservation Corps, one of the New Deal agencies, throughout Montana, Minnesota, Washington, and Oregon, where they dismantled buildings, emptied warehouses, and collected road-building equipment. More equipment was secured from the Works Projects Administration (WPA), which had also been responsible for many Depression-era construction projects. Hundreds of railway cars loaded with supplies were sent to Dawson Creek and Whitehorse (via Skagway), where they were used in highway construction. The PRA also moved quickly to set up an administrative system, opening field headquarters in Whitehorse and Fort St. John, with regional offices at Fort Nelson, Mile 510, Fairbanks, and Gulkana.

During 1942, PRA contractors worked on the pioneer road alongside the military. They upgraded the existing provincial road between

Dawson Creek and Fort St. John, and built the sections of the road between Whitehorse and Jakes Corner, and between Big Delta and Tanacross. They began work on improving the army's pioneer road from Fort St. John to Fort Nelson, from Whitehorse to the White River, and 100 miles eastward from Jakes Corner. They also began regrading the highway west of Fort Nelson, and the Alaska sections of the road, and built a number of temporary bridges.

Through the summer of 1942, camps had to be constructed, with large depots built at Valdez, Skagway, Gulkana, Gacona, Tanacross, Big Gerstle, Big Delta, Whitehorse, Carcross, Fort Nelson, Dawson Creek, and Fort St. John. Crushing plants and sawmills were located as near the resources as possible. The PRA contractors also completed a number of smaller projects for the army, including building headquarters facilities, surfacing the streets of Whitehorse, building hospitals in major centers, improving airfield surfaces, building a water reservoir at Fort St. John, and completing a number of winter camps for the army (at Haines, Champagne, Kluane Lake, Big Delta, Cathedral Rapids, Big Gerstle, Beaver Creek, Lewes River, Judith Creek, Squanga Lake, Carcross, and between Nisutlin and Watson Lake).

Overwhelmed by the size of the administrative part of the project, the PRA decided to subcontract some parts of it to companies experienced in the management of large-scale construction jobs. A fee-for-service arrangement was made, based on an estimate of the construction costs. All labor and supplies were paid for by the PRA, and contractors' equipment was rented. Five management contractors were employed. E. W. Elliott of Seattle was responsible for transportation and construction of highway camps. R. Melville Smith Company, run by the former deputy minister of highways from Ontario and based in that province, was to supervise the construction of 250 miles between Dawson Creek and Fort St. John, and Fort Nelson and Watson Lake;[21] the intervening 256-mile stretch was to be completed by Okes Construction of St. Paul, Minnesota. Dowell Construction of Seattle was to build 627 miles between Watson Lake and the Yukon-Alaska boundary; the final contractor, C. F. Lytle and Green Construction Company of Sioux City, Iowa, was to complete the 306 miles of road in Alaska. The five main contractors then hired an additional seventy-nine

Welding the Canol pipeline. (NAC, PA-171533)

companies, including sixteen Canadian and sixty-three American firms, to do the actual work. In most cases the subcontractors came from the same vicinity as the main contractors.

There were of course some changes to this plan as the work went ahead. Lytle and Green Construction, for example, completed its work ahead of schedule and expanded operations east of the Alaska-Yukon boundary. Oakes Construction completed two small sections on either end of the R. M. Smith contract. E. W. Elliott, which held the transportation and camp contracts for 1942, tackled two sections of the highway, one on either side of Burwash Landing. In addition, Utah Construction of Salt Lake City was contracted to complete several pieces of road between Kluane Lake and Beaver

Creek; to this company fell the honor of completing the reconstruction of the highway in the fall of the 1943. [22]

The PRA retained responsibility for the location and design of the highway. PRA engineers in San Francisco found themselves drafting plans for bridges over rivers that the highway crews had not yet reached; the agency's soils crews scoured the Northwest for building materials; its survey teams searched for the best route for the improved road. It had at first been expected that the PRA road would simply follow the route of the military road, but civilian engineers found the route unsatisfactory, so they began to design what was essentially an entirely new highway, one that was in places as much as 10 miles distant from the pioneer road. The army took offense, viewing the PRA's plan as a waste of time and money, and a slur on its work; it ordered the PRA to follow the original route. A bitter squabble ensued. Brigadier General J. A. O'Connor, commander of Northwest Service Command, put the army's case bluntly, recommending that the PRA contractors be put under military control:

The Public Roads Administration has been a hindrance to the execution of the completion of the Highway. There seems to be no question as to the ability of the P.R.A. employees, but their attitude is such as to slow up the work. . . . They cannot divorce themselves from the idea that their mission is to construct a finished highway of the highest peace time standard. Consequently, they do not push the contractors with the idea of putting through a road suitable for present requirements in the shortest time possible. [23]

His supervisor, Lieutenant-General B. Somervell, agreed in part, remarking that the PRA should be kept on the project, but if it did not soon "abandon its business-as-usual attitude, and serve properly as an agent of the Military Establishment," he would recommend the agency's removal. [24]

But by this time, the late summer of 1943, the Northwest defense projects were becoming irrelevant to the war effort, and the U.S. government was becoming reluctant to spend much money on a marginal project. One cost-cutting solution was to revise the specifications for the rebuilt highway, lowering its quality considerably. This angered the Canadian authorities and the men who were building the road, who viewed it as a breach of the original agreement: "All these changes and reversals have had a very damaging effect on the morale of both Public Roads and the contractors' personnel. They feel their efforts have to a considerable extent been wasted, and that their superior officers don't know what they want done."[25]

In 1943 the PRA tackled its main task of upgrading the pioneer road to a civilian standard. Early that year, the army's road carried the eighty-one civilian contractors and their equipment into place. The spring rains that followed devastated the primitive military road. Truck convoys were lucky to average 30 miles a day; the 900-mile trip from Dawson Creek to Whitehorse could take a full month. Worse followed in the Fort Nelson district, where June rains destroyed nearly all the original bridges and culverts, bringing travel and transportation to a complete halt. Throughout the summer and fall of that year, the civilian contractors rebuilt the road and the bridges. It was a tremendous job, since there were 133 bridges 100 feet or longer along the highway, with a total distance of 7 miles. Eventually 67 percent of the final road followed the PRA's rather than the original route. The Alaska Highway, built in 1942, had been largely rebuilt in 1943, yet the final product was less than project organizers had planned. It was still not up to proper standard, containing many poorly surfaced stretches, steep hills, and treacherous grades; it was, however, adequate for military purposes.

The rebuilding of the highway required a massive mobilization of manpower, equipment, and other resources. In 1943 the PRA had 1,850 of its employees at work in the Northwest. Civilian contractors employed 14,100 workers, of whom 10,400 were American and 3,700 Canadian. At the height of construction, the contractors had over 11,000 pieces of heavy equipment in the region, a quarter of which they owned and the rest rented from the U.S. government. The costs were, by the standards of that day, tremendous. A preliminary accounting, completed in October 1944, reported a total expenditure by the PRA of $130.6 million on the Alaska Highway (the figure included $7.8 million for work on the military road, $2 million for subsidiary roads, $6.2 million for maintenance in the winter of 1942–43, $58 million for construction of the final road, an additional $21.3 million for the erection of major structures on the final road, and $35.3 million for other expenses).

Lunchtime along the Canol route, Godlin River, NWT, 21 January 1944. (NAC, R.S. Finnie photo, PA-175982)

The Fort St. John section cost $60.3 million and the Whitehorse sector $38.3 million, while the Alaskan district spent $16.1 million. The various district office expenses amounted to approximately $830,000. The cost of the "final-type" road was $66,160 per mile, or $39,600 when "those costs not normally incurred in the construction of roads in the United States" were eliminated.

The major contractors operated little independent construction empires within their areas of responsibility. Each had its own headquarters, complete with administrative offices, repair shops, and other services. R. Melville Smith had its headquarters in Dawson Creek; Dowell Construction had a central shop in Whitehorse; Utah Construction's repair base was in McCrae, just south of Whitehorse; E. W. Elliott maintained a large repair shop at Kluane Lake and a number of smaller field stations; Lytle and Green Construction had its headquarters at Tok Junction. From these headquarters, they administered the operations of the subcontractors under their supervision.

It is difficult to say what profits were made by these private contracting companies. The accounts mention fixed-fee payments, management fees, and other costs. But since the cost-plus contracting system used during the war was notoriously prone to padding and inefficiency, there were many cracks through which substantial sums could and did slip, especially since cost-effectiveness was not a priority. As of July 1945, the contractors had received fixed-fee payments of over $4.8 million, with an additional $327,000 still outstanding. Most of the contractors came in far over budget, often two to four times the original estimate. This was usually because of unexpected costs, such as those associated with muskeg and permafrost.[26] For example, the highway segment supervised by R. Melville Smith came in at more than twice the original estimate, $30 million instead of the projected $13.5 million. There was naturally a good deal of padding on many contracts, a practice made easy because of the loose supervision. Shortages of labor compelled some companies to hire kitchen workers at skilled tradesmen's rates, and to pay them overtime though they worked only a few hours a day.[27] This practice was perhaps understandable, but more dishonest practices also occurred, though with what frequency it is difficult to say. According to a supervising engineer, one Canadian contractor delivered unusable equipment to its highway work site, repaired it at U.S. Army expense, and then tried to ship it out of the region; the same company stockpiled new tires, bought as project expenses, and put them on its equipment when removing the machinery from the Northwest.[28]

The other major addition to the Northwest highway network authorized by the U.S. government was the Haines Road, which connected the port of Haines, Alaska, with the Alaska Highway. The Haines Road (or Haines Lateral, as it was also called), followed a trail pioneered by Jack Dalton before the Klondike gold rush and first surveyed in 1912.[29] Its purpose was to relieve pressure on the overloaded White Pass and Yukon Railway by providing an extra link between the coast and the Alaska Highway. Trucks could thus supply the highway west of Whitehorse from the sea via Haines. The U.S. Army Corps of Engineers surveyed the route in the summer of 1942, and the decision to build the road (with Canadian permission) was made in November of that year.[30] It was a tough job, for although the road was only 154 miles long, it climbed quickly from tidewater to the summit of the Chilkat Pass, then ran across tundra, skirting the edges of what is now Kluane National Park before reaching a point on the Alaska Highway prosaically called Haines Junction.

By October 1943 the PRA had finished the major part of its work on the Alaska Highway, and most of the civilian contractors left the North, leaving the U.S. War Department with the responsibility for highway maintenance. By September 1944, 385 civilians were working for the War Department, and that number rose to more than 500 by February 1945. Reductions began at the end of the war, leaving 132 workers on the Canadian section of the highway by April 1946 (see table 5). Responsibility for the 208 miles of the highway in Alaska was transferred to the Alaska Road Commission.[31]

The Alaska Highway, punched through at high speed as a pioneer road in the fall of 1942, and finished a year later as a "final-type" road, continues to have a reputation as a feat of engineering and as a classic confrontation of man and machine against the wilderness. The reputation of the other major Northwest defense project, however, is markedly different.

Canol, which stands for Canadian Oil, was a pipeline project designed to carry crude oil from the Norman Wells oil field in the Mackenzie valley to a refinery in Whitehorse, where it would be used to supply the Alaska Highway, the Northwest Staging Route, and the Alaskan military establishment, and perhaps could fuel the economic development of the region after the war.[32] The project was entirely American; Canada had given its permission by granting the U.S. government a huge reservation for oil exploration in the region.[33] With the exception of a few wells drilled twenty years earlier near Norman Wells, none of the infrastructure for the project yet existed. There was no land route through the Richardson Moun-

Members of Company F, 341st Engineers, building the Beatton River
Bridge at mile 104 on the highway, 18 July 1942. (YTA, MM Collection,
3553)

tains between Norman Wells and Whitehorse, no pipelines in the
Yukon or Alaska to carry the finished product.

The Canol Project was the kind of scheme that could have been
realized only during a wartime emergency, and even then some realized that it was far-fetched; President Roosevelt himself noted, "It is
fully recognized that the project is not commercially feasible."[34] Like
the Alaska Highway, Canol rested on a cooperative military-civilian
effort. The U.S. Army Corps of Engineers was dispatched to complete the preliminary work; a private consortium, Bechtel-Price-Callahan, had been formed to build the actual facilities. The project was
top secret at first, though Edmontonians could guess from the troops
and equipment heading north through town that something major was
afoot in the Mackenzie valley. When the project was announced in
1943, it was greeted in the press with the kind of enthusiasm that
welcomed news of the Alaska Highway. Later commentators, however, have been uniformly critical of the project; the most detailed
study of the project describes it as a kind of bad joke:

Today, to be sure, it is not easy to take Canol seriously. Its 4- and 6-inch pipeline, puny by our standards, was puny by the standards of the 1940s as well. Moreover, some of Canol's technology was the crudest to be found in the modern repertoire: the wood stove, the pack horse, and the dog sled, proved after all to be still valuable adjuncts of life in the north. Then, too, for all the project's pretense of being an earnest wartime and a great undertaking for its day, it often proceeded like a situation comedy, with moments of bumptious slapstick, as when the Mackenzie River mud swallowed whole vehicles, or a workman drove a truck through a mess hall after a lunch he did not like.[35]

The Canol project involved four pipelines and a number of ancillary facilities. Canol 1, the main line, ran between Norman Wells and Whitehorse, a distance of nearly 600 miles. Canol 2 joined Whitehorse and Skagway, Canol 3 paralleled the Alaska Highway

Table 5 Highway Maintenance Camps between Dawson Creek and the Canada/Alaska Boundary

Dawson Creek	Camp Name	Personnel	Family Apartments
20	Kiskatinaw River	5	5
49	Fort St. John	5	5
101	Blueberry	6	6
163	Sikanni	5	5
201	Trutch	6	6
245	Prophet River	5	5
300	Fort Nelson Jct.	5	5
392	Summit Lake	6	6
456	Muncho Lake	6	6
543	Coal River	6	6
635	Watson Lake Jct.	5	5
733	Swift River	7	7
804	Teslin	6	6
883	Marsh Lake	5	5
956	Stoney Creek	8	6
1,016	Haines Junction	8	6
1,083	Destruction Bay	9	8
1,156	Koidern	8	6
Highway Emergency Crew (Whitehorse)		10	
Bridge Crew (Whitehorse)		11	
Total Personnel		132	

south to Watson Lake, and Canol 4 linked Whitehorse and Fairbanks. A large refinery was built at Whitehorse, existing facilities at Norman Wells were enlarged, and storage facilities built at Prince Rupert.[36] By the time the project began to wind down in 1944, the U.S. Army had also improved transportation facilities in the Mackenzie valley corridor, built a number of airfields, greatly expanded the Norman Wells oil field (twenty-three wells were drilled in 1942 and thirteen in 1943), and built a series of connector roads—all of this for a project of doubtful usefulness, plagued by bad planning, and with an insatiable appetite for public money.

Viewed from a "can do" perspective rather than one of common sense, however, the Canol Project had its moments of success, if only because of the obstacles that had to be overcome to complete it. Tons of pipe and other supplies had to be delivered to Norman Wells through an antiquated, small-scale transportation system developed decades before by the Hudson's Bay Company to serve its trading posts along the Mackenzie River. The material went by train over the Northern Alberta Railway to Fort McMurray (or Waterways) where it was transferred to barges for the 1,200-mile trip to Norman Wells, a journey broken by a number of barriers, including a 16-mile portage between Fort Fitzgerald and Fort Smith. The regional transportation system soon broke down under the onslaught of manpower and supplies, and "Task Force 2600," the military unit of 2,500 assigned to the project, had to improvise.[37] Pontoon bridge equipment was transformed into rafts, a system that worked well enough on the rivers south of Great Slave Lake but was poorly suited for use on the lake. Docking facilities were quickly erected along the route to facilitate the transfer of supplies, but not much got through in the summer of 1942; most of the material had to be sent north on winter tractor-trains, or held over until the navigation season of 1943. The army and the civilian workers kept busy building airfields (some of which had only a tenuous connection to the project), portage roads, and a rough road between Fort Nelson and Fort Simpson (the 1,000-mile Grimshaw Road, begun by the 388th Engineers and finished by Bechtel-Price-Callahan). Company B of the 38th Engineers worked on the main base at Camp Canol, which had to be moved several times in the search for a suitable site. Plans were laid for more roads—from

The pioneer road, finished in November 1942, had a number of "Suicide Hills." (National Archives of the United States, 111-SC-143373)

Alberta to Norman Wells and from the Mackenzie to Alaska via Rat Pass (near Fort McPherson), and winter roads throughout the district. The American invasion of the Mackenzie valley was far greater than U.S. authorities had led the Canadian government to believe, and it raised questions about American designs on Canadian resources.

An effort was also made to increase production from the Norman Wells oil field. By December 1942 crews from Imperial Oil, working for the army, had drilled nineteen new wells and tripled oil output. By the end of the war, a total of eighty-three wells had been drilled by Imperial Oil and by Noble Drilling Corporation of Edmonton, most of them near Norman Wells, but others farther afield, raising potential production to a level that far outstripped both the capacity of the pipeline and military needs in the Northwest.

The main part of the project, the construction of Canol 1, the line from Norman Wells to Whitehorse, took longer than expected. The Richardson Mountains, and particularly MacMillan Pass, presented a formidable obstacle; nonetheless, the line was eventually completed, and was opened with a celebration on April 30, 1944.[38] Delays with the building of the refinery and final work on the pumping stations prevented completion of the entire project until August 1944.

The other lines proved easier to build; the Skagway system was operating by December 1942, and was used not to deliver oil from the North, but to pump California petroleum projects from tidewater to supply the highway and other projects at Whitehorse.[39] The other two lines were finished by March 1944.

For a short time oil flowed (intermittently, between breakdowns) from Norman Wells to Whitehorse, but the project's working life was short. Plagued by slipshod construction, leaks and wastage of oil, low morale among the workers, and spectacular cost overruns, Canol attracted the attention of the Truman Committee, the U.S. Senate Special Committee Investigating the National Defense Program, where it became a horrible example of wartime waste and bad planning.[40] On March 9, 1945, the Whitehorse refinery was closed and the pumping stations mothballed. The 4600th Service Command Unit took over control of the project from the civilian workers and continued to operate the pipeline on a reduced scale, finally closing it in 1946.[41] The Whitehorse refinery was dismantled and shipped to Edmonton, site of major new oil discoveries. The pipe, telephone lines, camps, and other equipment were sold as surplus or salvaged. The project had cost more than the Alaska Highway, between $133 million and $144 million. Hailed by its promoters as the foundation of the region's postwar economy, it had become the quintessential white elephant of the wartime military-industrial complex, an object of derision to critics of military spending and to Canadian nationalists, who discovered, after the fact, the remarkably wide net spread by the Americans in the Mackenzie valley. P.S. Barry wrote its epitaph:

What began as an illusion, then, ended as an illusion. The extravaganza that Canol's hunt for oil became has peculiar kinship with other ambitious undertakings in the vast and thinly populated north. Whether civilian or military, the people who traded on Canol's emergency status and the screen the wilderness provided succumbed to the same visionary magic that has beguiled whalers, traders, fur dealers, and telecommunications engineers. From the bewitching dreams of easy possession that the great northwest continues to provoke, a magic working even yet, came the stimulus for Canol's extraordinary growth and the cause of its equally extraordinary demise.[42]

The invading force that came to build Canol was not as large as the military-civilian army that built the Alaska Highway. It was also more scattered, from Prince Rupert to Norman Wells, from Fort Smith to Fairbanks. The original military unit, Task Force 2600, numbered about 2,500. Additional troops were assigned to the project as necessary, and by January 1944 there were 10,618 military personnel working on the various parts of Canol. An equally large number of civilians also worked on it (see table 6).

Along with the two major Northwest defense projects—Canol and the Alaska Highway—there were dozens of smaller projects and assignments carried out in the region. A variety of scientific and geographic surveys were conducted, and a telephone system was built from Edmonton to Fairbanks and from Norman Wells to Whitehorse, providing a link from the North American communication network to a region that had previously relied entirely on telegraph and short-wave communication. Dozens of small generating plants were carted into isolated villages and camps throughout the region, providing them for the first time with electricity. A number of scientists—geographers, botanists, ethnographers— were permitted to carry out studies along the route of the highway, providing some fundamental knowledge of the region.

The projects, particularly the Alaska Highway, were well publicized during the war. They made great copy: Americans and Canadians, working together in the sub-Arctic, racing against time to protect the region against invaders. The fact that the setting was the same as the famous Klondike gold rush (or only a few hundred miles from it, which was close enough for southerners), added to the sense of drama and excitement. Numerous accounts, many written by army writers emphasizing the glamor and hardships of the task, and hinting at a new frontier in the postwar era, circulated

Table 6   Total Civilian Workforce, Canol Project Construction, 1942–44

Location and Types of Employees	Oct 1942	Mar 1943	Aug 1943	Jan 1944	Apr 1944
Crude Pipeline/Refinery					
Architects/engineers	59	132			
Contractors	100	1,499			
USED civilians	62	121			
Crude Pipeline					
Architects/engineers			204	194	164
Contractors			3,548	3,925	376
USED civilians			138	193	50
Whitehorse Refinery					
Architects/engineers			67	66	57
Contractors			1,486	1,136	1,331
USED civilians			38	76	40
Mackenzie River					
Architects/engineers			41	27	42
Contractors			327	567	330
USED civilians			35	70	76
Prince Rupert–Skagway–Whitehorse					
Architects/engineers		44	30	27	12
Contractors		494	649	395	78
USED civilians		10	23	0	15
Carcross-Watson Lake					
Architects/engineers		13	23	22	24
Contractors		88	853	221	64
USED civilians		10	15	15	19
Whitehorse-Fairbanks					
Architects/engineers	17	52	57	83	49
Contractors	15	324	2,112	872	87
USED civilians	22	41	79	114	20
Fairbanks-Tanana					
Architects/engineers		11	20		
Contractors		10	187		
USED civilians		13	22		
Oil production project					
Contractors		330	612	617	544
USED civilians		70	112	140	119
Marine operators					
Contractors				931	
USED civilians				87	

Continued

Table 6   *Continued*

Location and Types of Employees	Oct 1942	Mar 1943	Aug 1943	Jan 1944	Apr 1944
Grimshaw Road					
Architects/engineers			23	0	
Contractors			249	1,079	
USED civilians			14	88	
Canol composite					
Architects/engineers	208	284	419	379	270
Contractors	1,283	6,488	9,635	6,715	2,338
USED civilians	166	450	545	561	229

in the South, and culminated in the widely publicized opening ceremonies at Soldiers' Summit.

But not all the publicity was favorable. The losers in the battle
over the location of the highway continued to carp about it, and the
Canol Project was pilloried as an egregious example of wartime
stupidity. The criticism bore the sting of truth. Canol was a folly,
and was closed soon after it opened. The Alaska Highway, as the
U.S. military and Canadian officials had argued from the start, was
not of much use as a military supply road, and declined rapidly in
importance as the Japanese threat waned. The effect on the region
itself, however, was overlooked at the time and has not attracted
much attention since. The combined projects had involved a massive invasion of the Northwest, an invasion whose civilian and
military troops bore shovels instead of rifles and drove bulldozers
instead of tanks. They came by the thousands, initially mostly
soldiers, black and white, followed by civilian workers, largely
Americans, drawn northward by a mix of patriotism, adventure,
and the lure of high wages. They did not stay long—most of the
soldiers were gone by 1943 and the civilians the next year—but
they left a deep mark on a region that few of them had known about
two years earlier. History would judge the value of the projects,
but in the short term, the small and scattered population of the
Canadian Northwest was faced with an invasion rivaling that of the
gold rush.

3. The Native People and the Environment

HAD THE PROMOTERS of the Northwest defense projects paused to consider what effect they might have on the aboriginal people and the environment of the region, they would have painted a rosy picture. In the capitalist model of development, roads were the vanguard of progress. Native people had been held back from the benefits of progress by isolation; the road would bring good things to them, and make it possible for them to become better integrated into North American society. The region was rich in resources, which should be exploited for the advantage of all, and the Native people would benefit through jobs and the adoption of a more "civilized" way of life. As for the environment, it was there to be used—the trees to be cut down, the rivers to be bridged and dammed, the gravel and minerals to be taken from the ground, the game to be hunted for food and recreation. There were no conservationists among the projects' planners, and if there had been, they would have been ignored; as the cliché of that day put it, there was a war on, and what were a few trees and moose compared to the exigencies of continental defense?

No one, of course, asked the indigenous people of the Northwest what they thought about the Alaska Highway, or even told them in advance that it was coming. This was the way things had always been done. The Natives, whose ancestors had lived in the region for at least 8,000 years, had been compelled to adapt to successive waves of fur traders, miners, and administrators, and were now forced to cope with another invasion of their homelands. They would also experience an unprecedented assault on their land, as strangers tore a path through the countryside, blocking rivers, spilling oil, starting forest fires, shooting the wildlife, and generally attacking the fragile ecology of the sub-Arctic wilderness.

As outside scholars and the Native people themselves have shown, they are not and never have been the passive victims of such forces. They could adapt to change and in many cases make the best of it, seizing opportunities when they presented themselves. One option was simply to avoid the development corridor by moving elsewhere to continue working in the still-profitable fur-trading economy. Others, particularly women, took advantage of the employment possibilities the projects presented. Whichever option they chose, however, they all retained their deep attachment to the land, and continued to hunt, fish, and trap for sustenance. For many, the prewar pattern of a mixed economy remained intact, despite the many pressures put upon it.

The Native people of the Northwest had never been particularly averse to wage labor, though they had generally been unwilling to accept the limits and controls of the workplace—particularly on their time—for very long. Clifford Rogers, president of the White Pass and Yukon Railway, told Canadian journalist Gordon Sinclair that "the Indians were not a shiftless lot. They were strong, able and self-reliant, but the idea of working for a master made them turn up their snoots and drift into the bush."[1] But to the first contractors who arrived in the region in the spring of 1942, the Natives had a priceless asset—their knowledge of the terrain.

It was not surprising then that a number of contractors hired Native workers. Rogers, working with local people hired for their ability to manage Native workers, supervised the extension of the Whitehorse airport in 1941 as part of the Northwest Staging Route. His policy, unusual for that day, was that the Natives would receive the same pay as everyone else. To complaints that such a policy was "immoral, ridiculous, fantastic and all that stuff," Rogers replied, "Well, we won't have Jim Crow laws up here. If labor gets

$7.50 and labor is Indian, then Indian gets $7.50." A more common view of Native labor was reflected in the suggestion that their wages be held in trust for them so that they would not misuse or squander their money.[2]

For Gordon Sinclair, the peripatetic Toronto journalist who had made a national reputation for his colorful stories from faroff places, such sober common sense was not enough. He had come to the Yukon looking for the facile stories that had made him famous, and the kind of Indians he wanted were primitive and picturesque. He padded his copy with lengthy commentaries on how they had to be educated to spend their money, a problem solved, he claimed, when the women were introduced to silk stockings, girdles, and hairdressers, and the children to ice cream. He also commented on their insistence on being paid weekly, a demand he attributed to their fear of dying while being owed money.[3] All of this was rubbish: the Native people of the Yukon had been commercially active for half a century, and were well versed in the nuances of the market-place. The demand for weekly pay originated in the men's unwilling-ness to commit themselves to longer work terms, or was due to bad experiences with dishonest employers. Such shabby tales fed the public appetite for stories based on racist stereotypes of Indians as credulous savages, wondering at the marvels of ice cream and fancy clothing.

Sinclair was not the only journalist who wrote this sort of thing, however; most reporters saw the Native people of the Northwest as primitives whose sayings were cute and naive. Don Menzies, a staff reporter for the *Edmonton Journal,* began a story about the aboriginal people around Dawson Creek with the following: "Indians who have spent all their lives in northern British Columbia think the white man must be crazy. All they can say is a disgusted "ugh ugh," added to the usual "ugh."[4] Don MacDougall, who wrote an interesting and fairly accurate series of articles on the Alaska High-way for the same paper, adopted a droll tone when talking about Native people:

George Johnston, Thlinget [*sic*] Indian of the Teslin Bay band, thinks the Alaska highway is a fine idea. In 1933, George had a good year on his trap line and, with sudden affluence, decided on a purchase of an automobile. The car was shipped in by rail and water from the coast and landed at

Teslin Bay almost before George realized that cars require roads if they are to be operated with any degree of success. A little thing like that didn't dismay the husky George. He took up his axe and cleared out three miles of road . . . operated the car up and down his private road, charging his Indian friends for pleasure rides . . . when it is not being used in chasing wolves along the ice of frozen lakes and streams.[5]

The tone adopted in the press when writing about the blacks who were assigned to work in the region was much the same. An article in the *Edmonton Journal* entitled "Negroes on Alaska Highway Sing and Chant as They Labor" was full of stereotypes:

There are dark spots in the world coverage of the U.S. army today but they aren't ominous. They're the U.S. Army Negro Corps. . . . in London a big buck rolled his eyes over the scene and said "We sho' like it here." Now they've popped up on the Alaska highway adding their high tones to that already colorful project. . . . Light-hearted lads, heavy logs on their shoulders, come shuffling out of the brush to a red-hot vocalization of the "Chattanooga Choo-Choo."[6]

Examples of this sort could be quoted almost endlessly, but perhaps the prize might go to the writer who managed to combine black and Indian stereotypes in a single paragraph:

One place an Indian coming down his old pack trail met a cat[erpillar tractor] coming up. Just as he came into view the Negro operator rolled his old white eyes, shoved in the clutch and three jack pines flew into the air and rolled over the bank. The savage left and tarried not in the leaving. When he finally reached the trading post he was only able to gasp, "Big black devil him come!"[7]

Sporadic employment did not, however, prepare the Native people for the invasion that began in the spring of 1942. Many of them knew nothing about the construction projects until surveyors, or in some cases bulldozers, arrived in their communities. Virginia Smarch of Teslin recalled that a Carcross man visited their community with news of the building of the highway—an army battalion was moving cross country from Carcross to Teslin. They believed him, but still had trouble comprehending the scale or purpose of the project. Then the troops arrived in Teslin; the fact that they were blacks, the first most local people had ever seen, only added to their confusion and surprise.[8] Some of the most isolated aboriginal

Tent camp of the 18th Engineers headquarters at Whitehorse in a snowstorm, 4 May 1942. (YTA, Robert Hays Collection, 5692)

populations in Canada were, almost overnight, placed in direct contact with an American or Canadian construction workforce. Places like Fort Nelson, Liard, Aishihik, Snag, Watson Lake, Ross River, Burwash, Dezdeash, and nearby Klukshu, where the Natives lived almost exclusively off country produce and the proceeds from the sale of furs, suddenly had sizable non-Native populations.

Many Native people were employed in the early stages of the defense projects, but there was never any serious consideration given to making use of them over the long term, though the Canadian government was not opposed in principle to the idea. Some were hired by the U.S. Army and the Public Roads Administration (PRA) for the initial surveys and locating work, and Native guides and wranglers were invaluable in determining a route for the pioneer road in the early months of 1942.[9] But such work only confirmed the perception that their skills were "Native"—that is, their knowledge of the land and their ability to live off it. Beyond that, the stereotypes which portrayed them as indolent and unreliable prevented any real effort to integrate them into the civilian work crews.

Nonetheless, the seasonal employment the projects brought to the Northwest was important to its Native people. In some areas, particularly northern Alberta, the upper Mackenzie River valley and the Whitehorse-Carcross region, they had long played an important role in the transportation industry. They worked as laborers on the riverboats, cut wood for sale, and helped load and unload the vessels. They were accustomed to seasonal employment, generally in the summer, when there was little hunting and trapping to be done. For several generations the Natives of the region had mixed a harvesting and a wage economy, and the Northwest defense projects continued this pattern. After the army of occupation arrived, Native workers were employed unloading and loading trains, barges, and trucks; continued to serve as guides and packers; and found additional occasional work around some of the camps. In other regions the situation was different; along the British Columbia portions of the Alaska Highway, where there had been little contact between the Native people and the wage economy, they were seldom employed on the defense projects. Non-Natives working in northern British Columbia reported almost no contact with the local indigenous population, in contrast to those who served in the western Yukon, or in the Athabasca–Fort Smith area of the Northwest Territories.

The military and civilian workers also created an instant market for Native handicrafts, and one in which demand quickly exceeded supply. One surveyor, working near Burwash Landing, noted that "Natives would make caribou coats, muklucks, moccasins, caps, etc. decorated with sequins with very reasonable prices as we went north. On the way back though, prices had gone way up. They learned fast."[10] J. E. Gibben, the Indian agent in the Yukon, tried to encourage Native women to cash in on the handicraft market, but with mixed results. He had trouble getting the necessary supplies, especially beads, and found the idea hampered by a generation gap: "It appears that most of the work is done by the older women and it seems difficult to interest the younger generation in their traditional handicraft." But there was money to be made: the women of Moosehide, just downriver from Dawson City, grossed over $1,300 from the sale of one consignment of handicrafts to Whitehorse.[11]

The defense projects also created a number of openings for Natives in occupations not directly related to military work. The high wages paid in the construction camps drew dozens of non-Native workers from their jobs in the region, leaving openings in the retail, hotel, transportation, and mining sectors. This led some employers to consider (often for the first time) hiring Native labor as replacements. In the Dawson area, the Yukon Consolidated Gold Corporation, faced with a major labor shortage, hired indigenous workers from the area for the first time in its history. The Natives answered one of the company's concerns; they were not as mobile as non-Native workers and were not likely to go south to seek jobs with the construction companies. The company managers found that the Natives could easily handle the work given to them, but that they were "undependable." That is, they would not give up the traditional hunting part of their way of life for permanent wage labor. At the end of the war, J. E. Gibben observed, "I have endeavoured at all times to induce the Indians to become self-sustaining, but regret that I do not see much progress in this regard."[12]

Many of the workers who arrived in the Northwest in 1942 had never met or rarely seen Native people, and were willing to believe stories about them based on racial stereotypes and misconceptions. Nearly fifty years after the event, some of the workers described them as awe-struck by the white man's technology. Stories recounting Native surprise at everything from binoculars, photography, and doorknobs are commonplace: "We ran across some that had never seen a motor vehicle or been in a town. They came wandering into camp and were trying to open the door to the mess hall. I guess they hadn't seen a door handle and didn't know you had to turn it."[13]

One man who spent eighteen months working on the southern part of the highway reported only a single contact with the local Natives, which "occurred at the Beaton River Bridge. A group of 12–15 natives, 2–3 males on horseback with the women, children and dogs following on foot, stopped at the bridge. The males dismounted and approached the concrete structure. They felt the concrete, tapped it and evidently discussed the product. After a short while they mounted and continued on southward."[14]

In the short term, most of the Native people of the Northwest remained hunters and trappers. While time and a postwar slump in fur markets would later undermine the viability of this way of life, fur prices remained high throughout the war years, providing an alternative to wage labour on the construction projects.[15] The Canadian government recognized the importance of hunting and trapping in the lives of these people, particularly since the activities prevented the Natives from becoming a charge on the public purse.[16] The governments of British Columbia and the Yukon agreed with this view, and demonstrated flexibility in enforcing regulations on Natives who hunted back and forth across the territorial-provincial boundary.[17]

Arguably the worst effect of the invasion of workers was the diseases they brought with them. Native people across North America had always been vulnerable to "virgin soil epidemics"— imported diseases for which they had no natural immunity. Many times before 1940 isolated Native bands had been exposed to a new illness, often following the arrival of a stranger in their midst. The disease would usually spread rapidly, affecting particularly the elderly, the weak, and the very young; no one knew how many, since statistics were not kept, and medical care was limited or unavailable. Despite these waves of sickness, which had swept the region for over 100 years before the workers arrived, many Natives still had little immunity to their diseases, and the results of an invasion of newcomers were truly devastating.

J. F. Marchand, a doctor stationed at Teslin in the winter of 1942–43, noted that the community had in the space of less than a year suffered outbreaks of measles, dysentery, jaundice, whooping cough, mumps, and meningococcic meningitis.[18] David Johnson, a resident of Teslin working as a guide for an army survey crew, arrived home to find that the entire village was sealed off and his children were seriously ill. Ignoring the quarantine, he returned to his family and soon became sick himself.[19]

C. K. LeCapelain, Canadian liaison officer with the defense projects, painted a sad picture of the situation:

The Indians of the Teslin and Lower Post bands until the advent of this new era, have been almost completely isolated from contacts with white people and have had the least opportunity of creating an immunity to white

"The Whole Family Camped at the Beat[t]on, Alaska Highway." No
adult men appear in the picture. (Anchorage Museum of History and
Art, B84.82.4.51)

peoples' diseases. Consequently they have been distressingly affected by
the new contacts. No doubt a contributing factor has been the fact that to
a considerable extent the adult males have abandoned their normal nomadic
pursuits and have accepted work on various construction projects, both
American and Canadian.

The band of Teslin suffered epidemics of measles and whooping cough,
which in some cases developed into pneumonia, last year, and now are
plagued with an epidemic of meningitis and have suffered three deaths so
far from the latter. The bands at Lower Post were devastated last spring
with an epidemic of influenza which caused 15 deaths among a total population of about 150 of all ages. There is no doubt in my mind that if events
are allowed to drift along at will, but what the Indian bands at Teslin and
Lower Post will become completely decimated within the next four years.
The problem is how to prevent this, or at least to ameliorate conditions
as far as possible.[20]

At one point, 128 of the 135 residents of Teslin were sick with
measles. St. Philip's Anglican Mission school and church were used
as a hospital, and patients were cared for by army doctors and
RCMP constables, and later by two nurses sent from Whitehorse.
Bessie Johnston, a young Tlingit woman from the community,
assisted with the care of her people, helping with the cooking and
cleaning for sixty patients in the makeshift hospital while also caring

for her parents at home. Having worked herself to exhaustion, Bessie herself caught measles, lapsed into a coma, and died within twenty-four hours.[21]

Because reporting was so spotty, it is hard to assess the full impact of the epidemics that swept the Northwest during the construction period. John Honigman, an anthropologist working among the Native people near Fort Nelson, reported that the diseases had not appeared there.[22] At Watson Lake, 300 miles to the north, a major influenza outbreak occurred in April 1942, affecting a large number of whites as well as many Indians.[23] Perhaps the previous length of contact between the races had something to do with the difference; in the Mackenzie valley, where aboriginal people had been in regular contact with non-Natives since the early nineteenth century, there were fewer major outbreaks of epidemic diseases. Even here, though, the arrival of thousands of outsiders brought illness and suffering. In October 1942, a government official at Fort Norman reported, "Fewer Indians were seen during this month but at month's end word from Willow Lake had it that they were all very sick with influenza."[24] Along the Canol route, particularly at the isolated trading post of Ross River, the arrival of U.S. troops touched off major outbreaks of diphtheria. A local Native woman who had had some training as a nurse tried to treat the ailment, but several parents, terrified by the illness, would not let her near their children. Those unattended died; most of the others lived.[25]

The medical officers serving with the U.S. Army in the Northwest, and to a lesser extent the civilian contractors, gave what medical assistance they could to the Native people. Their aid was welcomed, though there was a brief squabble when the Yukon Territorial Council debated barring American doctors from treating Canadian patients. It was the military doctors, for example, who imposed the quarantine on Teslin, and who tended the sick there. In 1943, Dr. Lucey of the U.S. Army cared for the sick during an influenza epidemic at Watson Lake. He provided the RCMP with sulfa drugs, aspirin, and a thermometer for visits to the bush camps, for there was illness there too. A constable reported from one camp:

Most of the sick are up and around now but of course are extremely weak. Mrs. L—— T—— was found laying out on the snow and her husband, L—— T—— was persuaded to build a bunk of spruce logs and cover it with spruce boughs and cover her with blankets. Patrol remained at the camp until this was done. All are well supplied with food and cannot be suffering in any way for want of eatables.[26]

While the military and civilian doctors provided care freely to the indigenous population, one of their goals was to keep the epidemics from reaching the non-Native population, an effort that was largely successful. In 1943, the medical officer for the Whitehorse area reported that

the health of troops and civilian employees within the Post area during the past year has continued to be satisfactory. There have not been any serious epidemics, nor have any of the diseases endemic among the local Indians affected our troops. On the contrary, several epidemics of communicable diseases appeared among the Indians which they had apparently never before experienced. This was attributed by an investigator of the USPHS [U.S. Public Health Service] to the influx of outside contacts (carriers), both civil and military.[27]

Though it is difficult to be precise, what figures are available show that the diseases brought in by the construction workers led to a serious, though short-term, demographic crisis among the Native people of the Northwest. In 1942 deaths outnumbered births by nineteen, and by fifteen in 1943, among the Natives of the Yukon. By 1947 the trend was reversed; in that year births outnumbered deaths by forty-nine, and in 1948 by thirty-nine. It is also likely that the enumerators missed many deaths due to disease, especially among infants, when they occurred in the bush, where many Native families had retreated in an attempt to escape the invasion and the illness that accompanied it.[28]

The presence of American doctors cast a light into some of the darker corners of the Canadian Northwest. Elizabeth Carswell, a Canadian nurse working in a U.S. medical dispensary in the Lower Post district, contrasted the work of the Americans among the Native people with the Canadian neglect of them:

The work of the R.C.M.P. is greatly to be admired—but they get no support. They go to endless trouble tracking down a grapevine rumor of a sick Indian, unmindful of personal comfort or hazardous weather. But, although they are expected to care for illnesses found, they are allowed to keep no medicines on hand and each time an emergency arises are obliged to wait precious days until the necessary drugs are sent. This delay sometimes adds up to one more dead Indian. . . .

Another case involved a 30-mile trip by dog team to tend a woman acutely ill of pneumonia. To feed the hungry mouths of some 12 Indians, we found in that cabin one can of milk, some macaroni, a few prunes, a little tea. The R.C.M.P.'s wire to Whitehorse for permission to transport the patient up the 300 miles of highway to the nearest hospital, after a three-day wait, brought a reply in this vein: "Symptoms you describe are those common to 'flu. Do not bring patient in unless condition becomes worse." The woman is living today because the American army furnished life-saving sulfadiozine and American contractors contributed good meat, fresh vegetables and milk for the whole family.[29]

Though disease and death were perhaps the most dramatic marks left on the Native people by the invasion, there was also much official concern that the contact between them and the invaders would be harmful to them and might also hamper the construction projects by introducing an element of disorder into the camps. For both reasons efforts were made to keep the races separate. Official orders declared off-limits "all houses, tents, buildings, or shelters, owned, occupied, or used by Indians or mixed breeds regardless of the blood percentage," but such regulations were hard to enforce, particularly away from the major centers.[30]

The common ground for contact between the workers and the Native people was all too often alcohol. Until 1960, Canadian Indians were forbidden by law to possess or drink alcoholic beverages. This regulation, aimed at keeping Native people away from the worst features of white society, had the opposite effect. Natives looking for alcohol had to seek it out in the lowest levels of society, at the hands of bootleggers, or they could make homebrew.[31] There had always been a lively market in illegal liquor in the Northwest, but the influx of thousands of single, often hard-drinking men into the region changed the dynamics of alcohol consumption in the region.

In recognition of the unique conditions in the Yukon and Northwest Territories, liquor and beer were not as strictly rationed there as in the provinces during the war, though the distribution machinery proved inadequate for the influx of workers. Interminable lines at the liquor stores were a notable feature of wartime life in the region. Native people who wanted commercially manufactured liquor had to buy it from some non-Native person, and it generally

A "Texas oilman" inspecting the Canol pipeline, June 1943. The trees were bulldozed, and the pipe laid directly on the bare ground. (NAC, Harry Rowed/National Film Board photo, PA-174542)

came at a high price. The penalty for bootlegging or supplying liquor to registered Indians—a stiff fine and a prison sentence—was reflected in the price paid by the consumer. Much Native drinking took place at parties (often referred to in press accounts as "drinking parties") where the main purpose was for everyone to get as drunk as possible—just the sort of situation the government had passed laws to prevent. In such a setting the price of liquor was often sex rather than money—a pattern familiar enough in the North. John Honigman observed this pattern often, particularly among truck drivers, who had numerous contacts along the highway and the means of bringing in liquor from the South.[32]

The government was determined to check this situation, and to punish offenders of both races. To this end, it moved members of the RCMP from the territorial headquarters in Dawson to Whitehorse, and in 1944 moved the headquarters there as well. The increased number of police officers in the southern Yukon resulted in increased convictions, but did little to solve the problem (see table 7).

The arrival of the troops had increased the amount rather than the nature of interracial drinking. The authorities, particularly in the southern Yukon and the upper Mackenzie basin, tended to view the problem as an "Indian" one, and concentrated on trying to keep alcohol out of Native hands—a reflection of North American stereotypes of the aboriginal weakness for liquor—but without much success. The Native people who wanted to drink found willing suppliers in bootleggers and in men from the construction crews looking for money or sex in the Native camps.

Despite the popular mythology of the Northwest defense projects, accepted by most Natives and non-Natives in the region, the highway and the other defense projects dramatically affected the Natives' world, but did not overturn it. There were of course some serious dislocations, particularly the suffering and death resulting

Table 7   Native Alcohol-related Convictions and Police Manpower, Southern Yukon, 1940–49

Year	Convictions	Police Force
1940	3	4
1941	9	4
1942	28	4
1943	27	15
1944	34	25
1945	51	25
1946	75	30
1947	82	27
1948	61	21
1949	55(32)[a]	22

SOURCE: NAC, RG 18, Whitehorse Police Court Register.
NOTE: Convictions include those for supplying, possession, drunkenness, and breaches of Indian Act.
[a]Records to July 1949; 55 equals rate of convictions projected over the entire year.

from contagious diseases. But during the war, trapping and hunting remained the cornerstone of Native life throughout the region. When Natives took jobs for wages with the construction companies, they did so for periods that suited their seasonal way of life. The main impact of the projects on the hunting way of life was that the new roads made it easier to get to once inaccessible hunting and fishing sites. On the other hand, the disruption of construction work and hunting by work crews drove much of the game far from the roads, affecting traditional hunting patterns.

What really changed the lives of the Northwest's Native people were two postwar developments that had nothing to do with the construction projects. In 1947 the North American fur trade went into a prolonged slump that undermined the commercial viability of an industry that had been the cornerstone of the Native economy for over a century. Even more important was the advent of the Canadian welfare state. During and after the war the Canadian government abandoned its traditional laissez-faire policy towards its citizens—it was inhumane, and did not sell well at election time—and began to pour a cornucopia of benefits upon them, targeting Native people for special attention. The first gift was the Family Allowance, popularly called the baby bonus, a monthly grant given to all parents of children under the age of sixteen. But government cornucopias come with strings attached, and these severely altered the Natives' way of life in the Northwest. Native people in the Yukon and Northwest Territories got the baby bonus in kind rather than in cash, which gave the government the right to interfere in their purchasing habits. Though the original grant was only $5 to $8 per month, a family with eight children would get about $50, a sum not to be sneered at in a cash-poor subsistence economy. Other programs followed, many of them with conditions: compulsory education, pensions, housing projects, employment schemes, and relocation of Native people to residential reserves.

These programs really struck at the core of aboriginal life and forced fundamental, painful changes in the nature of Native society in the region. But because bulldozers are easier to comprehend than bureaucrats, especially distant ones, many Native people continue to regard the projects as the cause of the transformation of their way of life. Their place in the historical consciousness of the indigenous people of the Canadian Northwest was shown over thirty years later, when plans for pipelines across the North became the focus of aboriginal hostility.[33]

Years later, the two Canadian pipeline inquiries—the Berger Commission and the Lysyk Commission[34]—demonstrated the fear among the region's Native people of megaprojects imposed upon them from the outside. Several witnesses for the Berger Commission testified that the Alaska Highway and Canol Project had devastated their communities, and said that they opposed the pipeline on the grounds that it was likely to do the same thing.

The two commissions also focused on another vital aspect of northern construction—environmental impact. Even in the 1970s, little was known about the impact of heavy construction on the fragile sub-Arctic, a fact that highlights the even greater ignorance of the engineers who worked in the Northwest in the early 1940s. Then, the highway and pipeline builders had virtually no experience in dealing with muskeg and permafrost, nor had they much information on rainfall, ice movement, snow packs, soil types, and other basic geological and climatological information. The kind of environmental impact studies that were to become the norm in the 1970s were undreamed of in the early 1940s. There was no information available, for example, on how to contain oil spills in sub-Arctic conditions, nor any real sense of the impact such environmental disasters would have on the region—nor was there much concern when the spills occurred. Little thought was given to the effect of construction activities on fish and wildlife. The projects, in short, took place in a general state of ecological unconsciousness, in which planners knew little about the area they were "developing," and gave scant thought to the long-term environmental impact of their activities.

This ignorance and lack of concern are reflected in the historical documentation. It is difficult to assess precisely the damage wrought by the builders, since few scientists visited the Northwest during the war to record the ruin of creeks and rivers, the erosion of hillsides, the disturbance of wildlife migrations, and other damage to the environment. After the war the scientists did come, and the studies they conducted in the 1950s were to become the bedrock of knowledge about the sub-Arctic ecosystem. The engineers should not be held wholly to blame, since they were sent to a region they knew nothing about, and were ordered to do a difficult job with maximum speed; concern for their surroundings was not part of their mandate.

It is clear, however, that the massive construction projects did much harm to the Northwest's environment. Some of the most dramatic damage involved the regions where permafrost was found. Here, as elsewhere, the overburden was ripped off with bulldozers; when the season warmed, the permafrost melted and the roadway turned to thick mud. Land wounded in this fashion took decades to heal, and building roads and pipelines across it was a massive challenge. This problem and others were solved by trial and error, often by adopting or rediscovering techniques that had been pioneered during the gold rush forty years earlier. These experiments left even more scars across the land—scars regarded at the time as the inevitable results of progress and victory in war. And after all, where were the builders to go for advice? The Alaskans knew little more than the southerners, the Scandinavians were cut off by war, and to ask the Soviet Union—an ally, but still the hated bastion of communism—was unthinkable, even if the Soviets had had a reputation for being helpful.

Probably the most immediate and wide-ranging damage caused by the construction projects came from the many forest fires that swept the region during the war years. The occupying forces furnished a potent combination of incendiary elements: widespread cigarette smoking, notably among truck drivers, who often threw their butts and matches into the ditches as they drove; portable sawmills that produced large quantities of sawdust; poor storage of oil and gasoline products; heavy equipment, such as welding gear, that produced heat and sparks; poorly organized fire-fighting plans; and a general attitude that the forest was limitless and the task urgent. Clearing the highway right-of-way left large piles of slash along the routes—tinder ready to be touched off by smokers or a variety of other causes.[35] So many fires were started by carelessness that the U.S. Army launched a prevention campaign; a directive from the summer of 1943 prohibited "throwing of lighted material of any kind from motor vehicles." Efforts were also made to clear up slash piles and flammable wastes located near camps and maintenance yards.

Some of the fires started by the army of occupation were large enough to destroy thousands of acres of forest. When U.S. troops first arrived in the Fort Smith area, for example, a number of forest fires soon broke out, caused by soldiers setting smoky fires in an attempt to keep the mosquitoes at bay. Several of these fires combined to become a large, uncontrollable blaze, burning through moss and muskeg for months. The troops seemed indifferent to the damage they were causing; one man who was fighting a fire in June 1943 passed a small group of U.S. soldiers sitting around a small campfire. When he returned a few minutes later, the fire had gotten out of control and was 75 feet in diameter. A small group of volunteers fought hard to keep the fire from reaching the Roman Catholic mission near Fort Smith. After working for hours on a fire break, they found to their dismay that some of the Americans had left smudge fires burning behind them, rendering their efforts useless. Much of the mission property and hundreds of acres of timber were destroyed before the fire burned itself out. Official indifference appeared to favor a policy of "let[ting] the country burn, it's no good anyway, and with that attitude in view fire suppression is a hard job indeed."[36]

Rather uncharacteristically, the Canadians actually took the Americans to task on the subject of fires. Commenting after the war, R. A. Gibson, director of the Canadian Lands, Parks, and Forest Branch, wrote, "You will remember the difficulty which we had with the United States Army before we finally had a show down with the American authorities here. . . . All we asked the Americans was that they should put out the fires that they started."[37] The Americans responded by ordering their military personnel to put out fires they had started and to "co-operate to a reasonable extent in fighting fires in the country tributary to the highway."[38] As with so many aspects of the invasion, rumors about fire damage, some true, some wildly exaggerated, circulated in and outside the Northwest. In the fall of 1943, a story reached Ottawa that a series of deliberately set fires had destroyed huge stretches of timber around Kluane Lake. RCMP officers who patrolled the

"Moose Shot at Camp #2." (Anchorage Museum of History and Art, B84.82.4.61)

region reported the facts, which were that many small fires had indeed been started along the construction corridors, but that most had quickly been brought under control.[39]

Fire was not the only threat to the forests of the Northwest, for there was a tremendous demand for wood to be used for heating, building construction, bridges, telephone and telegraph poles, and temporary bridges. A number of sawmills were hastily set up near the main communities and construction camps to supply the demand. By the fall of 1943 there were about sixty cutters working in the forest, supplying at least fourteen sawmills in the region. The appetite of the construction projects for cordwood was tremendous; the RCAF operations at Whitehorse alone required 10,000 cords of wood, and at Watson Lake 8,000 cords for the heating season, a combined total representing a pile 4 feet high, 4 feet wide, and more than 27 miles long. A Canadian official observed that "it does not take much of a mathematician to figure out the effects in denuding the country of timber over a period of years, and this is not half of the total requirements."[40]

Little could be done about the cutting of timber, since the original agreement that set the projects in motion had guaranteed the Americans free access to whatever natural resources they needed; Canadian officials, while recognizing this fact, nonetheless felt "we have a right to expect that conservation principles will not be violated."[41] Their objectives were minimal: they hoped that the military and civilian contractors would cut timber so as "not to impair the scenery or cause hazard to the stand any more than is absolutely necessary," but there was little they could do to make this wish a reality.[42] Towards the end of the war, many of the camps were converted from wood to oil-stove heat, with the result that thousands of cords of wood were abandoned near the camps. An estimate in August 1945 was that 8,000 cords, cut into 16-foot lengths, remained in the bush, presenting a fire hazard. Local residents were urged to make use of this timber, but few did so.[43]

The matter of timber did raise the whole question of conservation in the Northwest, a region where the issue had never been given much thought. C. K. LeCapelain, the Canadian liaison officer, remarked that "up to the present moment there have been no conservation thoughts in the timber cutting regulations. These were concerned principally with collecting revenues and not with conservation." He thought that the war was not a good time to initiate conservation measures, since they would be difficult to enforce on the contractors, but he did recommend that a timber inspector be hired to survey timber use in the Northwest, particularly with a view to fire prevention. For the present, he recommended, "If we can adequately protect the scenic values and beauty spots along the Canadian Alaskan Military Highway from spoilation we should be satisfied for the present."[44]

The same attitude, that little could be done while the war was on, also prevailed on the subject of wildlife preservation. Areas along the highway and pipeline corridors, particularly near the camps, were often badly overhunted, and the noise and construction also drove animals from traditional habitats.[45] One result was that by the end of 1942, the Natives were reporting severe shortages of game in some areas. Observers differed on the actual size of the losses; some suggested that the stocks had not been depleted at all, but that the animals were avoiding the construction corridors; others, like Joe Jacquot, argued that in some areas the game was all but wiped out:

With this influx of activity, game moved away from the highway. It was rare indeed if a Moose crossed the highway and if it did it would not hang around long. If it wasn't scared off by the noise it more than likely would be shot and many times left to rot. There was an attitude of "Don't give a damn," probably because of the war and the fact that the soldiers were constantly rotated and had very little recreation facilities. . . . Fishing holes and many spawning grounds in the rivers were dynamited and ruined never to be used again, by people who didn't give a damn. In many cases the fish weren't even picked up. It was a horrible waste. In our Trading Post we would not sell any ammunition to non-residents or people that we knew would waste the game.[46]

The Canadian government did not want to upset the pace of construction, or to annoy the Americans. The Canadian and Yukon policy was to permit the visiting U.S. forces to purchase residents' hunting licenses in the Territory, a privilege not granted to nonresident Americans in Alaska for another year. The policy was different in the Northwest Territories; there the game resources, which were much sparser than in the Yukon and Alaska, were reserved exclusively for the Native population.

There was a particular problem in the southwest corner of the Yukon, an area noted for its game, especially the Dall sheep. Hunting pressure, and the American decision to set aside a large section of southeast Alaska for a game preserve, convinced the Canadian government to establish a new game preserve west of the Alaska Highway and the Haines Road. The idea was proposed by C. K. LeCapelain in September 1942:

Almost all along the highway the scenery is lovely and the views along some of the lakes for instance are beautiful but they can be duplicated in many other areas in Canada. That stretch of the road running from Bear Creek, a tributary of the Dezdeash River to the White River in southwestern Yukon offers something that you cannot get anywhere else in Canada; a view of the St. Elias Mountains containing the largest glaciers and highest mountain peaks in Canada. Therefore, I respectfully suggest that the areas . . . bounded on the east by the Alsek River, on the north by the Canadian-Alaskan Highway and White River and west and south by the Alaska Boundary be reserved for consideration as a National Park. This area is well-known for its big game including White Bighorn Sheep (Ovis Dalli), mountain goat, Osborne caribou, moose and grizzly bear.[47]

His advice was adopted, and the Kluane game preserve was established that same year. The local Native people, who were not consulted, found themselves barred from an area they had relied on for generations. Fortunately for them, however, the boundaries were not enforced at first, permitting a local guide, Eugene Jacquot, to continue taking hunting parties into the area. A year after the sanctuary had been designated, a police officer traveling through the area reported, "Most men in the various construction camps do not know they are in a game preserve," a statement that reveals the difficulty of enforcing regulations.[48] Signs identifying the game preserve were posted along the Haines Road and Alaska Highway, but the hunting restrictions remained difficult to police.[49] The move was nevertheless a preliminary step in the eventual creation of the Kluane National Park (later named a UNESCO World Heritage Site). An additional result was to deprive the local residents, particularly those from Burwash Landing, of a rich and valuable hunting area. In 1946 they petitioned the government for redress, but to no avail:

It is not the Indians that are a threat to the game and fur trade of the country, but it is them that are punished. Before the whites came in this country, game and fur were abundant although the Indians were in much greater number than they are today. . . . Hunting and trapping are our only resources—the whites have a thousand ways of earning money for a living. . . . We have no objection to the development of the country, on the condition however that we be left free to live and develop ourselves also.[50]

In the first year of construction, most of the workers were too busy to hunt more than a short distance from the construction sites, areas the game avoided.[51] In 1943, however, most of the military and civilian workers were able to take several days off to go on extended hunting trips. Though regulations governed the possession and use of firearms, generally no one was around to enforce them, and there were reports of the wanton destruction of game. One man working on the Canol pipeline reported a number of incidents and claimed that "there are guns in every camp killing everything from the smallest to the largest. . . . The soldiers kill anything. What are your people going to do. Stand by and see your game destroyed? It hurt a lot of us to see these trusting animals killed."[52]

There were already three large game preserves in the Northwest Territories (out of the way of the projects), and there was much debate in Canadian official circles on the advisability of establishing others in the Northwest Territories and in the Yukon. LeCapelain, after an informal survey of game resources in northern British Columbia and the Yukon, wrote in 1942, "I seem to be coming to the point of recommending no sanctuaries or preserves in the Yukon, other than the possible National Park and, probably a game sanctuary in northern British Columbia along the Liard River or rather in the mountains south of the Liard River to preserve the band of elk in that area."[53] But Kluane remained the only preserve set up during the war.

Wartime hunting eventually became part of the mythology of the Alaska Highway, along with the stories of millions of dollars' worth of wrecked and abandoned equipment. Numerous stories circulated based on the Americans' alleged desire to shoot anything that moved, using everything from heavy machine guns to pearl-handled revolvers. One long-time Whitehorse resident remembered that "the Americans shot everything in sight, from Whitehorse to Lake Laberge."[54] The Native people of the Northwest unanimously reported disruptions of the local game supplies. In contrast, Robert McCandless argues in his history of wildlife use in the Yukon that most reports of overhunting were exaggerated, and that disruptions were comparatively slight.[55]

Four young Native men, photographed somewhere in northern British Columbia during highway construction. (Anchorage Museum of History and Art, B84.82.4.52)

The reality lies somewhere between official wartime assurances that hunting activity had slight impact and the folklore legends of Americans strafing moose and caribou from fighter planes, leaving hundreds of carcasses abandoned in the bush. The Americans did hunt—some with permission, others without—and were enthusiastic about the prospect of having fresh meat to eat. One Oregonian even proposed an organized game hunt to feed military and civilian workers.[56] One man who served as an officer with the 93rd Engineers (a black regiment), recollected how "we would shoot game when we could until the RCMP got on us. We were supposed to get a licence or something before we did it but they didn't really bother us. But eventually we scared all the game away from the road so we didn't get that much, but we did shoot caribou, mostly if we could see anything . . . not really that much."[57] There were also incidents of simple foolishness:

I happened to be driving and [they said] "Jim, stop the car. There's a moose." I stopped and they jumped out and the two of them ran down to where that moose was supposed to go in. They got down there and they saw something move and they shot it. And the first thing I knew they come running out and they said "Get out of here." I said, "Well, what about the moose?" "It wasn't a moose, it was a farmer's cow." . . . He came down and told our company commander. . . . So, we had to pay for the cow. But the farmer wanted to keep the cow. We say no. . . . So we went out and got the cow and brought it home and hung it out in the cooler.[58]

There were areas where overhunting did take place, particularly in the sheep-hunting areas of the southwest Yukon. It is true that game became scarce throughout the construction corridors, though it did return after the building was finished. Canadian officials at the time usually discounted the stories about American overhunting. C. K. LeCapelain, who knew as much about what was going on as any Canadian, acknowledged early in 1943 that there had been considerable unregulated hunting, but agreed with the B.C. Game Commission, which did "not feel such killing to be excessive."[59] In some cases the killing was for the protection of the workers, particularly in the summer of 1942, when bears became a nuisance around the highway camps:

We first noticed them hanging around our abandoned camps in the rear, which they found good pickings because of the garbage pits, which they raided. Not satisfied with this, they then started visiting our forward camps, particularly the small ones occupied by men at watering points and small guard detachments. Here they became quite bold, entering men's tents in search of food, ripping open barracks bags, and causing confusion generally. It has become so bad that Col. Ingall had finally, and reluctantly, given men permission to shoot bears that come into camp, as the only way of preventing some one from getting mangled. It seems a shame, they are such friendly harmless seeming animals. We have had to shoot a number already, and the score undoubtedly will grow, as they seem to be having their national convention at our expense.[60]

Only a small percentage of the army of occupation had the time, the equipment, the permission, or the bush skills to hunt in the region. A greater number, however, brought their fishing tackle north with them. Most of the construction camps were located near lakes or rivers, where lake trout, grayling, pike, and other species provided ample rewards for fishermen. In short order much of the water near the camps was overfished, resulting in a serious depletion of stocks and reducing the supply available to local residents who depended heavily on this resource.

The idea that the Northwest was bursting with exploitable natural resources attracted a number of would-be developers, people who hoped to cash in on the easier access to the wilderness. One American proposed hunting along the highway for the commercial market. A company from Saskatoon asked for commercial fishing licenses for the area; the owner planned to catch fish in lakes such as Teslin and Swan Lake, now accessible via the Alaska Highway, sell all he could to construction workers, and market the surplus in Canadian cities.[61] Yukon member of Parliament George Black opposed the project on the grounds that such commercial operations would soon exhaust the resource. Canadian government officials agreed, believing that the resource should be used by the Natives of the region. The RCMP in Whitehorse estimated that it had received nearly 100 inquiries about commercial fishing licenses in 1942–43, a sure sign of the high prices and the demand for fish. The police believed that the northern lakes were already being fished close to capacity and could not tolerate large-scale commercial operations. Inspector H. H. Cronkite of the Whitehorse detachment proposed tough new restrictions on commercial and private fishing, leaving only Native fishing rights intact.[62]

In fact, many of the region's lakes and rivers had not been fully exploited before the war, and when the highway workers went fishing, they were rewarded with large catches and many trophy fish, particularly in northern British Columbia and the southern Yukon. As a result, fishing trips rank among the happiest memories of many members of the army of occupation. Over time, however, the waters close to the highway suffered as a result of fishing pressure. Once-rich streams became much less productive, a matter of only passing concern to the transient workers, but a serious problem to the local people who depended on the resource. Eventually the fish stocks increased again, but much more slowly than in southern waters, where there was more food and where the fish reproduced and grew at a faster rate.

As well as the dramatic environmental problems, like forest fires and depletion of wildlife stock, there were hundreds of small incidents of injury to the environment. Although both the Canadian and U.S. governments were at pains to reassure the public that controls were in place, the projects were so vast and diverse that effective policing or pollution control was all but impossible. There were hundreds of incidents like the following: A man driving a fuel truck arrived at his destination to find that storage tanks were nonexistent. Having fulfilled his mission, and under orders to be back at the refinery at a certain time, he simply dumped the fuel on the ground and drove off. Similarly, bridge construction proceeded with little care for the fish in the rivers; careless work by bulldozers disrupted the riverbeds and spawning activities, and eradicated the fish life in some of the smaller streams. Joe Jacquot described how spilled oil harmed the environment in the 1950s; the same kind of thing happened during the war:

When the line was cut the fuel ran into pockets and disappeared. Some went into peat bogs that acted as a large sponge. When the spring breakup came and the spring run-off was in effect, fuel flowed not only into the lakes but into the streams. The migratory birds heading north at this time became unknown victims. The muskrat and beaver died. Some of those lakes still don't have rat houses on them. Up until about 4 years ago [1972] the people couldn't eat the fish in Swede Johnson Creek because they tasted of fuel oil.[63]

Some of the smaller companies were inexcusably careless with their effluent. One witness lodged a complaint in August 1943 against Foley Brothers' Camp on Kathleen Creek, claiming that "the toilet is built over the stream. Not thirty feet below this I have seen several taking out big catches of fish and eating them." She also claimed that a sawmill company was dumping large quantities of sawdust into Miller Creek. The police officers who investigated reported that the larger camps avoided such obvious problems, but that "smaller, disorganized units, of a temporary nature," were more likely to pollute the waters near their establishments.[64]

These events took place in a time of national crisis, and one in which the North American conservation movement, though active, was not yet the powerful political force it is today. Nevertheless, they did not pass without comment, and sometimes protest. The news accounts of highway and pipeline work, which often gave brief comments on environmental matters, raised serious questions about the impact of construction activity. Reports of overhunting, particularly in the picturesque southwest corner of the Yukon, resulted in a number of written protests, in which outsiders, even those with little direct knowledge of the region, expressed their concerns to the Canadian government.[65] In the fall of 1942, Ira Gabrielson, a member of the U.S. Fish and Wildlife Service, reported stories "that United States soldiers in Yukon kill large numbers of big game animals unlawfully, and take large numbers of fish with dynamite." He expressed the hope that Canadian agencies were taking "corrective measures" to "stop this destructive waste of wildlife."[66] The response to Gabrielson's inquiry reveals a great deal about Canadian attitudes to game in the area. Acknowledging that the Americans "varied their fare with a certain amount of wild meat," Gibson concluded:

We have not been greatly worried about serious depletion of the game resources because not many of the men showed a disposition to wander very far away from the right-of-way of the road and some numerous stories were told of the unfortunate experiences of some who went hunting and got lost for days at a time. However, we must admit that we have not the full information we should have about the game situation in the country tributary to the road and we must take steps to remedy this situation.[67]

Gabrielson's inquiry bounced around the Canadian and American civil services for several months, leading to considerable discussion as to how the hunting activity might be regulated.[68]

Gabrielson continued his efforts to publicize the lack of protection for wildlife in the Northwest, expressing concern that the Porcupine caribou herd would be overhunted by Natives eager to capitalize on the market for meat in the area.[69] He was particularly anxious to warn Americans that Alaska was not "a land teeming with unlimited quantities of big game," and was worried that the new roads and airfields would open the region to an influx of population that would crowd out the wildlife. In public lectures and press releases, he argued for new game reserves and more game wardens. Most important, he argued:

In order to place the management of the wildlife resources on a permanent basis of self-perpetuation it will be necessary to change the concepts of the people of Alaska and of most of the people who are going to Alaska, regarding the extent to which wildlife may be utilized. Only by successfully changing the popular viewpoint may we maintain Alaska as the source of the most valuable salmon fishery in the world, as the home of the greatest

Three black soldiers and two white civilian workers constructing log buildings for the Canol Project in the NWT, 11 May 1943. The man in the foreground has acquired a hooded deerskin jacket, probably from a local Native. (NAC, R. S. Finnie photo, PA-175984)

bird colonies in the country, and as the last reservoir of the great game herds to be found under the American flag.[70]

Gabrielson was supported in his campaign by P. J. Hoffmaster, the president of the International Association of Game, Fish, and Conservation Commissioners, who, alarmed by the construction of the Whitehorse oil refinery, asked R. A. Gibson for assurance that the refinery effluent would not damage the local wildlife. Gibson replied that "the subject will be kept under active observation and review and that the design and operation of this refinery will include all provisions necessary to avoid harmful pollution of the Lewes River."[71] Fortunately for Whitehorse, the refinery did not operate long enough for its effluent to become a serious problem.

These questions, particularly when raised by foreigners, tapped a vein of guilt in Canada. The national and regional governments had to face the fact that they knew next to nothing about the environment of the Northwest and that they were relying for what they did know on pioneering work done by the Geological Survey of Canada.[72] During the war, they began to make up for this neglect by taking advantage of the new transportation facilities to send a number of scientists into the region, where few had ventured before 1941.[73] In 1943, Dr. A. L. Rand of the National Museum of Canada conducted the first major survey of mammal and bird life along the Alaska Highway.[74] In the same year, Hugh Raup of Harvard University's Arnold Arboretum led a small team on a survey of soil and flora conditions along the highway, with particular attention to the prospects for gardening and agriculture.[75] In 1944 Rand and A. E. Porsild traveled into the Mackenzie Mountains, using the Canol Road to reach an area that had previously been inaccessible to scientists, and Dr. W. A. Clemens of the University of British Columbia conducted a biological survey of the province's northern waters on behalf of the British Columbia fisheries department, "with special reference to the new Canadian Alaska Highway."[76] The same year, Dr. C. H. D. Clarke of the Lands, Parks and Forest Branch, with T. M. Shortt of the Royal Ontario Museum of Zoology, received permits to collect specimens of mammals and nonmigratory birds along the Alaska Highway and in Kluane National Park.[77]

Perhaps the most important result of this activity was that it forced a reassessment of one of the Northwest's most durable myths—that it contained limitless wildlife resources ready for exploitation. The scientific studies showed how fragile the region's ecosystem was, how vulnerable to damage and overharvesting. In the last years of the war and the postwar period, the ethic of conservation appeared in the Northwest, marked by the establishment of the Yukon Fish and Game Association, the banning of the commercial sale of wild meat in 1947, and other measures designed to bring northern wildlife practices into line with those of the rest of the continent. In this way—and with disregard for the needs and way of life of the Natives and other long-time residents—the frontier relationship between the people and the environment began to break down. Over the next decade the Canadian government accelerated the process, urging the Native people to move off the land, regulating hunting and fishing, and changing the relationship of people and the environment from one based on consumption to one based on recreational use and the conservation of dwindling game stocks.[78]

By 1945 the Canadian government was also reconsidering its policy towards the Native people of the Northwest. For decades it had believed that they were "best left as Indians," and did little to try to integrate them into the national economy and society. Just as northern wildlife practices were brought into line with national standards, so the government began to draw the Native people into a complex web of national programs, a process that began with the introduction of the Family Allowance in 1945 and accelerated rapidly thereafter. By the mid-1950s the Native people of the Canadian Northwest were being drawn into the provincial and territorial educational systems and encouraged to integrate as much as possible into Canadian society. The wartime projects did not initiate this process, which proved painful and difficult for many of the people it was supposed to benefit—the postwar welfare state and changed attitudes towards Natives did that—but the construction of highways and airfields made it much easier for the government to impose a new agenda upon its Native clients.[79]

The U.S. invasion of the Northwest had a dramatic effect on the two constants in the region: the ecology and the Native people. The people were ravaged by epidemics, displaced by construction activity, abused in some cases by outsiders, and forced to compete with them for dwindling resources. In some areas, notably northern British Columbia, the Natives avoided the construction areas, and played only a small part in the wartime activities. In other places, especially the southern Yukon and the upper Mackenzie valley, some Native people found jobs, mostly casual and unskilled. Throughout the region the greater availability of alcohol, sexual relations with non-Natives (see chapter 5), and increased involvement with the legal system (largely through the enforcement of discriminatory regulations on alcohol use) disrupted the equilibrium of Native life in a way unmatched since the Klondike gold rush. Much the same was true of the northern environment. Forest fires ravaged large areas, destroying timber and wildlife habitat. The outsiders damaged streams, polluted the land, and put severe pressure on fish and game stocks.

Native life, and the environment on which it was based, were severely strained by the arrival of tens of thousands of southerners. Although many of those who came to the region in 1942 did not stay long, the mark they left on the land and its people proved to be permanent. The challenges to Native life in the region, and the threat to the sub-Arctic environment, both of which hit new peaks during the war, would gather strength over the next decades. The disruptions of the war proved to be a beginning (in the Yukon, a second beginning), not an end of this process.

4. Law and Order in the Occupied Northwest

BEFORE WORLD WAR II, law enforcement in the Canadian Northwest was handled mainly by the Royal Canadian Mounted Police, which had jurisdiction over northern Alberta, the Yukon, and the Northwest Territories. The British Columbia Provincial Police enforced the law in the northern part of that province. Most of the police detachments were in Native communities, where the officers not only enforced the law, but also served as the representatives of all the government departments; in remote areas the mounted police took the census, served as health officers, distributed welfare, and in general served as the contact between government and people. The mounted police interpreted as well as enforced the law (as all police forces do); in the Northwest, serious cases were dealt with swiftly and firmly, but minor offenses were often ignored.[1] The police were rather slow to react to the American invasion. In 1942 the Whitehorse detachment had only three members, increased to seven in the next year. The RCMP's Yukon headquarters was in Dawson City, where it had been since 1896, and it remained there after construction began far to the south. It was not until 1943 that police gradually moved the center of their operations to Whitehorse (see table 8).

The arrival of tens of thousands of American soldiers and civilians

Table 8   Strength of the RCMP in the Northwest, 1940–44

Location	1940	1942	1943	1944
Yukon				
Dawson	11	12	12	3
Granville	1	1	1	—
Mayo	1	1	1	1
Old Crow	2	2	3	3
Selkirk	1	1	2	1
Teslin	1	1	2	3
Carcross	—	—	2	2
Burwash	—	—	2	—
Kluane	—	—	—	1
Watson Lake	—	—	2	2
Whitehorse	3	3	7	17
Total	20	21	34	33
NWT and Northern Alberta (selected communities)				
Fort Smith	6	7	11	11
Fort Good Hope	1	2	2	2
Fort Norman	3	2	5	2
Port Radium	2	—	1	1
Rae	2	3	4	3
Reliance	3	3	3	4
Resolution	3	3	5	3
Yellowknife	2	3	2	1
Norman Wells	—	—	—	1
Camp Canol	—	—	—	1(1945)
Edmonton	149	163	156	128
Athabasca	1	1	1	1
Fort McMurray	1	2	3	2
Peace River	11	11	10	9
Slave Lake	—	2	1	1

SOURCE: Canada, *Report of the RCMP*, 1940–1944, statistics for March 31 of each
year.

in the Canadian Northwest posed a tremendous number of administrative and legal problems. Would the soldiers come under the
jurisdiction of their own military authorities—that is, would Canada
grant extraterritoriality to the U.S. troops, as Britain and other
countries did during the war? More important, how could such a

large number of people, scattered throughout a relative empty land, be kept under some sort of control? A suggestion came from an observation made by a lawyer working for the U.S. Northwest Service Command (NWSC): "In times of war, jurisdictional powers ordinarily dormant in peace times must often be exercised. Such an emergency now confronts the American armed forces, in Canada."[2]

The arrival of the defense workers also brought dramatic changes to the nature of law enforcement in the region. The number of offenses increased beyond the capacity of the local police to deal with them. Because of the overlapping jurisdictions it is difficult to be precise about the number of crimes committed in the Northwest during the war, but it is clear that the crime rate did increase (see table 9).

The American military brought their own police with them—

Table 9   Charges laid by B.C. Provincial Police for various offenses in Peace River Subdivision (Pouce Coupe, Dawson Creek, and Fort St. John), 1940–45

Offense	1940	1941	1942	1943	1944	1945
Theft	9	2	1	20	39	38
Carrying weapons	4	1	2	3	1	1
Obstructing police	—	—	3	7	—	5
Vagrancy	11	7	10	61	44	33
Furious driving	4	4	9	16	6	11
Assault, common,	9	6	9	17	15	10
bodily harm	1	1	1	1	6	5
Disorderly house, gambling	—	—	1	111	81	—
Receiving stolen goods	2	2	2	8	21	5
Govt. liquor act	3	11	39	238	159	82
Motor vehicle act	13	11	53	31	76	95

SOURCE: British Columbia, *Report of the Commissioner of the Provincial Police . . . and Inspector of Gaols* (Victoria, 1941–46).
NOTE: The charge of vagrancy was commonly laid against women suspected of being prostitutes, since it was easier to prove in court than prostitution. The table does not include offenses committed by military personnel, since these were handled by the Americans. Nor does it include offenses for which only one or two charges were brought.

the tough, no-nonsense MPs, who were particularly effective in controlling activities on military bases.[3] At first, policing was somewhat haphazard, but by 1943 substantial numbers of military police were stationed in the region. In February 1943 Colonel K. Bush recommended that an MP Company of 5 officers and 200 men be sent to Edmonton, of which one platoon would be sent on to Dawson Creek. These would police American activities in Edmonton, the southern part of the highway, and the trains bringing supplies and personnel to the Northwest.[4] The presence in the Northwest of units of the RCAF provost marshall's office and the U.S. Air Corps Military Police complicated the question of jurisdiction, and frequent meetings of people from all these agencies were necessary to keep relations smooth.[5]

Of all the aspects of Canadian-American activities in the North west during the war, the question of legal jurisdiction was perhaps the most troubled, since law enforcement is such an obvious sign of sovereignty, and quarrels in this area can take on nationalistic significance. The U.S. authorities insisted that their troops be answerable only to American military law, which meant not only that small offenses could not be tried in a Canadian court, but that even very serious ones, such as rape or murder, were beyond the jurisdiction of Canadians. This meant, to take an extreme case, that an American soldier who raped or murdered a Canadian civilian on Canadian soil was answerable only to an American court. This was a situation that could be understood in a conquered country like postwar Japan or Germany, but one that required some swallowing on the part of a friendly country. Nevertheless, Canada did swallow it, though not in a single gulp.

Surprisingly, the question of who should have jurisdiction over crimes committed by U.S. troops in Canada was not discussed at the time the defense projects were being planned.[6] It was not until April 1942 that the subject was first considered by the Permanent Joint Board on Defence, though no action was taken at the time. The Canadian government had already taken the step, in April 1941, of issuing the "Foreign Forces Order, 1941," which provided for "limited exercise of jurisdiction in Canada by forces of certain designated countries," and this was made applicable to the United States at the end of June 1942.[7] This order gave American military courts power in Canada to deal with all offenses except murder, manslaughter, and rape, which remained entirely under Canadian control. It also stated that the Canadian courts "retained concurrent jurisdiction over offenses committed by U.S. military personnel against any law in force in Canada."[8] The Americans pressed their case for increased power on Canadian soil—for concurrent jurisdiction in murder, rape, and manslaughter—a case that was strengthened by the fact that they were at the same time negotiating an agreement along those lines with Great Britain. In July 1942 Canada agreed to this as well. The United States then requested complete criminal jurisdiction over its military personnel serving in Canada. By a Privy Council order of December 20, 1943, the Canadian government granted this request; as of that date the U.S. military courts had "jurisdiction to try all members of its forces in Canada in respect of every offense committed by any of its members in Canada."[9] Since all American civilians working in the Northwest were also subject to military law, this meant that the great majority of those who worked on the defense projects in the region fell outside the jurisdiction of the Canadian courts. Canadian civilians working on American projects could also be arrested by the U.S. Military Police, and in theory tried by U.S. military courts, though in practice they were turned over to Canadian courts for prosecution. The only right the Americans did not claim was the authority to arrest Canadians who did not work for the projects, except those who "may be apprehended only under general rules pertaining to arrests by private individuals."[10]

The rules as they applied to civilians working in the Northwest were summarized in a U.S. War Department General Order of July 1943:

1. Regardless of citizenship, civilian employees of the United States Government, or of contractors, working under and in physical proximity to the United States Army, including those United States citizens in the above categories discharged from their employment who are awaiting transportation to the United States, are persons accompanying or serving with the armies in the field and are subject to military law and discipline under

Article of War 2 (d) and triable by general and inferior courts-martial . . .

2. As a matter of policy, Commanding Officers will turn over civilian employees of Canadian citizenship to Canadian authorities for trial unless such authorities expressly waive jurisdiction.

3. Other civilian employees, regardless of citizenship, subject to the Articles of War, will be held and tried by Courts-Martial unless Canadian authorities insist upon their delivery for trial.

4. Requests by Commanding Officers to Canadian authorities for delivery of civilians, regardless of citizenship, except Canadians, for trial by Courts-Martial will be made but not insisted upon.

5. In cases of requests by Canadian authorities for delivery of military personnel as defined by Article of War 2 (a) to them for trial, such requests will be submitted to this headquarters by the most expeditious means practicable, the authority requesting such delivery being advised of such action and the individual retained in United States Military custody pending decision.[11]

Canadian nationalists who recoil in horror at such a loss of sovereignty often forget that such arrangements were common in other allied countries, and in fact the United States passed legislation extending similar privileges to Canadian troops (though not civilians) stationed in the United States—of course, there were not many of these.

Within this legal framework, the authorities in the Canadian Northwest worked out their own arrangements, sometimes informal ones. Minor offenses, like drunkenness and fighting, were quite often dealt with informally, without any charges being laid. And in practice the lines of jurisdiction were often blurred, as Canadian and U.S. authorities cooperated to bring what was sometimes ad hoc justice to the region.

The fact that American civilians working on the defense projects—even those who had left their jobs but remained in Canada—were subject to military law gave the authorities an unusual degree of control over their workforce. Lieutenant Colonel T. J. Hayes, district engineer, observed, "Generally, it would not be considered desirable to resort to court martial in case of offenses but if this office has authority to notify employees they are subject to military law and, in particular, to Article of War 89, a very desirable control would be thus attained over contractors' personnel."[12] Civilian workers could not be charged with offenses that were purely military in nature, such as mutiny, and they could be turned over to the Canadian civilian authorities if the crime and situation seemed to warrant doing so. In addition, the military had the right to garnishee the wages of any civilian sentenced to pay a fine.

The reaction of Canadians to this state of affairs varied with the individual. Some adopted the old argument that an honest person had nothing to fear from the law: the commissioner of the B.C. Provincial Police argued that the regulations were "no more restrictive to the average citizen than is the law of Canada. Decent people, behaving decently, would never know [they] existed."[13] The Canadian government had reservations about accepting this extension of U.S. authority over civilian personnel working on Canadian soil. While not conceding the legal right for the U.S. government to exercise this authority, Ottawa was prepared, as a matter of policy, to allow this system to operate. "It was a different matter," an External Affairs memo noted, "in the case of locally hired employees or persons who are not United States citizens," although even here Canadian authorities were reluctant to press their case too far.[14]

The rationale for extending military law to the civilians was simply that the end justified the means: "where the security of our forces and the accomplishment of our mission are threatened such measures should be taken with relation to apprehension, trial and punishment of civilian offenders as may then and there be necessary to assure success of our operations.[15]

As this and other statements make clear, the legal system was to a degree an adjunct of the overall management structure in the Northwest, helping to keep the workers dedicated to the work at hand. That the private contractors saw the advantage of this arrangement is clear from the fact that they all seem to have accepted it without complaint.[16]

This judicial structure consisted of General Courts-Martial, established by the Service commander, and Special Courts-Martial and Summary Courts-Martial, appointed by post or camp command-

Lining up in the snow outside the Government Liquor Store in White-horse, winter 1942–43. (YTA, Preston Collection, 85/78, #68)

ers.[17] In August 1944, there were General Courts in Whitehorse and Edmonton, plus Special Summary Courts established by each commanding officer.[18] The system was flexible, permitting post commanders to establish courts when needed, and did not require a large permanent legal apparatus.

It is not easy to characterize the administration of justice on the Northwest defense projects. The system changed during the war as the Americans assumed more control over it, there was much local variation, and the clash of jurisdictions—U.S., Canadian, provincial, territorial—sometimes led to confusion. This was particularly true when "concurrent jurisdiction" was involved. In many instances the authorities cooperated and matters went smoothly, but at other times there was conflict. The provincial governments of British Columbia and Alberta in particular resented the loss of provincial authority over legal matters. In the fall of 1942 a rape case in Alberta involving an American serviceman brought a protest from Lucien Maynard, the province's attorney general. The case had dragged on, with Canadian federal and U.S. authorities unable to decide what should be done. In a meeting with an American lawyer, Maynard demanded to know when officials would reach a decision, afraid that "the Provincial Government [would be put] in a position where the people of the Province felt their Government was negligent."[19]

The idea of shared legal responsibility through concurrent jurisdiction might have seemed fine in theory, but it caused problems in practice. Alberta's deputy attorney general complained that the U.S. military's legal system was too different from Canadian criminal law for the two to harmonize effectively. The U.S. military caused endless delays, did not have the proper charges in the code to cover the range of offenses committed in the Northwest, operated under different rules of evidence, and had very different penalties than did the Canadians for the same offenses. Under U.S. military law, the maximum penalty for rape was death; in Alberta the offense carried a five- to ten-year sentence. The Alberta official also noted that "it is contrary to the well established principles of criminal law that an accused person should be placed in jeopardy twice for the same offense which is the situation under our present arrangement." He requested preliminary consultations on all such cases, with the suspect liable to only one legal system.[20]

Another irritant was the Canadian suspicion that the Americans were not taking offenses seriously enough. Late in 1943 a series of incidents occurred in which the offenders, American service personnel, were arrested by the U.S. Military Police and either were spirited out of the country before proceedings could begin or were tried by military courts and given sentences that were considered far too lenient.[21] In one instance, a man tried for rape on strong evidence was convicted instead of the much lesser offense of giving liquor to a minor. After a series of confrontations over the matter, Canadian officials in December 1943 declared their intention to force the issue by holding the next American charged with a major offense.[22] The Americans responded by making an effort to remind the troops that they were guests in a foreign country, suggesting more recreation and athletic activity as antidotes to the impulses that led to rape, and calling their attention to the "ill effects of such offenses upon [the] reputation and interests of the United States."[23]

These events occurred during the period when Canadians and Americans had concurrent jurisdiction over much of the law enforcement in the Northwest, and when the Americans were pressing for complete power in this area. The compromise of concurrent jurisdiction pleased neither country, and means were sought to resolve the situation.[24] In the spring of 1943 the matter was put before the Supreme Court of Canada, but the five justices who considered the case gave four different opinions, and the question finally was solved by the Canadians giving the Americans everything they wanted.[25]

There was criticism of this move, particularly from Alberta, which charged that it would deprive Canadians of some of "the protection of Canadian law and Canadian courts, and subject them to American military law and the administration of U.S. courts-martial" in cases where members of the U.S. forces committed offenses against Canadians or their property.[26] Special commissioner Major-General W. W. Foster dismissed Maynard's complaints as "cheap politics"; the U.S. consul in Edmonton commented that "it is considered good political strategy in this part of Canada to bait the Dominion Government on every occasion."[27] Whatever the political ramifications of this decision may have been, the practical effect was to establish parallel legal systems in the Canadian Northwest, one for U.S. soldiers and civilians and Canadian civilians working for Americans, and the other for the rest of the population.

American citizens resident in the region who were not working for the military or one of the defense contractors fell, of course, under Canadian civil jurisdiction. When such people found themselves in trouble with the law, their interests were cared for by the U.S. consular service in Edmonton. When, for example, an American waitress working in Dawson Creek was charged in January 1944 with murdering her husband, she was arrested by the Provincial Police and arraigned in a provincial court. The consular office found a lawyer for her and arranged to have an American official present at the hearing. It was necessary to do this, "since the Service Command had accorded a like privilege to Provincial officers where trials concerning Canadian citizens took place before military courts."[28]

No agreement, however amicable, could eliminate all the difficulties that were bound to arise in a situation where two parallel legal systems existed, and it was difficult for the Canadian police to accept the fact in practice that Americans working on the defense projects were beyond the reach of Canadian courts (after December 1943; before that date the matter could be negotiated), even if they accepted it in principle. It galled the RCMP and the Provincial Police to have the power to arrest a suspect off his base, but then to have to turn him over to the American authorities, though in such situations, Canadian authorities were permitted to have an observer at the trial.[29] If an American soldier reached the sanctuary of a U.S. military establishment, Canadian requests to surrender him were firmly but politely denied. However, the Americans gave guarantees that if prima facie evidence of a crime was presented, the suspect would be arrested and tried by court-martial. American civilian workers faced a curious kind of double jeopardy; they could be tried under either Canadian or American law, depending on how the authorities decided to dispose of the case.

The existence of several police forces, a dual court system, and a confusing system of complementary and overlapping jurisdictions did not necessarily mean that the Northwest was in any sense a police state. There was a degree of tolerance, a willingness to accept certain forms of behavior that would not have been acceptable in more settled areas. The occasional incident of binge drinking was winked at and even tacitly encouraged in the camps, so long as it did not become endemic, but drunks who publicly misbehaved in Whitehorse or any other town could expect quick punishment.

Perhaps the most remarkable feature of the system of justice in the Northwest was its flexibility. Before the Canadians and Americans had agreed on division of legal responsibilities, and even after, police and other legal officials had problems in deciding who should enforce what law, and on whom. A case at Camp Canol in the Northwest Territories in the summer of 1943 is an example of the operational flexibility of justice in the Northwest. An American civilian worker assaulted another man, giving him a bad beating.

Under the Canadian-American agreement then in place, the man should have been charged before a U.S. court-martial, but the Americans chose not to proceed in that fashion. The accused, who had a previous conviction for sodomy, was unpopular in the camp, so the U.S. authorities turned him over to the Canadians, who brought him before Dr. J. P. Harvey, justice of the peace at Fort Norman, for arraignment.[30] Another example is the case of Eugene Patterson, a civilian working for the U.S. Army, who was charged in October 1944 with the murder by stabbing of Lester Cieluch, a resident of Whitehorse. This case took place after the Americans had won exclusive jurisdiction over such matters, and Patterson was arraigned in Whitehorse before a General Court-Martial of five American officers. He was, however, defended by a Canadian civilian—George Black, the Yukon's member of Parliament, whose experience with courts-martial consisted of a series of Canadian cases after World War I. Patterson was found guilty of the lesser charge of manslaughter and received a ten-year sentence.[31]

Most residents of the Northwest were not interested in the complications of a joint legal system. What rubbed them the wrong way was the substantial and sometimes aggressive presence of the U.S. Military Police in their country. The MPs seemed to be everywhere—controlling line-ups in the liquor store, patrolling the streets, and asking politely or not so politely for identification from drivers who were proceeding on innocent errands, minding their own business. A minor refrain of the war in the Northwest was the question, "Just whose country is this, anyway?"

One of many examples of the friction that could arise involved a man named T. H. Callahan, a Canadian working for the R. Melville Smith construction company in Fort St. John. While driving on the highway in the fall of 1943 he was stopped by the military police and charged with exceeding the speed limit. Over his protests he was taken to a U.S. Summary Court in Dawson Creek, where he was ordered to pay a $10 fine. To make things worse, his attempt to pay the fine in Canadian dollars was rejected; he was told to pay in American money, or failing that, to pay $11 Canadian. (The Canadian dollar was worth a good deal less than the U.S. dollar during the war.) Callahan paid, again under protest, and went to complain to the Provincial Police; he found them "much insensed [*sic*] over the authority which these United States military police have taken upon themselves."[32] Nonetheless, no formal protest was made. Many American soldiers also disliked the MPs, of course. One man characterized them emphatically nearly fifty years later as "HORSE'S BUTTS"; the RCMP, on the other hand, he believed were "fine, professional people."[33]

Incidents of conflict between the U.S. Military Police and Canadian civilians seem to have taken place quite frequently, though most of them were fairly minor. C. K. LeCapelain visited Dawson Creek in the summer of 1943 and reported ten incidents that had occurred in just over a month, indicating, he said, "a regrettably strained situation." Among them were the following: In July 1943 a Canadian police corporal and two constables, all in uniform, were stopped by the U.S. MPs, told they were speeding, and ordered to report to military police headquarters, which they did not do. In the same month a suspected bootlegger was arrested by the MPs for trying to sell liquor to them. He stated he had not done so, but had been beaten and clubbed by the police and had been taken to their headquarters where he was again beaten. On July 1, the Canadian national holiday, Provincial Police Constable J. Gunn stopped his car on the provincial highway about two miles from Pouce Coupe and then drove it off the side of the highway while he spoke to a friend. He then was checked, reprimanded, and insulted by a U.S. Military Highway Patrol officer who stated, "As long as we are controlling these highways law and order is going to be kept." A local resident who drove his car to the top of a hill on a country side road near the town in the evening in order to improve his radio reception, was challenged by a U.S. MP, who told him to move on. The bridge superintendent for one of the construction companies arrived in Dawson Creek from the Liard River not knowing of the increased activities of the U.S. Military Police. He borrowed a light delivery truck, the property of the U.S. government, to pick up a suit from the cleaners. While he was in the store, an MP entered and demanded to know what he was doing there. Taken by surprise, he asked what it was all about, upon which the soldier manhandled him, arrested him, and took him to Military Police headquarters where, he claimed, he was beaten with a club,

Black troops of the U.S. Army Corps of Engineers building a bridge over Goose Creek, twelve miles north of Teslin, Yukon. (Anchorage Museum of History and Art, B62.X.15.6)

called "yellow," and told he should be in the army. On August 10, the head electrical engineer for the R. M. Smith Co., stopped his truck outside the Alaska Restaurant in Dawson Creek and went inside. While there he noticed through the window an MP searching his truck. He went outside to see what was going on and noticed a pair of gloves was missing from the cab. He mentioned this to the soldier, who thereupon grabbed him by the throat, threw him around, and said "Don't you accuse me of stealing you Son of a Bitch." On July 29, ten restaurants in Dawson Creek were placed "out of bounds" for all U.S. Army personnel and civilian contractors' employees, owing to their dirty and unsanitary condition. Most of them were tidied up and placed back in bounds. When the ban was placed on these restaurants, military police pickets were posted at the doors and anyone attempting to enter was asked for proof of identity. This led to much resentment and a very explosive situation; many customers simply brushed the soldiers aside and walked in. "The chief complaint seems to be and, I believe it is justified, in the manner in which a few soldiers carried out their instruction, behaving somewhat in the manner of bullying thugs."[34]

The most notorious case of American bullying of civilians took place in Whitehorse in January 1945. A group of MPs stopped a car driven by Dr. Franks, a local dentist. He and the other people in the car were forced out, manhandled, and placed under arrest. Both the women in the car sustained slight injuries. When the men protested, they "were told that if they didn't get into the car they'd be shot." Eventually they were released and went to the RCMP detachment to complain. While they were there, a young Canadian civilian, George Klinck, was brought in unconscious, his face bruised and bloodied. No charges were laid against any of the Canadians. Protesting the "injustice," George Black wrote, "It is patent that the conduct, if as described, was that of thugs and gangsters, amounted to criminal assault and those responsible for it should forthwith be tried by Court Martial." This case was too flagrant to be ignored, and the officer in charge of the detachment of MPs at the time was disciplined for "disobedience of standing orders and for inefficiency." Apologies were offered to the people involved in the incident. Nonetheless, Black was informed that the Americans were "exempt from prosecution by Canadian authorities for criminal acts committed while in Canada." Black was not mollified, and continued to protest, on one occasion referring to the "U.S. Army Gestapo . . . still being obnoxious," but to no avail.[35] He and others would grumble about American insensitivity and aggressiveness until the final military police officer of the army of occupation left the Yukon in 1946. In fairness it should be added that not all the complaints about the U.S. Military Police were valid. In March 1944, two MPs stopped a car being driven erratically along the Alaska Highway. When the police questioned the driver, his wife and the other passengers bombarded them with abusive language; the wife called them "scum." Reporting on the incident, the sergeant in command of the local RCMP detachment commented, "Our relations with the U.S. Army 254th Military Police Company here have been excellent, and I have found all of their men to be courteous and efficient. Very close cooperation is maintained between this Det. and the Military Police, and the system has worked very well to date."[36]

On some levels there was a good deal of cooperation with the MPs. A basic fact of law enforcement in the Northwest was that despite jurisdictional disputes, the Canadian and American police were more allies than competitors—in fact, as Major-General Foster commented in reply to C. K. LeCapelain's list of irritants, the Canadians had asked the Americans to increase the strength of their police in northern British Columbia to "control what was felt by the . . . authorities to be a serious menace."[37] Although the official policy was that the military police could not arrest civilians, the RCMP found the MPs very helpful in assisting it with some of its cases. One Canadian official praised them for their helpfulness: "It is well known that in various parts of northwest Canada American Military Police work in very close and harmonious cooperation with Canadian civil police and that on numerous occasions American MP's have simply offered their friendly assistance to the Canadian police in maintaining civil law and order. The civilians picked up by the American MP's are promptly turned over to the civil police."[38] Others suggested that local businesses welcomed the assistance of the military police in helping to maintain public order. In the case of crowds waiting to get into the liquor stores, for instance, "ninety percent of those concerned are Americans and if the M.P.s were not present half of the customers would never be served—a fruitful cause of irritation and fights." Police Commissioner Parsons commented on the situation in northern British Columbia: "On the whole police are doing very well, and although 40,000 people have passed through the area during the past 18 months—there has not been a single murder and only some 4 or 5 assaults upon women— all dealt with. Almost if not quite a world record?"[39]

Given the circumstances of the war, the police found themselves with a diverse range of tasks. Canadian and U.S. agencies readily exchanged information and conducted joint investigations into people applying for jobs where security was sensitive, those reported to have made unpatriotic comments, and those of questionable ideological viewpoints. Smuggling was a perennial problem. The police were convinced that most of the smugglers and bootleggers in the Northwest were civilians, though the soldiers provided an eager market for their wares.[40] Customs investigations were frequent, and the searches often uncovered contraband. Many of the smuggling offenses were minor ones, such as sending post exchange (PX) supplies home through the mail, and penalties were small. The Northwest provided almost unlimited opportunities for theft and pilfering; there was so much material lying about, and records of supplies were so poorly kept, that it was impossible to prevent the disappearance of tools, equipment, and other materials. Although little could be done to control petty theft, the authorities acted quickly to investigate reports of large-scale criminal rings. One rumor concerned a ring supposedly formed at the end of the war to exploit large caches of abandoned construction supplies; the ring was said to use a concealed detour, which permitted its members to bypass highway checkpoints.[41]

The greatest problem facing the police in the Northwest, however, was the control of alcohol. The use and misuse of liquor disturbed the authorities for several reasons: bootlegging defrauded the Canadian treasury; drunkenness harmed productivity and the war effort and posed the possibility of social disorder; and bootlegging rings might bring organized crime to the region. Cases involving liquor were numerous; liquor offenses outstripped all other forms of illegal behavior in the Northwest during the war years. The official attitude towards the consumption of beer and liquor by military and civilian workers was ambivalent. On the one hand, it posed dangers, but on the other it could, if controlled, provide a useful form of recreation. Since the workers were denied most of life's pleasures, it might benefit them and the projects if they were able to let off steam once in a while. This was the reasoning behind the more or less officially sanctioned "beer bust," a periodic feature of camp life, in which large quantities of beer were brought in and everyone got drunk. In retrospect it sounds rather dispiriting, but it was considered therapeutic at the time. What the authorities would not permit was unsanctioned drinking, which is why public drunkenness, particularly in permanent civilian communities, and the supplying of liquor to Indians were swiftly and severely punished.

One factor controlling drinking in the Northwest was the shortage of alcohol. Though neither the Yukon nor the Northwest Territories were subject to the formal wartime liquor rationing in force in the Canadian provinces, difficulties of supply and transport meant that stocks were never sufficient to meet the demand, and quotas had to be introduced. These, however, were much more generous than those in the provinces. At first, the Yukon liquor stores were allocated 300 bottles of spirits per day, and each customer was permitted to buy one bottle, with no limit on the purchase of wine and beer. (The Canadian liquor bottle of that premetric day was called the "26er"; it held 26 imperial ounces or somewhat more than the American quart.) In the Northwest Territories the limit was one bottle per day to a monthly maximum of 165 ounces; two bottles of wine could be purchased per day, but only ten per month. A case of beer could be bought each day, but not on the same day as spirits were bought.[42] Residents of British Columbia had a much smaller quota: 40 ounces of liquor, 1 gallon of wine, and 12 pints of beer per month; the figures for Alberta were 25 ounces, half a gallon, and 12 pints. But these generous allotments were too much for the supplies, and the limits had to be reduced on several occasions;[43] eventually the ration in Alberta was 13 ounces of spirits, 1 bottle of wine, and 12 pints of beer per month. Such were some of the byzantine regulations that governed the consumption of alcohol in Canada two generations ago.

Other restrictions were imposed as well. In an attempt to curb the booming black market in liquor, officials in the Yukon began issuing liquor permits, a system already in existence in some of the provinces.[44] The idea was to make sure that no customer exceeded the quota, but the result was to increase the length of the lines in front of the liquor stores. As George Jeckell noted, "We find out that the patronage of Liquor Stores has greatly increased since the introduction of rationing. Many many people who were never known to enter a Liquor Store now have individual permits and appear to get the maximum quantity."[45] The permit system did not end bootlegging, but rather democratized it, as nondrinkers realized the profit to be made in obtaining and reselling their liquor allotment. In 1943 it was estimated that $15 worth of liquor (three bottles at 1943 prices) bought in Pouce Coupe could be sold in Dawson Creek for over $100.[46] One man reported being offered $100 for a "mickey" of liquor (a bottle holding 13 imperial ounces, worth about $2 in 1942) in Dawson Creek.[47] Though wages were high in the North, the fact that a bottle of liquor could bring such prices—two days' wages or more—shows how strong the demand was. Liquor permits were often sold on the black market; one man was found carrying fourteen of them. In Fort Smith in 1942, a local resident, known to be a nondrinker, was found purchasing liquor at the local store and reselling it to American soldiers. He was charged and convicted, and put on an interdiction list for two years.[48]

The U.S. authorities lent a hand in the control effort by requiring each permit holder to have his permit authorized by his immediate superior; civilians working under the authority of U.S. law had to appear before the provost marshall at Edmonton, Dawson Creek, Fort Smith, or Whitehorse for authorization. There the American men had to produce draft cards, the women Social Security cards, and Canadians their Registration Certificates before the permits were issued.[49]

The main factor keeping the price of bootleg liquor high was the fact that supply fell so short of demand.[50] Under the terms of the Wartime Alcohol Beverages Order of 1942, the Yukon's allotment for 1942–43 was based on shipments of liquor to the Territory between November 1941 and October 1942. Given the tremendous increase in population in the region in the spring of 1942, this amount was hopelessly inadequate. Thus black market prices rose, and homebrew appeared in the camps and civilian settlements.[51] The price of a bottle of "hooch" was $25, about half the cost of smuggled commercial spirits.[52]

Shipments of alcohol were regularly pilfered, particularly on the railroad between Skagway and Whitehorse.[53] Truck drivers on the highway were in a good position to profit from the black market, and the temptation to do so was great: secret compartments on trucks could easily hold ten bottles, bought for $50 and retailed for $1,000. Some entrepreneurs hollowed out loaves of bread and hid small bottles in them. One of the primary functions of the checkpoints on the Alaska Highway was to check for illegally transported liquor. Pilots and their crews, particularly those working for civilian companies, were also able to earn extra money smuggling liquor.[54] There was also a certain amount of small-scale bootlegging for

Special efforts were made to rescue this truck, which had come to grief in the Tahkini River in the summer of 1942. It was loaded with beer for the July 4 celebrations at a construction camp. (YTA, Robert Hays Collection, 5689)

individual use. One man who worked for the PRA recalled that his boss, the resident engineer, had a still in the back of his office where he made alcohol from dried fruit he got from the kitchen.[55]

One result of the shortage of alcohol was, as one observer recorded, that "whiskey became the only medium of exchange—a bottle with the seal still intact no matter what size was worth a new motor or whatever you needed from the army."[56] A few bottles of beer could be a lifesaver on the road:

On November 11th, 1942 my brother and I left Edmonton with a 1940 Chev sedan that I wanted in Whitehorse for my own use . . . under frozen conditions I thought we could get the car to Whitehorse. Beer was pretty scarce in Whitehorse so although neither of us drank beer, we bought a dozen quart bottles and packed them in blankets in the back seat. I had a letter from the Department of Transport authorizing me to use the facilities at any airport along the way. . . . About 20 miles before getting to Fort Nelson I found out why I was carrying quarts of beer in the back seat. My gas gauge was just about on the empty mark when we came to a U.S. Engineering Department camp. I pulled in and asked one of the G.I.'s on duty if he could sell me a couple of gallons of gas to get me to Fort Nelson. He was quite brusque in telling me he "Couldn't sell me nothing!" and that was that. I then suggested that I had a leftover quart of beer that I would be willing to trade for a little gas. He brightened up and said "You got a quart of beer for gas?" I dug out a quart of beer and he filled the tank right to the cap. From then on I knew why I was carrying a dozen quarts of beer. It was the best legal tender a fellow could have and it was good at any U.S.E.D. camp for fixing flat tires etc.[57]

There was some squabbling about how to deal with those who broke the liquor laws. When soldiers on the Canol Project began buying liquor from local civilians who had purchased it legally, the RCMP decided they would prosecute only the sellers and not the buyers. Dr. Urquhart, the local magistrate, disagreed with this policy, and announced that he would dismiss all cases where the seller and purchaser were not both charged. Local-level negotiations ensued, resulting in Urquhart backing down.[58]

There was also some resentment among Canadians in the North over the U.S. Army's policy of giving its officers preferential access to liquor. Early in 1943, when George Jeckell was away from his office, territorial officials agreed to the army's request for a special allocation above the standard 300 bottles for the NWSC mess, and the U.S. Army and RCAF officers' messes in Whitehorse.[59] This meant that the officers did not have to line up with enlisted men and civilians to buy their ration of liquor. George Jeckell, who was perennially concerned about how local people might react to the presence of the Americans, revoked the arrangement as soon as he heard of it, and let it be known that he was opposed to treating officers as "a preferred class."[60] Responding to Jeckell's criticism, U.S. officials reported that they did not want special allocations, but did not want their officers to have to stand in line with civilians and enlisted men.[61]

Most of the crime that took place in the Northwest during the war can be categorized as crimes of social control—nonviolent offences, chiefly involving liquor or gambling, which threatened to impair the efficiency of the war effort or to offend conventional standards of behavior. There were comparatively few crimes of violence and little real public or military disorder in the region. For an area in the midst of a wartime upheaval, the Northwest was remarkably peaceful and orderly. It was also notable how heavily the hand of the American occupation lay on the region in the sphere of law enforcement, and how tenuous was the presence of Canadian representatives in this respect.

5. Men, Women, and the Northwest Defense Projects

IN THE RELATIONSHIP between an occupying force and the occupied population, sex inevitably plays an important role. Sometimes it is peaceful and friendly in nature, sometimes violent and exploitive, but it is always there. During World War II, as in all wars, pregnancy, abandonment, sexually transmitted diseases, love, exploitation, and all the other facets of human sexual relations were thrown into sharp relief. The countries that welcomed the largest numbers of Allied soldiers—Britain, Australia, and New Zealand—have the strongest folk memories of the sexual aspects of the occupation. "Over-paid, over-sexed, and over here" is perhaps the most memorable cliché surviving from the Allied occupation of Great Britain and Australia. The sexuality of the Canadian troops also became notorious in Britain.[1] Contact between the sexes ran the full gamut from affection to prostitution to rape, from brief encounters to successful marriages. The subject is as complicated as warfare, or as human nature itself.

From London to Sydney to Tonga, wherever the armies of occupation went, their sexual habits often aroused intense resentment among the local male population. The Americans were invariably overpaid by local standards and had access through their PXes to luxury goods not available to civilians. They were able to offer inducements to women that the local men could not match, and the idea that a pair of nylons could make a local girl a willing sex partner was not entirely a barrack-room fantasy. Parents tried to keep their daughters away from the soldiers and often complained to the authorities if the young women fell for a man in uniform, especially if he was a foreigner. Others welcomed such relationships, and still others, no doubt, were indifferent.

Of course the relations between the armies of occupation and the local female population was not at all the same thing as the rape of a country by an army of conquest. There was nothing in the relations between the U.S. Army and the Allied countries in which it was stationed that even remotely resembled, for example, the horrible scenes of wholesale and repeated rape that characterized the Soviet invasion of Germany at the end of the war, or even the sexual domination asserted by U.S. soldiers over the Germans after V-E day.[2] Nor were these relations like the dionysian scenes of mass fornication that took place in London and other cities on V-E day or in liberated Europe as the Americans advanced across it.

The personal relations between the soldiers of the friendly armies and the local women often were a major factor in determining public attitudes towards the occupation. In most cases the situation was mixed. Relations were generally friendly at first, smoothed by the civilians' relief at being under military protection and by widely publicized accounts of romantic love and wartime marriage between soldiers and civilian women. But as time went on, harsher notes intruded as occasional acts of rape, violence, and disrespect towards women occurred.

From another perspective, wartime fiction and postwar memories are full of stories of men serving their country overseas and returning to find that their wives had had affairs, or had borne a child by another man, as well as stories of men receiving what the Americans called a "Dear John" letter while on active service. The popular attitude toward such events was ambivalent; on one hand it was bad form for a woman to cheat on her soldier husband with some attractive, well-fed Yankee, but on the other hand one could sympathize with those who fell prey to temptation.[3] The ambivalence suggests that such events were quite widespread. Since there was no Dr. Kinsey in England in 1943 to quantify the sexual contacts between the occupiers and the occupied, it is difficult to be precise about the question, but the tremendous amount of anecdotal evidence suggests that there was indeed an increase in sexual activity in Britain and the other occupied countries during the war.[4]

There was more to this sexual revolution than the act of sex itself. Women on both sides of the battle lines found themselves recruited for jobs formerly held exclusively by men, earning independent incomes, drawn into industrial or other labor in cities, having their husbands or boyfriends off at war, living in a state of uncertainty about the future. One measure of the change, perhaps, was the amount of propaganda needed to reverse it—propaganda directed toward women at the end of the war to persuade them to quit their jobs, go back to the kitchen, and prepare to make "homes fit for heroes."[5]

The question of race complicated the sexual equations of wartime.[6] Black troops made up a significant percentage of the U.S. servicemen overseas, and although the authorities were at pains to send them where they were most likely to be welcomed (or least likely to be resented),[7] the racial attitudes most Americans carried with them caused problems overseas. The prevailing image of the American black contained a strong sexual component; mating with white women was popularly supposed to be every black man's highest ambition. To the horror of many white American troops, many women in the occupied countries, British women included, were largely free of racism, and related to black men simply as men, a situation fraught with tension.[8]

Another factor that affected sexual relations during the war was the sexual aspect of war itself. The male environment of the typical military base, as it was forty-five years ago, was much like a locker room, in which the arts of war, masculinity, and sexual prowess were mixed, as the vividly sexual nature of soldiers' speech gives evidence. A relatively mild example from the Northwest is two stanzas from a poem describing the arrival of the 18th Engineers in Whitehorse:

> Two hundred people and six thousand dogs,
> Trillions of "skeeters," and millions of bugs.
> Five or six women were in the town,
> (There may have been more,—I wasn't around).

A lady came out and tripped in the slush
And seventeen soldiers were killed in the rush.
Right down on her back, her skirts flying free
(She made sixteen dollars before you could see).[9]

The male bonding process integral to military training has always served to generate a sexist and dominant attitude towards women. Armies at war have traditionally been preoccupied with sex, partly because it tends to be in short supply for soldiers, partly because military service frees men from many restraints of civilian life, and partly because of the complex psychological relationship between sex and death.[10] Armies attract large numbers of prostitutes, who satisfy the physical need for sex and provide an opportunity for the men to demonstrate virility without emotional vulnerability. Brothels play an important role in warfare, especially behind the lines where the soldiers are not always on the move. By the 1940s the authorities had learned to depend on physicians and psychologists to shape the military attitude towards sex: the former as guides to physical health, and the latter as guides to mental health in sexual matters.

The assumptions underlying the military attitude toward sex were clearcut. Sexual activity was natural and necessary for men on military service, though not, it seems, for women in uniform. Men would always find women, and many would inevitably catch sexually transmitted diseases, which were often difficult or impossible to cure in the days before penicillin. Thus prevention and treatment of what was then referred to as "VD" (venereal disease) was an important part of military medical practice, and no medical station, particularly in the rear echelon, was without its stock of prophylactics; in the larger centers, medical facilities were set up specifically for the purpose of providing prophylactic care to men returning from leave. Mandatory attendance at graphic films on VD was part of military life, as were "short arm" inspections and lectures on the perils of vice.

In sexual as in other matters, the situation in the Canadian Northwest did not precisely echo that of other occupied countries. Once the initial threat of Japanese invasion faded, the region was spared the possibility of battle; notably absent was the turmoil of life that seems to have had an aphrodisiac effect in London during the blitz—or in Sydney and Auckland while the Americans prepared for the push toward Papua–New Guinea, the Philippines, and Japan. While times were somewhat chaotic, there was little of the violence and possibility of imminent death that contributed to or rationalized the sexual intensity that existed closer to the front lines.

Unlike the armed forces in Great Britain or Australia, however, the army of occupation in the Northwest overwhelmed the local population and created a variety of tensions that did not exist in more populous regions. The predominance of Native women among the female population was an important consideration, as was the number of men among the non-Natives—both of these conditions had existed since the early days of the gold frontier in the 1880s. Because of the differences of race, gender, nationality, and occupation in the wartime Northwest, there were a number of possible sexual combinations: civilian-military, Native-white, Native-black, black-white, Canadian-American, northerner-southerner, to name only some of the more conventional possibilities.

An important point is that there was not nearly as much sexual activity involving the army of occupation and the local people as there was in a more populous region, such as Great Britain. It was not that the invaders were particularly virtuous or restrained; rather, the limiting factor was simply the scarcity of women. The narrow construction corridors did not have a large population, and there had been not enough women of any race to meet the demand, even if all of them were willing to do so, which was certainly not the case. There was a good deal of consensual sex, and some that was forced, but the Northwest was never a sexual paradise for the army of occupation, in the way that some of the South Pacific regions and the occupied urban centers were rumored to be. "Rumored" is an important word here, for the information available to the historian on sexual activity is spotty. Interviews with veterans of the period (which must be conducted with considerable tact) seldom yield much data on the subject, though some people are willing to provide information on the activities of others. Much of the written material in the archives dealing with sex originates with the legal process, usually charges of rape or prostitution, and thus gives only one side of the picture. Therefore the story that emerges is biased towards violent, clandestine, or otherwise illicit activities; there are few stories of sexual relations that contain the word *love,* and for reasons involving scarcity as well as race there seem to have been few, if any, war brides from the Northwest outside the urban centers like Edmonton.[11]

Another question that must be dealt with in a consideration of this subject is the nature of the male sex drive.[12] Generations of sociologists and sexologists have wrestled with the question, which also worried the military brass and civilian planners in the Northwest. They assumed that men could not survive on the frontier without sex (though "decent" women apparently could, and were expected to), and they worried that lack of sexual opportunities would damage morale and efficiency. Armies generally operate on this assumption, which is why regular furloughs, or what the Americans in Vietnam called "R and R" (rest and recreation), were regularly provided for, after the initial construction period ended. Despite the sermonizings of chaplains and Red Cross workers, chastity was not considered a serious option. The authorities were clearly uncomfortable with the issue and did not confront it unless it became a problem, as when VD rates rose or prostitution became a nuisance.

Yet the thousands of men who came to the Northwest had many attitudes towards sex, which were in turn shaped by the circumstances of the region in which they found themselves. Some had stronger sex drives than others; some were influenced by pressure to conform to a masculine, "macho" image. Others were loyal to their wives or girlfriends; still others were repelled by the thought of sexual intercourse with Native women, whom they considered diseased or dirty. Some were simply too tired most of the time to bother to look for sex. Some, no doubt, were homosexual, a subject on which the records are generally silent—understandably, given the military abhorrence of homosexuality.[13] Finding a partner and engaging in clandestine homosexual behavior must, like masturbation, have been no easy thing to do, since the men lived in large open bunkhouses where privacy was nonexistent. Even the privies were communal; the men sat and defecated in rows, a novel experience for most civilians. The sex drive, though persistent, is not the strongest one, as anyone who has been exhausted, starving, or terrified can attest, and there is no reason

Table 10   Sex Ratios in the Canadian Northwest, 1941

Location	Men	Women	Men/Women
Yukon Territory	3,153	1,761	1.79:1
Northwest Territories	5,092	3,795	1.34:1

SOURCE: Census of Canada, 1941.

to doubt the comments of many wartime workers that sex was not a major consideration in the Northwest. This is an important point, for there is a tendency to think of all soldiers and frontier workers as satyrs. It seems not to have been true in the Northwest, though perhaps limited opportunity was as important as the other factors mentioned above. It may also be significant that the workers were on average several years older than men on active service, a difference that may have made sexual deprivation somewhat easier to endure.[14]

The Northwest overall had a tiny population with a disproportionately small number of women, most of them Native (see table 10). The Native communities were closer to the demographic norms, but here too were factors that skewed the balance of the sexes. For several decades, some Native women had married outside their communities, choosing a fur trader, prospector, miner, missionary, trader, or other non-Native man as a legal or common-law husband.[15] These relationships were criticized by church and government officials, but while some were short-lived, others proved lasting. Based on the sketchy evidence available, one might say that this pattern caused many Native women to marry quite young, while some Native men had difficulty in finding a suitable mate (almost none married a non-Native woman). Even before the invasion, therefore, Native communities were having to adjust to the appropriation of their women by outsiders, and the influx of thousands of men, who brought only a few women with them, inevitably made things worse.

The women who did come north as wives and girlfriends of the army of occupation had their own difficulties to overcome. There was initially no regulation keeping them out of the region, since the Northwest was not a theater of war in which armed combat could be expected. The project organizers, who believed that the frontier camps were "no place for women," kept most of them in the main centers—Edmonton, Dawson Creek, Fort St. John, Whitehorse, and Fairbanks—and relegated them to office and kitchen duties. A few went farther afield; about 100 women were hired, for instance, as office workers at Camp Canol in the Northwest Territories, 100 miles south of the Arctic Circle. [16] A small number of civilian workers brought their wives with them to the highway work camps, where they found work as typists, laundry workers, or cooks.

The main reasons why the authorities balked at the thought of permitting substantial numbers of women to work in the more remote camps were, first, that there were no facilities for them, and, second, that they would be an unsettling influence there. Yet some did come, with the result that toward the end of 1942 Canadian immigration officials began to block the entry of American women, pending proof that they had a home to go to when they reached the Northwest. [17] The U.S. adjutant general decided in December 1942 that "due to the shortage of housing accommodations for dependents in the territory embraced by the Northwest Service Command . . . officers, enlisted men and civilian employees of the United States Forces assigned for duty in the Northwest Service Command will not be accompanied by their dependents." The army also announced that it would take steps to remove those dependents already in the area, and moved to evacuate the women and children "in a considerate and orderly manner so as not to work undue hardships on the individuals concerned," the costs to be borne by the government. Officers in the field were given three weeks to draw up a plan for the evacuation of all dependents under their authority. After some confusion it was announced that this order did not apply to civilian employees of the PRA. [18]

The officers responsible then drew up lists, planned for the evacuation, and either listened to the anguished appeals from their men or ignored them. The resulting flurry of official correspondence provides a good indication of the number of women and children, most of them American, who were in the Northwest in 1942–43.

The lists drawn up for Edmonton, for example, suggest that in mid-January 1943 there were between 150 and 200 American wives in the city.[19]

Nine employees of Miller Construction had wives with them in the city, and four of these had brought children. Nineteen workers with J. Gordon Turnbull and with Sverdrup and Parcel lived with their wives, one of whom was a Canadian; five of these had brought children with them. The U.S. Engineer Office reported twenty-three families in the Edmonton District.[20] In the Fort St. John sector, officers reported that there were thirteen dependents of enlisted men, one of a warrant officer, and twelve of officers. There were fourteen married women employed in clerical positions in Skagway.[21]

The order to leave was later expanded to include dependents of U.S. citizens employed by civilian contractors as well; the U.S. government once again provided financial assistance, and it made arrangements with the Red Cross for the care of families en route to the United States. The only exception was for "dependents directly employed by [the contractors] where replacements from the United States would be required if separated from their current employment." To ensure that the problem did not recur, "Canadian Immigration authorities have been contacted and advised that dependents of military personnel or of employees of the U.S. Engineer Department, or its agencies, will not be allowed privileges of passage into Canada." All dependents were to be gone by March 1, 1943.[22]

Some of the women lodged vigorous protests against this policy. Ada Smith, a Canadian woman who had gone with her husband to a remote military radio station on northern Vancouver Island, described her useful contributions to the war effort:

I am a loyal wife! When my husband was posted to this uninhabitable "no mans land," I packed my belongings and infant son in a large polka-dot bandana 'kerchief and hied me to my hubby's retreat far removed from civilization.

At present I cook, sew, knit, fill kerosene lamps, carry water, help saw wood, entertain forlorn and weary comrades of my husband who are grateful for the good things I bestow on them. My home-cooked meals are unsurpassed and greatly in demand—in short, I am a "Florence Nightingale" in a forgotten land. All of these things I accept as my lot in life and I am content.[23]

Other appeals pointed out that although housing was in short supply, and many families lived in cramped quarters with few facilities, "persons now located here have adjusted themselves more or less satisfactorily to the conditions; they could well remain here."[24] There were numerous requests for exemptions.[25] The Northern Commercial Company, which operated a parts and supply depot in Whitehorse, had hired Lenore Hone, wife of Staff Sergeant R. C. Hone of the Headquarters Medical Section. Company Manager W. P. Janes petitioned the NWSC, pointing out that if Mrs. Hone, an accountant and bookkeeper, was evacuated the company would have to recruit a replacement from the south, a costly and time-consuming exercise.[26] Since this was the kind of case that exceptions were made for, she was presumably permitted to stay, though the record is silent on the matter.

This policy seemed particularly silly when applied to Edmonton where, though housing was in short supply during the war, the number of American dependents was only a tiny part of an urban population of more than 100,000. The American consul general in the city noted "the friendly local feeling toward Americans in general, together [with] the real regret felt in Edmonton over the coming departure of American women."[27] The Edmonton Chamber of Commerce even petitioned the NWSC to lift the order, "to permit such dependents already here and provided with housing to remain," but in most cases, to no avail.[28]

The evacuation took place early in 1943. Dependents working in authorized positions were permitted to remain; all others prepared to leave. Of the eight dependents of employees of the U.S. Engineer Office in Whitehorse, four were able to stay because of the nature of their jobs, and one working woman was permitted to delay her departure until May 1. The others flew out of Whitehorse, two of them traveling to Juneau.[29] U.S. authorities made one major exception to the policy. The Canol refinery, under construction in Whitehorse, was planned as a major permanent facility, and hence required a stable workforce. The evacuation orders would not, authorities claimed, affect women working at the refinery: "when pipeline and refinery housing facilities are available there will be no objection to bringing employee families to the site."[30] By 1944 company policy was to permit "an employee to have his family with him after one year's continuous service," and the company paid the cost of moving the family and household effects to the work site. At that time, Standard Oil had homes for 5 families in Skagway and another 40 in Whitehorse; work was under way to convert government buildings to civilian housing for an additional 100 families by 1945.[31]

The barrage of complaints from the workers eventually forced a change in the policy of removal.[32] In March 1943 the order for the evacuation of dependents was suspended, permitting wives and children of American soldiers and civilian workers already there to remain in the Northwest, though the provision barring workers from bringing wives and children to the region remained in force. The importation of dependents continued nonetheless.[33] Some of the workers arranged to have their wives hired by contractors operating in the same place, an arrangement that the government tried hard to discourage.[34] In July 1943 two women who had been hired for office work in Dawson Creek arrived to join their husbands there. The commanding officer objected to their presence, arguing that it "affects adversely the discipline and morale of the personnel, many of whom wish to bring dependents here. If Mrs. Braun and Mrs. Vermeer are allowed to remain then I feel in all fairness to three other officers and some twenty em [enlisted men] that I should rescind the order in its entirety." He went on to threaten, "Unless I am upheld in my administration which is in accordance with War Dept. and NWS Command directives, I feel that my usefulness as a post commander ceases."[35]

Faced with such complaints, in July 1943 the authorities modified the policy again, stating that "Commanding Officers are authorized to evacuate all dependents regardless of time of arrival when in their opinion the conditions under which the dependents are living are such as to create a health hazard, are not up to normal standards, or if housing conditions in the community are congested or for any other reason which makes their presence objectionable."[36] Women who arrived after the posting of the orders restricting the immigration of dependents were to be removed from the district at their own expense.[37] Those who held jobs in their own right were, as before, permitted to remain—an arrangement that, given the endemic shortage of female labor in the Northwest, left a large loophole in the regulations.

The local authorities had considerable latitude in determining who should leave and who could stay. One important factor was the sexual aspect of the situation. On one hand, some commanders felt that if a few men had their wives with them, other men would feel jealous or angry, a situation bad for morale. It seemed better to leave everyone womanless than to permit a few to have their wives with them. On the other hand, many older, veteran civilian workers would not tolerate lengthy separation from their wives and families and might simply pack up and leave, a situation that posed a delicate problem for the camp commanders.[38]

Eventually the problem solved itself; the housing crisis in the larger communities was alleviated by military and civilian construction, and as the projects wound down, the majority of the workers left for the South. By 1944 the search was on for a smaller permanent workforce, and the restrictions of the previous year were lifted.[39] At the height of construction there had been more than 65,000 workers in the Northwest; by January 1944 the number had been halved, and by the fall of that year it had halved again. The space created could be used to house the dependents of the workers remaining in the region. A senior officer noted, "It is apparent that if dependents are now permitted to live in Western Canada, the resources of this country will not be over-taxed. Permitting dependents to live in Canada will add greatly to the morale and efficiency of all military personnel stationed here."[40]

One of the most effective means of preventing dependents from coming to the communities of the Northwest was to deny them permission to travel on the Alaska Highway, a practice that had forced some women to evade the check posts and patrols. This restriction was lifted in February 1944, when it was decided to "permit dependents of maintenance personnel to accompany the employees for purposes of visiting or residence."[41] Later that month, regulations governing the employment of dependents were altered to make it easier for women to find work:[42]

It has been found that this prohibition resulted in a rapid turnover of personnel and also limited the field of employment to men who were prepared to work separated from their families. As a result, there was a tendency for married men to work for short periods of time only and then leave the job, or for a less desirable type of employee to come in who was prepared to accept the isolated conditions which prevailed in order to get steady employment at a good salary.[43]

By December 1944 a total of 177 families had joined Alaska Highway employees in the camps. Of these, fifty-four were in Fort St. John, fifteen in Fort Nelson, and twenty in Whitehorse. The rest were scattered among the other twenty-five maintenance camps along the road. The families had a total of 170 children, 83 of whom were of school age.[44] In general, however, "the tendency is for young couples without children to accept employment on the Highway."[45] The transition to a peacetime labor force, in which women and children were encouraged to accompany their husbands into the Northwest, had begun.

In the meantime, however, for want of female companionship, many of the men in the camps had to make do with fantasy. A memorable image of the construction era, repeated in many locations, was the erection of a homemade sign reading "Help Wanted Female" (in imitation of the newspaper job ads of the time, which were divided according to workers' gender). A number of newspaper articles, intended to inform and amuse, instead revealed the sexual tensions and the racist attitudes toward women prevalent in the camps. One began with the headline "Alaskan Highway Workers Treasure Pictures of Girls: Many Have Not Seen Any Women Except Squaws in 9 Months," and went on to describe the men's limited contact with women. The camps were apparently still buzzing about a visit by a female performer with the United Service Organizations (USO): "even men hopelessly stranded in the wilds were excited on learning that she was only 200 miles away." There were always pinups, of course, and the ubiquitous Betty Grable appeared in the Northwest as elsewhere: "A sweater girl clipping becomes something of a shrine . . . something to rest one's eyes on after a bitter day among the great groves of spruce that lead to nowhere. The chorine who has posed for some picture magazine would be proud if she knew how many good-looking young men had dozed off in a Yukon tent with her face and legs as their last walking [sic] memory."[46] Perhaps she would have been less proud had she known what the men were thinking as they looked at her picture, or how many were using it as an aid to masturbation. One report stated that "the walls of officers' quarters, quonset huts, stout houses and tents in the remote interior posts . . . are plentifully decorated with the nudest possible art."[47] In any case, photographs were a poor substitute for the real thing, and the journalist reported one lieutenant's racist observation that "these Indian girls look whiter every day."

The antidotes suggested for all this frustration were work and exhaustion, and the article ended with the observation that there was plenty of that in the North. Some men, particularly those stationed in or near the urban centers, did manage to find sex partners, and the army responded by opening prophylactic stations in several places. In May 1943 soldiers used the facilities at the rate of 72 per 1,000 men in the command, not a particularly high rate.[48]

The tone the newspapers took on this subject was reminiscent of male virgins in a high school locker room trading misinformation about sex, but the reality was often cruder. Many men in the region were accustomed to female companionship and regular sex, and they bitterly resented the segregation and isolation. An American soldier in Fort Smith, asking a resident about the availability of the local women, remarked that he had not "had a piece of tail since he left the United States and said he would like to meet a girl from whom he could get a piece." According to the informant, "He asked me if they used rubber safes around here."[49] In the absence of sexual opportunities, talk on the subject was endless. In June 1943 a rumor spread all over the Northwest that a "platoon of Geisha girls" had been captured on Attu Island, and there was widespread prurient speculation on what the victors would do with them.[50] The Canadian anthropologist Diamond Jenness repeated a tale that "in 1943 coloured employees of a firm that had contracted to build an oil pipeline in the region openly offered a prize of $500 to the first Indian woman who should give birth to a baby with black kinky hair."[51]

Another picture of the social situation in the Northwest, this one intended for public consumption, was given by an American journalist who traveled through the region in 1944. He reported

Halloween dance, U.S. Army Air Force. The men outnumber the women by two or three to one. (Courtesy Marion (Ambrose) Clark)

that in Edmonton, women were not permitted to attend dances unaccompanied, so they "line[d] up outside waiting for fellows to buy their tickets and get them by the doorkeeper. . . . One of the favorite GI pastimes in the town is marrying Canadian girls." The rest of the North, he wrote, consisted of "dreary airbases in a dreary womanless country." "It would be possible" he continued, "to glamorize these places with accounts of their history, geography, flora and fauna; but to pretend that life at any of them is much fun would be to invite a rotten-egg barrage from the soldiers who live here." The exception was Whitehorse, where "no shortage of women exists . . . any more." For the rest, including the Alaskan camps, the main drawback to life was the "low 'chicken' count."[52]

With such a shortage of women in most places, and with the presence of so many lustful men, the women who did work in the more isolated spots led carefully protected and regulated lives. Married couples were given, or in some instances built, their own accommodation. Unmarried women were not brought into camp singly; instead, they were hired in groups and housed together in separate, though spartan, quarters. As one woman described it, "in the dorm where I lived we each had a little cubicle of a room, with a single bed, dresser and maybe a chair. There was a 'common room' where we could meet and be together, and a long bathroom with a number of sinks and showers. There was also a sewing machine, and we bought material and made curtains for our room."[53]

Relations between these women and the construction workers were generally guarded and proper. The camps had rules, especially ones prohibiting men visiting women's rooms, to guard against improprieties. The women interviewed forty years later about this aspect of their northern experience usually commented that they were treated with decency and respect by the men. There were instances of men trying to force their affections on the women, but not out of proportion to the incidence of such things in the general population.[54] Admittedly, some women did have bad experiences. One woman working for the Melville Smith Company at Fort St. John had been led to expect private quarters, but instead found herself in a "shack" with eight other "girls." Her boss, the camp cook, was "very abusive," there was much drunkenness in the camp, and one evening "the doors were forced off their hinges by drunken men who wanted to come in despite our protests and screams." She did not lay all the blame on the men; her roommates did "stay out until the early hours of the morning," and there were reports of "misbehaviour."[55] In another camp it was the officers who were at fault: "We have several reports from the female barracks that the conduct of some of our officers is not the best. . . . If the officers can't go in the female quarters and behave themselves, they will have to be barred altogether."[56]

But stories like this are rare in the records; more common are reports of romances and even a few marriages. Project managers in the larger centers, where the sexual balance was far more even than in the isolated camps, made strenuous efforts to encourage orderly social contact through dances, musical programs, and recreational outings. At the Dawson Creek base, for example, facilities were erected in 1943 "where our ladies could meet their gentlemen friends. . . . No men are allowed in the ladies dormitories and vice versa. It is not desirable for guests or visitors to enter the dormitory area, and they will be liable to the embarrassment of questioning by the guards and others. This is especially true in the evening."[57] A subsequent regulation made it clearer what was meant by "orderly social contact": "Men and women will not go past the outer door of the barracks of the opposite sex."[58]

On the whole, relations between the workers and women of their own race were marked by adherence to accepted social norms, the advances of amorous drunks notwithstanding. The authorities frowned on anything more erotic than dances and friendship outings, and disapproved of the marriages that took place between the workers and local women in the urban centers:[59] "In view of the War Department policy not to approve enlisted personnel acquiring dependents outside the continental limits of the United States, requests for marriage by personnel of the Northwest Service Command in Canada and in Alaska will not be approved."[60] The government could not prevent civilian workers from marrying Canadian and Alaskan women, only the military, but the directive provided clear evidence of the official line.

Some men, however, stepped over the line of acceptable behavior. The few soldiers and civilian workers who assaulted non-Native women were severely dealt with; a major incident, which particularly outraged the authorities because the offender was black, involved a white female resident of Fort McMurray. In June 1942 the soldier, a member of the 388th Engineers, was charged with assault with intent to commit a felony; he was swiftly court-martialed and sentenced to twenty years at hard labor. The authorities were pleased with the dispatch shown by Colonel T. Wyman, Jr., the local commander, but they soon found that the court-martial had been invalid on procedural grounds—Colonel Wyman lacked the authority to convene it. Concerned about the "intensity of local feeling" in the community and the "supersensitiveness . . . because the accused is colored," they tried the man once more, found him guilty, gave him the same sentence, and shipped him to Leavenworth to begin serving it.[61] This was the maximum sentence under military law, and the quick, harsh reaction of the U.S. authorities shows their concern about the occurrence of such incidents as the soldiers and construction workers moved north. The RCMP at Fort Smith reported the same month that they had warned "most of the local people . . . not to get too friendly or talkative with the coloured troops," in an attempt to "discourage a possible too intimate situation between the local inhabitants and the coloured troops."[62]

Another reason why such sexual offenses were severely punished is that they embarrassed the U.S. authorities, particularly when they occurred at diplomatically sensitive times. The U.S. authorities wanted to avoid giving offence to Canadians and wished to be seen as good neighbors and allies. To ensure that all military personnel in the Canadian Northwest understood the seriousness of the situation, the army published its regulations covering rape. The offense, soldiers were warned, was punishable by death or life imprisonment, and assault with intent to rape carried a sentence of twenty years; men who had intercourse with minors faced a fifteen-year penalty for the first offense, and thirty years for its repetition. In issuing the regulations, Colonel C. R. Hazeltine, acting chief of staff, asked his subordinates to stress "the importance of maintaining friendly relationships with the Dominion of Canada . . . with stress upon the disgrace and dishonor such offenses visit upon our own nation." Officers were also ordered to provide suitable recreational activities, religious supervision and advice, and the inevitable lectures and films on the "dangers involved in promiscuous sexual contacts."[63] In April 1943 the War Office in Washington sent a coded message to the Northwest Service Command in Whitehorse suggesting measures to be taken to avoid giving offense in this regard:

Impending negotiations whereby we seek recognition by Canadian government of exclusive jurisdiction of the United States forces over own personnel and general good will are being embarrassed by several recent charges against United States military personnel in Canada of sex crimes against Canadian women, rape, assault with intent to commit rape, and carnal knowledge of girl below age of consent. . . . [F]ollowing are some measures which should [be] adopted as far as practicable: dissemination among personnel of information of ill effects of such offense upon reputation and interests of United States, influence of immediate commanding officers and chaplains, and provisions for athletics and recreation. Information should reach all personnel that rape is punishable by death or life imprisonment and that according to law . . . no milder punishment may be imposed; that punishment of confinement up to twenty years may be imposed for assault with intent to commit rape and that carnal knowledge of a girl under age of consent may be punished by confinement up to five years.[64]

The level of racism in the Canadian Northwest during the 1940s was about the same as in the northern American states. Though there had been blacks in the Yukon since the gold rush, there were so few of them by 1940 that the death of the last black in the

Dawson district was noted in the local paper in 1942.[65] There was no evidence of overt hostility toward blacks—most racial feeling in the region was directed toward the Native people—but there was a fair amount of what might be called casual racism. The newspapers, for instance, were still printing "darky jokes" as late as the fall of 1942, at a time when there were thousands of black troops working on the Alaska Highway.[66] The arrival of the black troops, however, altered the equation; the combination of frontier conditions and prevailing stereotypes about black sexuality led to particular concern about controlling them.

The greatest controlling device, for both blacks and whites, was lack of opportunity. There were very few eligible non-Native women in the Northwest during the war years, and only a certain percentage of those were prepared for a brief fling with an American soldier or civilian worker. There were organized activities where "decent" women could be met—dances, picnics, church gatherings, and the like—but the local women were wary of the foreigners, and those who were willing to be friendlier than the rules of picnics and singsongs dictated could afford to be extremely choosy. One woman who came from Edmonton to work in Whitehorse during the war remembers being much in demand:

I loved it up there, it was paradise for a young girl, with all these men around. It would get that you had a date with a different fellow every night. One night I'd forgotten and was washing my hair and this guy comes up for a date. One of the girls came up to tell me "Your date is here." "Oh, my gosh." . . . We were flown into different air force stations around for weekends. They arranged for all these girls to come up and they'd really show us a great time, and they were so nice, and we'd have banquets and dances and go on hikes and whatever there was to do.[67]

For some, male and female alike, platonic relationships were not enough, but there were many roadblocks in the path of the amorous—the circumstances of life in the Northwest during the war complicated the logistics of romance, or even of casual sex. Military and civilian workers lived in dormitories, as did the female workers. Living space was at a premium. In Whitehorse, hotel guests were required to share their rooms, and people had to double and triple up in the small houses and cabins that provided most of the region's housing. The climate and the insect population tended to discourage outdoor sex for much of the year. Of course, love laughs not only at locksmiths but also at thermometers and mosquitoes, and amorous couples will put up with a good deal of inconvenience and discomfort. A tremendous amount of sexual intercourse in wartime London took place at night with the participants standing in the doorways of public buildings; certain highly favored locations were littered with used condoms every morning. No doubt there were many strange things done 'neath the midnight sun along the Alaska Highway and the Canol route, but their frequency was limited by the fact that there were far fewer women in proportion to the number of invaders in Whitehorse than in London.

Assessing the nature of those sexual encounters that did occur is not easy, since information on the subject is rare, and when available, impressionistic. It is also tilted towards the pathological side of sex, in particular to rape, prostitution, and venereal disease; there are no statistics at all on friendly, disease-free, consensual sex. One survey, compiled by the U.S. Army Medical Corps in Dawson Creek between March and June 1943, dealt with women found to have VD and subsequently treated by army doctors. It represented only one part of the region's sexual activity—how large a part is impossible to determine—based on people having several sexual partners, or having as partners people who had had more than one sexual partner (see table 11). This study gave a good impression of one aspect of sexual activity in the Northwest, particularly that in which payment was involved. Initial contact was made in public places—in bars, in cafes, or on the street. Once paired off, the couple headed for the woman's home or to a hotel room. Lacking this, they sought privacy where they could find it—in a barn, in an automobile, in the lane behind the cafe, or in the train station. Another report mentioned a local baseball field.

It was in fact VD as much as any aspect of sexual activity that concerned the authorities. Unregulated sex, particularly prostitution, carried the risk of disease and lost productivity, and prevention of VD thus became a major preoccupation of military and civilian authorities.[68] Isolated cases of disease had occurred in the region before the war, though it was not a serious problem, and significantly, most of the cases had originated in the South. A. C. Duncan,

Table 11   Sexual Contacts Resulting in Venereal Disease, Dawson
Creek, B.C., March–June 1943

Where Met		Place of Exposure	
Street	3	hotel	17
Brothel		brothel	5
Train station	1	car	5
Dance hall	3	home	19
Tavern	7	train station	1
Cafe	9	outdoors/outbuildings	4
Taxi	1	not given	5
Not given	29		
Total	56		56

SOURCE: RG 36/7, vol. 40, file 28-23, pt. 2, Summary Table of Data on File in
Dawson Creek Dispensary, U.S. Army Medical Corps, March–June 1943.

a Dawson City doctor, commented in 1940 that "for the past year
there have been some 12 cases of gonorrhea and no cases of
primary syphilis in Dawson. The majority of these few gonorrhea
cases were brought into Dawson by the annual spring migration of
labourers from Vancouver. During this period I know of no cases
that were communicated in Dawson."[69] This pattern continued
throughout the war. The post surgeon at Whitehorse reported in
1943 that "most victims of venereal diseases were those returning
from furlough with history of contact either in the States or in
Edmonton enroute to the North back to their stations. The majority
of these were discovered during the physical examination required
of every soldier upon arrival at Whitehorse."[70]

Isolation proved the best prophylactic. In April 1942 the 35th
Engineers Regiment reported only 11 out of 4,200 men receiving
treatment for VD, and there had been no new cases for a month.[71]
The same was true in Alaska, where soldiers in 1943 continued "to
maintain their amazingly low venereal disease rate, which for the
past six months has fluctuated mildly between three and five new
cases per thousand per annum." This rate was approximately 10
percent of that for the U.S. Army as a whole, which experienced
over forty-two cases per thousand.[72] The low rate was explained
as being the result of health checks on incoming workers; it was also

due to the very few furloughs granted to soldiers in the Northwest in the first two years of construction.

Far from being soothed by the comparatively low rate of VD cases, the military authorities, who had more control over their workers than the civilian contractors did, made strenuous efforts to control the spread of VD. Not only were films and lectures on the subject mandatory, but newly hired kitchen staff had to take the Wasserman test for syphilis before they started work.[73] To support this effort, the Yukon Territorial Council passed an ordinance making it an offense to have VD. Women who became infected—the law was not applied to men—were forced to remain in hospital until cured.

The Northwest did have a small corps of full- and part-time prostitutes, women who, in the tradition of the frontier, "mined the miners," though unlike many southern army towns, there were no red-light districts. In Dawson City, for example, the local madam, Ruby Scott, was a community fixture, generally tolerated, and subject only to occasional harassment during periods of moral fervor. The semi-official policy in Dawson, as in the rest of the North, was that prostitutes provided a necessary service that contributed to social stability.[74] When in 1940 one man complained that Scott was connected to a "vicious clique of French prostitutes placed there and controlled by a certain old country French gangster Sindicate [sic] operating in Montreal and New York State," the RCMP investigated. The officer replied, "Whilst there may have been prostitution taking place, I consider that to go any further in this investigation of the women mentioned . . . would amount to persecution. There is no evidence of white slave traffic."[75] In any case the construction projects passed Ruby by, and she stayed in business for another twenty years. In Whitehorse the police reported that "no complaints at any time have been received of accosting on the streets, and they usually work under cover. I am satisfied that this traffic is very small."[76]

The arrival of the construction workers in 1942 created a boom market for commercial sex, and also led to a hardening in the official attitude towards it. What the authorities feared was an influx of southern prostitutes under the control of pimps, which they felt would lead to disorder, crime, and the spread of disease, and they took what steps they could to discourage the growth of the trade. In Whitehorse, an RCMP corporal observed that "it will be appreciated that it is very difficult to obtain evidence of prostitution in a place where there are so many transient people. Most of the prostitutes have employment of some sort as a cover up. At the present we are aware of at least three prostitutes operating in the town of Whitehorse. In due course, evidence will be obtained against them and they will be prosecuted.[77]

In northern British Columbia the police discovered that a miner had brought his "niece," a well-known prostitute, with him to Liard Crossing, and was pimping for her with the American soldiers. The Provincial Police made sure "that she was on the next bus going south."[78] In other places, if local women were suspected of soliciting for the purposes of prostitution, their homes were put off limits to the troops, and in at least one case the army posted guards outside a home to keep the would-be customers at bay.[79]

In June 1943, Major Sinclair, the VD control officer for the Pacific Command of the Canadian Department of National Defence, made an extensive investigation of prostitution in Dawson Creek. His report provides the best available survey of the nature and extent of the trade in the Canadian Northwest. Dawson Creek was not a typical construction camp, since it served an existing farming district and was a substantial community before the army of occupation arrived. However, it was the site of several military and civilian headquarters establishments, and was an important stop for travelers in the region. Conditions in the town were, therefore, quite similar to those in Whitehorse, Fairbanks, and Fort St. John, and on a smaller scale, to those in Edmonton. The report makes it clear that the apprehension about prostitution was based not on moral qualms but on the fear that the spread of VD would disrupt the construction work. During a meeting held that June it was reported that Dawson Creek had three brothels; there had been others, but they were closed as soon as they were discovered.[80] Women suspected of being prostitutes were arrested and charged as such. Women found to have VD, prostitutes or not, were arrested, charged with vagrancy, and "sent back to their parents." There were fifty-six cases of women found to have VD in the town between

March and June 1943, of whom only ten were prostitutes; eighteen of the women worked in restaurants.

Sinclair then investigated the town's brothels, particularly "the house on the hill," Dawson Creek's most notorious address. It was located on a ranch, where horses were available for hire, and it was rumored that for an extra fee, one could hire certain horses that invariably took the rider to a particular house behind the town. The local police told him that the house had been occupied by prostitutes, but had been closed in March 1943. Major Sinclair's main discovery was that the problem of VD lay mostly with promiscuous nonprofessionals, with waitresses singled out as the main culprits. When the owners of a local sandwich shop returned from a short trip, they found that their two female employees had continued to operate the business, but had "spent their nights entertaining soldiers in their quarters behind the establishment."

Sinclair visited a restaurant in street clothes and asked a customer about the local sex trade. The man, a civilian construction foreman, denied that the town had brothels, but thinking that Sinclair was looking for a sex partner, "pointed out two waitresses either of whom he claimed would probably oblige after hours," and offered to "fix it up" for the officer. Sinclair declined, and during a subsequent "mild fracas" in the establishment, left alone. On returning a few minutes later, he discovered that a number of women patrons had picked up soldiers. He left again to fetch the military police. When confronted, the soldiers in the restaurant were "unable to bring forth any evidence or statement that would suggest the operation of a brothel."

Sinclair spent four days in Dawson Creek conducting interviews and watching soldiers on the prowl for sex. His conclusion was that there had been a brothel in the town, but that the police had put it out of operation. There was some prostitution in the town, but the problem, from the perspective of disease, lay with "sexually promiscuous individuals, who, however, have legitimate occupations and whose promiscuity is confined to after-work hours on a strictly amateur basis."[81]

Similar investigations were conducted in other communities. In Seward, Alaska, the red-light district, known as the "Line," was a

A truckload of local women going to visit the patients at the army hospital, Fort St. John, summer 1943. (Courtesy Margaret (Percival) Stuart)

notorious source of VD. In the summer of 1943 it was closed, to a chorus of complaints from men in the region. The closure raised the classic dilemma of the role of prostitution in military life:

Closing of this source of amusement has resulted in an increase in association between soldiers and questionable women, a condition which is hardly desirable. When the choice lies between organized segregated prostitution, more or less under control, and uncontrolled promiscuity through the community in general, the first seems decidedly preferable. There's no doubt as to how the inhabitants of the line feel about the matter—they'd give almost anything to be able to do business again on the old scale.[82]

The attitude of officials towards prostitution during the war was an uneasy balance of acceptance and prohibition, with prevention of disease the main guideline.

Sexual interaction between the workers and the Native women of the Northwest fell into yet another category of the complex social relations of wartime. It was not uniform throughout the region; in some places, such as Edmonton, Native women formed only a small minority of the female population, while farther north they made up a large majority. In places like Teslin, Carcross, Fort Smith, Whitehorse, and along the highway corridor in Alaska, opportunities for fraternization between workers and Native women were considerable, and the usual official attitude was to discourage it as much as possible. In Whitehorse, for example, "Indian Town" was put off limits to all U.S. Army personnel in May 1942, a regulation enforced by the MPs.[83]

Sexual contact between indigenous people and whites had been commonplace on the North American frontier for centuries. Sometimes exploitive and transitory, as was often the case on the mining frontier, these relationships could also be lasting, as with many that resulted from the activities of the Hudson's Bay Company.[84] A major problem with the mingling of the races was that it was not bound by the rules of non-Native society—that is, the normal rules of morality and responsibility did not always apply to non-Native men involved with Native women. The attitude toward sexual relations with Native women generally started with racist assumptions, particularly that they had a different attitude toward sex, placed little value on virginity, thought nothing of promiscuity, and so forth—all ideas that relieved non-Native men, in their own minds, from any responsibility for their own actions. A telling example of the prevailing attitude was a lecture given during the war to a group of soldiers on the moral nature of Native women in the Canadian Northwest. The speaker, an army sergeant, tried to impress on the men "the seriousness with which offences with native women were regarded in this country," and explained "that the natives were wards of the Canadian Government . . . although they were often morally weak and willing."[85] George Jeckell, comptroller of the Yukon, observed that "among all the newcomers, and the Half-breeds and Indians who appear to have congregated at Whitehorse, there are many immoral women of a greater or lesser degree."[86] An Alaskan official was even blunter: Commenting on the spread of VD, he said that "it is often difficult to determine who infected whom, for they sometimes have six or seven contacts within a period of a few hours."[87]

Because of the widespread disapproval of interracial sex (hence the pejorative term *squaw man*), the men who did form relations with Native women were clearly acting against the conventions of society. They were doing more than easing sexual tensions; in a real sense they were acting out some basic frontier myths and assumptions. Casual sex with Native women (and girls too, for some were barely into their teens) was a powerful assertion of gender and race dominance. If the Native women flouted the teachings of the missionaries and government officials, so did the men. The latter were "sowing wild oats," "acting like real men"; by thinking of their partners as immoral creatures to whom sex meant nothing, they absolved themselves of all responsibility for their actions. The difference between the women in the restaurants and the Native women was that the waitresses were viewed as a particularly promiscuous subclass of white women; all Native women, on the other hand, were considered to be sexually available.

The nature of the relations between invaders and Native women varied, of course. At one end of the spectrum, some Native women and non-Native men formed monogamous, romantic attachments, though many of these women were abandoned when work ended for the men. At the other end were a significant number of rape cases (only a minority of which were formally reported) and cases of sexual relations with minors, including a notorious incident involving two soldiers and young Native girls from the Carcross Residential School.[88] In between these extremes there were liaisons displaying a greater or lesser degree of affection, of longer or shorter duration, in which the women were cared for or exploited.

A marked feature of these interracial relations was their connection to alcohol. Canadian Natives were prevented by law from consuming liquor, a provision designed to prevent them from abuse at the hands of whites. In many cases this law had the opposite effect, and what were generally termed "drinking parties" provided an opportunity for sexual exploitation. At Fort Simpson, to take a prewar example, dances often turned into drinking parties: "One very unfavourable feature of these dances was the number of young Indian girls attending these functions. There were at least four girls present at these gatherings whose ages ranged from fourteen to seventeen years. They appeared to be in much more demand by the white men than the older white and Indian women."[89] Though most non-Natives thought that the willingness to exchange sex for alcohol was part of the nature of aboriginal people, it was instead an individual response to the situation. Some Native women, like Native and non-Native men, drank heavily and were willing to do almost anything to get liquor. Some were indeed promiscuous, and had many sexual partners; some were prostitutes. One woman from Dawson City moved for a time to Whitehorse, where she became "notorious for her promiscuous friendships with U.S. Military and civil personnel . . . her friendships during the past year were too many and varied." A Native woman who brought a charge of rape against a black soldier saw her complaint dismissed because "The reputation of ——— is questionable in this instance as it is a known fact of her having had intercourse with other Negro soldiers."[90]

Many of these relationships were consensual and developed along lines that would not have seemed strange in the South, though they did not conform to the social code prescribed by government and church officials. A married Métis woman from the southern Mackenzie River valley did laundry for a U.S. Army private. He began to "spend a lot of his spare time with her." About three months after they first met, the two began sleeping together—not a hasty romance. After several weeks of this, the soldier found he had VD, which he believed he had contracted earlier at Waterways, Alberta. The woman was sure that she was not at fault: "She was of the opinion that if she was infected, her husband would also have contracted this disease from her."[91]

Another Native woman from the same area conformed more closely to the stereotype. While her husband was overseas with the army, the twenty-five-year-old had a regular boyfriend, a black military policeman. At a community dance, the two had an argument, and the woman left with some friends. She found herself alone with an American soldier who "started to kiss and hug me. He asked me if I would do him a favour and then when he told me what the favour was, I said, 'O.K.' and we had intercourse on the Davenport. He then asked me if I would marry him and go back to the states with him." She refused and subsequently "had intercourse with other soldiers since that time."[92]

This kind of thing had importance that went beyond the rather grubby facts of the case because it reinforced widely held stereotypes about Native women. The majority of them were not often drunk and did not fornicate with every soldier who approached them with a bottle or a five-dollar bill, but a few did, and their actions colored the reactions of the judicial system and provided some men with a rationalization for forcing themselves on Native women. Stereotypes about Native women, the existence of women who were indeed actively promiscuous, frontier expectations, the military and masculine ethos of the wartime projects—all created an atmosphere of sexual tension, which pinup photos and the occasional visit of USO entertainers did little to relieve. With alcohol as a catalyst, it was not surprising that some men would turn their sexual attention towards Native women.

Sexual relations of this type, complicated by the unusual power relationships in the area and the male sense of dominance, sometimes became abusive. ———, an eighteen-year-old Native woman from the Whitehorse area, was a case in point. According to the RCMP, she had been involved in several cases of trouble between soldiers and Natives, was known to have contracted VD, and was allegedly being prostituted by several local Native men. When she went to the police to report an assault by an American soldier, they refused to press charges, preferring to have the matter dealt with by the U.S. military authorities, on the grounds that "experience of this headquarters has shown the testimony of Indians to be very unreliable in court" and that the woman had "been seen walking the streets with American soldiers."

The details of the case illustrate the relationship between drinking and sex—in this case unconsummated, though accompanied by force. ———, in town with several friends, was approached by "Tex." He produced a bottle of alcohol and a tin of fruit juice, which were mixed and shared around. The woman reported, "I began to get dizzy and I told them I had enough." Her male friends then left, at which point Tex became aggressive.

Tex was kissing me and asked me if I loved him. . . . I told Tex to be a gentleman and leave me alone. I got up then as I was mad at him. . . . Later we met Tex on the highway around the B.P.C. Co. Tex asked me to go over in the woods with him, and I told him, no. He said nobody would see us, but I told him no again. ——— and I started to run towards my mother's tent and he, Tex grabbed me by the arm and pulled me back. We were on a trail in the woods by this time and he knocked me down on the ground. I screamed for help, but he put his hand over my mouth. He told ——— he gave me $20.00 and that I promised to do something for him in the bushes.

Her story was confirmed by several friends, who saw Tex wrestling with her and calling her an "Indian Bitch."

Not surprisingly, Tex told a different tale. He said that "a girl came up to me and said she wanted $20.00. I said how far would she want to go for $20.00. She said not more than three times a week for one month. I said allright and gave her one $10.00 and two $5.00, all in Canadian money. Then she pulled her skirts up to her ass and ran away." He denied providing liquor to the Indians or assaulting the woman.

After an investigation, the police concluded that Tex had indeed provided the Natives with alcohol, and had assaulted the woman, who was insistent that charges be laid. But the police refused to proceed with the case, believing that the woman's character would result in Tex's acquittal, particularly because a Native man was supposed to be acting as her pimp. Inspector D. J. Martin of the Whitehorse Detachment of the RCMP concluded, "We could hardly object (if we were inclined to) if [Tex] were to be acquitted, and particularly if [she] herself is disreputable, as alleged by the Provost Marshall." The U.S. Army proceeded on its own, and Tex was eventually fined $20 and confined to his company area for two months.[93]

Another incident involved a Native woman from Whitehorse who was arrested in May 1942 for public drunkenness. Anxious to know how she had obtained the liquor, the police questioned her closely and heard a familiar story:

Enquiries have now revealed that this woman was accosted on a street in the Town by several U.S. Army personnel, who persuaded her to accompany them into the bushes where they gave her several bottles of beer, in the expectation no doubt, of later having sexual intercourse with her. This supposition appears to be borne out by the fact that she stated to myself that one of these soldiers asked her if he could "make love to her." No effort was made by any of those concerned to force her to comply with their request, due no doubt to the fact that she was unwell at this time.

The woman was sentenced to jail; the men were not prosecuted.[94]

Sometimes the women were quite sober when approached, yet liquor was usually offered as an inducement to sex, which speaks volumes about American assumptions about Native women. In June 1943, three Native women from the Watson Lake area were approached by an American soldier, who "asked my sister . . . to go to his camp and he would give her some beer and she could sleep with him. He said the same thing to me as well." When one of the women objected, the soldier brandished a knife. The women complained to the police—for one, it was the second such incident within a year—and the RCMP agreed that charges should be brought. Canadian officials tried to press the Americans on the matter, but could not discover if any action was taken against the man.[95]

The incidents continued, as they were bound to do, given the racial attitudes of the Americans of that era. In the fall of 1943, a group of surveyors stopped to purchase some mittens at the cabin of a Native woman and her thirteen-year-old daughter. A short time later, the jeep driver returned and entered the cabin. He "suggested to her that he have sexual intercourse with her or her daughter for which he would give her ten dollars later on. During this period he had unbuttoned his pants and displayed his person to them." The woman and her daughter, both of whom spoke little English, proved to be poor witnesses, and the RCMP decided not to press the case. The private denied the entire episode and claimed that he had urinated outside the woman's home; she had come outside just as he finished. A U.S. military court found the man guilty and sentenced him to KP (kitchen police) duty twelve hours a day for seven days, restricting him to barracks while off duty.[96]

For the Native women and their communities, such incidents were, of course, highly traumatic. Women who came forward to complain (and there were very few, consistent with the conventional wisdom that only a small percentage of rapes are reported) had to explain the circumstances in detail. They had to face cross-examination by the police, particularly into their sexual and drinking habits, and help locate the accused among the military or civilian workforce; if the case went forward, which it often did not, they had to repeat the process in court.

Though the records show that the women were usually treated gently by the police, this did not mean that they were always taken seriously. Though it may be dangerous to generalize from a few examples, these cases do exhibit a pattern in which the police showed skepticism towards the Native women's claims of abuse and downplayed the damage done. An example is an incident that occurred at Fort Smith in 1942. A local "Native half-breed" woman stated that she was working at home when a soldier entered the house. He played a guitar for a few minutes, and then, she testified,

I told him to leave me alone and then he pulled me over onto the bed and threw me down on the bed and lifted up my dress and lay down on top of me and then he pulled the left side of my bloomers right off my leg and the right side of my bloomers came down to my knee. I was trying to get up. He pulled out a pocket knife out of his pocket and opened the blade and it was a pointed blade and said "If I did not keep quiet he was going to kill me."

The man began to rape her, only to be interrupted when her sister entered the house.

The story was corroborated by two witnesses, the sister, who said she had seen the knife in the man's hand, and a man who reported that the accused had asked him "where he could find a piece of tail" in town. But the police were skeptical. The investigating officer noted the complainant's inability to identify the soldier from a troop parade, wondered why her underwear had not been torn and why she had not cried for help, and questioned other points of her statement. In his report he noted that "Both Mrs. ——— and Mrs. ——— are native half breeds," and speculated that "it is possible that if Mrs. ——— had not seen the offence being committed, that no complaint would have been made." His commanding officer, commenting on the case, concluded that the woman "was a willing party to the alleged offence" who had created the story to protect herself from a jealous husband.[97] Nothing was said about the knife. The point is not whether the police were right or wrong, but that they seemed always to judge the woman's reaction on the basis of how a non-Native woman would have been likely to react—with screams, a struggle, and perhaps tears.

There were a number of other such incidents—an orderly who climbed into bed with a woman in the Bishop Bompas Hospital in Fort Norman, Northwest Territories, and a romantic affair that turned violent near Fort Smith. (The fact that several incidents occurred in the Mackenzie valley was attributed to the large number of black soldiers there.) In the latter case, the woman initially charged the man with rape and a few days later recanted and agreed that she was at least partially responsible for the incident. After investigation, Superintendent R. Bettaney of the RCMP reported that "the circumstances of the case make it probable that the full offense was committed." He did not, however, wish to press prosecution in a Canadian court and wrote that "so long as the offending soldier was charged in a Military Court, found guilty and receives an adequate sentence I would consider then that the ends of Justice were served." Importantly, Bettaney made it clear that the woman's private history had some bearing on his decision; "I make this statement having in mind the reported notoriously loose character of the complainant."[98]

It should be noted that this attitude was sexist as well as racist. In southern courts, women complaining of rape were also routinely subjected to cross-examination about their sexual habits, and there was a general feeling that a woman who dressed provocatively or was overly friendly in her manner was "asking for it," a belief that has by no means been eradicated from society.

Whether the sex was consensual or forced, there was always a possibility that it would result in pregnancy. For a number of reasons it is impossible to quantify the incidence of pregnancy resulting from interracial sex during these years, not the least of which is that so few of the fathers took any responsibility for their children.

Some, of course, did not know that they were fathers, and in some documented cases the mothers did not know who the fathers were. Even in relations of longer duration the fathers generally shirked responsibility. One American had formed a relatively stable relationship with a Native woman from Whitehorse. "He went with one of my daughters proposing marriage then when she found out she was going to have a Baby he told her he was already married and couldn't marry her we went to see him and he agreed to support her." When he left the North and failed to honor his promise, the woman's parents applied to the Whitehorse RCMP and the Edmonton police for help, but they were unable to find him, nor did the U.S. authorities offer any assistance.[99] The upshot of this case and others like it was that the Canadian government bent the regulations of the Indian Act, which stated that the children of Native women and non-Native men were officially nonstatus, that is, ineligible for benefits as Indians. Instead, in cases where the father could not be found or refused to acknowledge paternity, the children were assumed to be Native in the eyes of the law.[100]

The nature of sexual relations in the Northwest during World War II reflects the unusual combination of stereotypes, of demographic and racial imbalance, local poverty and lack of contact with the outside world that marked the region during World War II. The sexual tensions of life in the military and on the frontier combined with the isolation of the region and the racial temper of the time to form a potent force. Yet despite the cases cited above, the small number of women and the isolation of the men limited the actual amount of sexual activity that occurred. Some men abused women, particularly Native women, but the total amount of sexual activity in the region paled in comparison with the major cities and other places where armies of occupation came in contact with the local population.

6. The Transformation of Northern Communities

"FORT ST. JOHN was the most dismal little settlement I had ever seen. The one street, lined by dilapidated and unpainted frame buildings, was a slough of mud which had the consistency of axle grease. There were no sidewalks, and the floors of all public buildings were nearly as deep in mud as the street."[1] Thus the *National Geographic* magazine described the town for its readers early in 1943. But peaceful armies of occupation have a tremendous power to transform the communities in their path, as Fort St. John and other Northwest settlements were to learn. The roads, the bridges, the airfields that the occupiers build inevitably give new direction to a region's development. Communities bypassed by the armies can wither; the best example in the Canadian Northwest is Dawson City, which began to decline in importance when the U.S. Army based its operations in the rival town of Whitehorse. Those attached to the new network flourish and take on a greater importance; the examples in the Canadian Northwest are Dawson Creek and Norman Wells. In the long run this benefits the community (if growth is considered beneficial), but in the short term the army of occupation can put a tremendous strain on the community and its people. The army can tax services to the breaking point and test the resolve and patience of local residents who see their towns and villages transformed in a matter of weeks.

Historians have often noted the capacity of war to transform society, though they have paid little attention to the impact of war on smaller centers.[2] In his study of World War II and the American West, Gary Nash has shown how wartime spending, military activity, and construction sparked a massive growth of population, encouraged urban development, and altered the racial composition of the region.[3] The same thing occurred on the Canadian prairies, though on a smaller scale. The construction of airfields and other facilities for the Commonwealth Air Training Program, the establishment of military centers and localized manufacturing facilities altered the nature of life in the region and expanded the role of many obscure prairie communities (for example, Rocanville, Saskatchewan, which produced oil cans for the Allied forces).[4] The construction of the Project Crimson airfields at such previously isolated outposts as Chimo, in northern Quebec, and Frobisher Bay, on Baffin Island, provided a core around which modern communities would eventually develop.[5]

The Canadian Northwest provides a particularly striking example of these forces at work. The Alaska Highway swiftly changed the settlement pattern of the country northwest of Fort St. John; construction camps and maintenance yards, often built near existing trading posts and seasonal Indian camps, provided a new regional focus, and the thousands who lived in them soon outnumbered the local population.

The community that experienced the first boom was Edmonton, which served for a time as the headquarters of the Northwest Service Command. It was also the major transshipment point for all the defense projects; thousands of people and tens of thousands of tons of equipment passed through the city to the Alaska Highway and Canol projects. The city's airport was also an important refueling and repair depot for the lend-lease network delivering airplanes to the Soviet Union. A wartime article in the *Vancouver News Herald,* headlined "Edmonton, Gateway to a New Frontier, Bustles with Northern Project Affairs," was full of enthusiasm about the hectic activity in the city. Business was booming, skilled workers were in great demand, hotels were filled to capacity, every available building had been pressed into service, "and all because of thousands of Americans—engineers and servicemen—working out from Edmonton on those projects which have been undertaken by the United States Army in the program of defence." "The whole picture is BIG," wrote reporter Laree Spray. "In unpretentious offices, the requirements of thousands of men are learned. And from these offices, the orders go out and deliveries are arranged. Almost every day huge convoys, involving hundreds of trucks, roll out from Edmonton, headed north. . . . It's a hectic, mushroom-growing city, but an optimistic, happy one."[6] It was an urban booster's dream come true.

Edmonton was already a sizable city, with a population in 1942 of 95,000, so the invasion did not completely overwhelm it.[7] Nevertheless, the city experienced a period of dramatic growth and change as the American military and civilian authorities went on a binge of building, buying, renting, and hiring. By the spring of 1943 its population had increased to 119,000, building permits issued had tripled over the previous year, and the local paper was touting the town as the "Young Chicago of the North."[8] The local Jesuit college building was bought by Bechtel-Price-Callahan for its headquarters, and new buildings were put up to handle equipment and support staff; while the work was being completed, the company was given free temporary office space in the basement of First Presbyterian Church.[9] This purchase and subsequent renovations played a minor role in the scandal over the Canol Project cost overruns. In January 1944 the American broadcaster Fulton Lewis, Jr., reported on the expenditures connected with the project, singling out the "luxurious" accommodations at the former Jesuit college for particular criticism. Some of the new facilities there had been built not with sober, cost-effective plywood, but with imported California redwood, which says a good deal about the cost-plus contract system.[10] Historic buildings, including the family home of Frank Oliver, one-time member of Parliament and minister of the interior, were taken over and converted into office space.[11]

Acute shortage of space of all kinds was the order of the day. When bad weather halted the flow of planes to the Northwest, grounding several hundred American pilots, hotels quickly filled, and the overflow had to be billeted in private homes. [12] New quarters were quickly thrown up, including a makeshift hotel with a capacity of 200. When Bechtel-Price-Callahan surveyed its employees on the housing situation, nearly half were unhappy with it. The unhappy ones were the married men looking for housing for their wives and children, and this was the main reason why the authorities discouraged those dependents from coming to the Northwest. Despite all efforts, there was a serious housing shortage in Edmonton throughout much of the war. The classified advertisments in the *Edmonton Journal* were full of pleas from "American Official[s]" who were looking for a "well-furnished house or apartment. For long- or short-term lease. Guarantee care of property. Pay any rent for suitable home."[13] At the end of 1942, the newspaper reported that

One official said more than 100 people "are putting up with temporary accommodation—three or four of them living in one room . . . we could use a thousand suites. We could rent them in about a week. Long-time residents of the city, living in large homes, don't seem to realize the seriousness of the situation. Surely some of them have one or two rooms they are not using." Working in co-operation with the Y.W.C.A., the Edmonton emergency accommodation bureau, in the past few months, has found living quarters for thousands of persons.[14]

Some landlords took advantage of the shortage, as a letter from "Two Americans" revealed:

We come from one of the most congested areas in the U.S. . . . Yet the maximum rent allowed under the O.P.A. is $14 per month for a nice double room cleaned and made up each day. But here . . . the two of us have been charged $25 to $40 for a basement or attic room, and $10 for a heated garage! At one place, the tenants, who paid $27.50 for the six-room house, sublet to us a tiny upstairs room with no door, for $25 which proved a perfect vent for all their greasy cooking and tobacco smoke. . . . Another time we paid $22.50 for 18 days in an 8' × 10' room containing only a chiffonier and double bed, sublet to us by tenants who were paying only $52.50 per month for the completely new 4-room apartment. . . . We can't understand how a city like Edmonton . . . can allow such conditions to be imposed on the citizens of a country that is your ally.[15]

Because of its large population, Edmonton was not an example of the way in which the army of occupation overwhelmed the locals;

Vehicles and equipment being loaded onto barges at Dawson City, on their way down the Yukon River to Alaska—one of the few episodes in which construction activity touched the old territorial capital. (YTA, C. Haines Collection, 1949).

rather, it was a situation in which the relations of the Allies were on a much more equal footing than in a place like Whitehorse or Norman Wells. Long-time residents of the city complained a good deal about the dislocations of the wartime activities—the housing shortages, the labor shortages caused by the generous pay offered by the Americans, the dust and noise of the construction equipment, the raffish ways of the soldiers. But Edmonton had not only served this kind of function ever since the Klondike gold rush, it had actively sought it. Although the invasion of 1942 was far greater than that of 1898, it fit neatly within the city's self-proclaimed role as the gateway to the Northwest, so the reaction of the citizens to it was bound to be ambivalent.

The Americans, for their part, had a variety of reactions to Edmonton. Some were not impressed. "Edmonton," one American observed, "like many Canadians insist, has become an 'American town.' It doesn't seem so to Americans. By American standards, there isn't much doing in town."[16] New York mayor Fiorello LaGuardia, a member of the Canadian-American Permanent Joint Board on Defence, observed somewhat slyly during a visit that Edmonton was "a most attractive city from the air."[17] Other Americans were anxious to flatter the locals. One New York journalist wrote a piece in the Edmonton paper in the time-honored style of Americans who thought Canadians would be pleased to hear that there was no difference between themselves and their southern neighbors: "If I had been knocked on the head in New York City a couple of days ago and had just come to here I would have thought I was still in New York City. You have all the things we have in New York, street cars, automobiles, raids, juke boxes and even hamburger emporiums."[18] This mixture of condescension and gee-whiz ingenuousness (automobiles! golly, you mean they don't drive dogsleds down the main street of Edmonton?) which is standard fare for American writers has always amused and irritated Canadians, but during the war the official Canadian reaction was generally upbeat. As one Canadian writer put it, "Edmonton is a test tube in which to study the impact of the new American Abroad on a friendly neighbour, and the effect on the American himself. The mix is working well."[19]

Of course the possibility of misunderstanding and conflict was always present, and the U.S. authorities were at pains to avoid awkward situations. After a number of articles appeared in the U.S. press about the critical housing shortage in Edmonton, workers on the Canol Project were ordered not to make any statements "relative to conditions in Canada and concerning the project."[20] As a symbol of Edmonton's new status, the rank of the U.S. diplomatic representative in town was upgraded from consul to consul general, and the staff allocated to the Edmonton consulate was increased.[21] John Randolph, the U.S. consul general who arrived in Edmonton in April 1942, kept a high profile in the community and traveled throughout the region to keep abreast of construction activities.[22] In his first month on the job, Randolph called on Premier William Aberhart and the entire Alberta cabinet, the city's mayor, the Chamber of Commerce, the Chamber of Mines, senior members of the local press corps, and a bevy of other notables, including military and police officials, university officials, businessmen, and bank managers. He also joined the Edmonton Club, "the leading men's social club of the city," in order to keep in touch with civic leaders.[23] Community boosters were only too anxious to welcome their allies. The Rotary Club, eager to educate the newcomers about Canada, issued a pamphlet entitled "Welcome, American," which described the country's geography, population, economy, and constitution—all in three pages. It ended with stirring words:

This, then, is Canada, big in area and resources, varied in terrain and products, small in population, active in trade and industry, independent in status, democratic in government, loyal to the British Commonwealth of Nations, and saturated with the same freedom that you yourselves treasure. To this Canada we bid you a warm welcome, with every good wish for your sojourn among us and God-speed on your return home.[24]

A less sanguine picture of the American presence was given by Pierrepont Moffat, U.S. ambassador in Ottawa, who visited Edmonton in July 1942 and reported "a disturbing increase of friction between Canadians and Americans, particularly in regions where American troops are so numerous as to give them the feeling of having certain proprietary rights." There was, he wrote,

first of all lack of discipline in the city. Perhaps it is because no one treats Edmonton as a foreign service station. Men in uniform are racing around in jeeps, on what is obviously pleasure bent [sic], often with girls riding in the jeeps. Despite the critical shortage of housing, nearly everyone who could do so has brought in wife and children. One of the big contractors has been trying to buy a large apartment house with a view to evicting its residents into a city where alternative accommodation is unobtainable.

Moffat expressed alarm at the fact that few of the American officers had ever visited Canadian civil authorities or tried to enlist their cooperation. The fault, he said, was not all on the Americans' side, for Canadian construction work was "dishearteningly slow," they were "short in most modern construction equipment," and "their labor is casual and at times dishearteningly apathetic." Nonetheless, he found that the Canadians had a "strong will to cooperate," and were "pathetically hopeful that out of the intermingling of Canadians and American a greater friendship will grow." He made two recommendations:

First, to put a senior officer in overall charge, who has authority and tact, who realizes that he is functioning in a foreign country and that depending on his attitude he will get either full cooperation or else only grudging help, who will appreciate the importance of discipline and observance of Canadian regulations as well as respect for their susceptibilities. Second, I believe that Edmonton should be treated as a foreign post on active service, that wives and children should be sent home, and an attitude of being on campaign should be inculcated.[25]

In response, the U.S. authorities denied that there was any significant friction. A senior Canadian officer remarked that "any personnel that have caused some unpleasantness at times have been civilian"; the mayor of Edmonton said that the conduct of the Americans was "exemplary"; and the police chief said that it was "excellent from a police point of view."[26] For their part the Americans tried to be better neighbors and visitors. Senior American military officers ordered their staff to support local activities and otherwise ingratiate themselves with Edmontonians. In September 1943, for example, Lieutenant Colonel C. M. Clifford of the U.S. Army Corps of Engineers issued a memo encouraging his staff to contribute generously to the Community Chest Club (the forerunner of the United Way), which was then raising funds on behalf of local charities.[27]

Part of the reaction of Edmontonians to the army of occupation was based on relief and gratitude that the United States was helping with the war, and part was based on American efforts to behave as good guests. But much of it was a reaction to the massive injection of money into the community that the American presence represented, in contrast to the Canadian government, which Edmontonians felt had always neglected the city. Soldiers and civilian workers assigned to the city spent millions of dollars there, and more millions came from men on temporary leave there from more distant camps. The Americans were great employers of local labor. Even larger expenditures came through purchases of material. A good part of the supplies for the southern end of the Alaska Highway and Canol routes was purchased in the Edmonton–Fort St. John corridor. A Canadian investigation carried out in August 1942 disclosed that although the Americans had brought in some of their food (especially meat) from the United States, they had bought over 70 tons of fresh vegetables since the spring of that year in Edmonton and 4,000 sacks of flour in Calgary. They had bought locally 400,000 board feet of lumber, $30,000 worth of tools and other hardware, and tens of thousands of gallons of petroleum products. With the Public Roads Administration just getting its operations under way in the region, it was clear that the projects were bringing a bonanza to the business sector.[28] Regional businesses geared up to cash in on this bonanza as much as they could, though they were somewhat constrained by the wartime regulations governing prices, wages, supplies, and labor. Canadian Pacific Airlines, for example, moved its western headquarters from Winnipeg to Edmonton to handle the "enormous volume of air transportation being required by the Governments of Canada and the United States."[29] Overall, Edmonton managed to absorb the invasion without major upheaval, and its result for the city was increased prosperity rather than serious disruption.

The same was not true of the smaller centers to the north and northwest of Edmonton, where the arrival of the army of occupation brought prosperity, but also considerable dislocation. For some people in the remote areas the Americans were like saviors. One such was Dorothy Mackintosh, a resident of Bear Creek, 100 miles west of Whitehorse. Her husband had operated a small trading post there. After he died in 1938 she had tried to keep it going, but was just about ready to abandon it and leave the community. Suddenly, thousands of Americans descended upon her, cleaned out her stock, and built a road linking her to Whitehorse. Instead of a difficult annual trip to town for supplies, she could now drive there in a few hours: "Until the road was built she often went months without seeing a white person and she was always alone when the Indians were on their traplines." Now she was kept busy at all hours making tea and cooking meals for hundreds of soldiers and civilian workers who stopped at her picturesque cabin at the foot of the St. Elias Mountains.[30] For Mrs. Mackintosh, the frontier had truly been rolled back.

For young people in the Northwest, the American posed no threat; they were friendly, rich, and generous. One man, who was a boy of twelve when the Americans arrived, remembered their generosity with food: "The diet was terrific and . . . they used to have the C rations there. Little brown boxes and the soldiers didn't like them. They'd prefer anything else so they'd swindle the cook into making them bag lunches. . . . They didn't like the C rations or K rations. . . . So I used to bring those home. . . . We used to give the stuff to other kids who didn't have enough to eat." There were other opportunities for a boy with his wits about him. On one occasion in July 1943 a troop train was derailed near Dawson Creek and the troops were ordered not to leave it.

So I thought, what a market. These guys are all complaining about the thirst . . . I raced into town, got a couple of cream cans . . . chopped up a bunch of ice in a local ice house, threw it in the can, went to the well and pumped it full of ice cold water, went flying down the road, six inches off the ground, down to the train wreck, and the soldiers just gathered round. I didn't charge them . . . just make a donation . . . I got American dollars left and right, and I got, I don't know, $20 a can for that water . . . you know, my pants were hanging down, loaded with money from these rich Americans who were just delighted with a drink of ice cold water.[31]

Before 1942, most of the communities north and northwest of Edmonton, from Waterways to Norman Wells, from Fort Nelson to Burwash, were primarily fur-trading posts, their tiny permanent population swollen on a seasonal basis by nomadic Native families. Except for regional centers like Whitehorse (see chapter 7), Fort St. John, and Dawson Creek, they had no government facilities or services, beyond the ubiquitous detachment of one or two members of the Royal Canadian Mounted Police. Not all of these tiny, obscure places were touched by the army of occupation, of course, but those that were experienced a tremendous upheaval as they were hauled in the space of weeks into the maelstrom of the mid twentieth century. Housing stocks everywhere were totally inadequate to accommodate the influx of people, a deficiency only partly alleviated by the rapid construction of military and civilian quarters. Where there were municipal services such as piped water, these also proved hopelessly inadequate. Such hotels and boardinghouses as existed were crammed; in some places customers rented a bed, not a room, and were guaranteed only eight hours' occupancy, since the beds were used in shifts. Knox McCusker, who led a survey crew in the early stages of highway construction, remarked on the change in Fort St. John between the spring and summer of 1942: "At Fort St. John, in our absence, everything had changed, from a one-restaurant town where the proprietor was his own best customer, the place supported seven eating places unable to handle the business. Sleeping places were almost impossible to get with parking spaces in the feed barn loft selling at $1.00 a night. The neighbour's field was an army camp. His hogs wore a bilious look presumably from imbibing too freely of army swill."[32]

Efforts were made to alleviate the crush on the small settlement. U.S. authorities established a strict permit system for travel along the Alaska Highway and Canol pipeline route. Government accommodations were not available without authorization, and permits were required before travelers were even allowed to enter the region.[33] Rules posted in September 1943 stated that "all personnel traveling on commercial aircraft whose destination is Watson Lake or Fort Nelson airport will be required to have in their possession a letter authorizing their presence at the airport in question."[34] Americans could have no quarrel with such regulations, but Canadian civilians did complain, fruitlessly, about American rules that limited their freedom to travel in their own country.

The U.S. Army responded to the accommodation crisis by taking buildings from forty former Civilian Conservation Corps camps, which had been dismantled and stored in warehouses across the American West, crating them, and shipping them to the Canadian Northwest, where crews reconstructed them.[35] Workers in the Fort Smith area were ordered to make do with more rustic quarters: "In the event adequate housing does not exist you will immediately proceed to construct log houses for your personnel utilizing poles, moss and earth for roofing."[36] A shortage of logs at Fort Simpson was filled by a local entrepreneur who bought and set up a small sawmill to supply the local demand for building material.[37] In December 1942 the Army Corps of Engineers shipped 300 carloads of "knocked-down houses" from Dallas, Texas, to Edmonton and points north.[38] While these kept the rain and bugs at bay, they were hopelessly inadequate for a sub-Arctic winter and caused much misery for those who had to live in them.

The Standard Oil Company made the same mistake when it drew up plans for its northern refinery staff based on "California type bungalows with flat roofs."[39] Not only the buildings but also the services provided for them were improperly insulated, requiring the shivering residents to keep the taps flowing all winter to prevent the pipes from freezing.[40] At war's end, these buildings were turned

A snapshot of the fire that followed the Dawson Creek explosion, February 1943. (Courtesy Joe Garbus)

over to the Canadian Army, which in 1949 was still trying to get enough money to insulate them properly, remarking that those stationed in them "suffer severe privations in winter."[41]

By any standard previously known in the Northwest, the scale of wartime construction was truly massive; only the Klondike gold rush was comparable, and it had been focused on a very small region, in contrast to the far-flung activities of wartime. In September 1942 the Northwest Service Command announced its construction plans for Dawson Creek, Whitehorse, and Fairbanks. Housing for more than 2,000 men was to be built in each of the three centers. In addition, storage space was to be built: in Dawson Creek, 240,000 square feet; in Fairbanks, 230,000; and in Whitehorse, 80,000. Forecasts called for 3,000 more men in each place and a total of between 1 million and 2 million square feet of storage space altogether. Requirements for steel huts (the ubiquitous quonset hut, named after the Rhode Island naval base where the design was first used) included 266 for Dawson Creek, 279 for Whitehorse, and 263 for Fairbanks. Three million dollars was allocated for the first phase of this construction.[42]

The port of Prince Rupert experienced a "literal invasion":

Shipping facilities were increased by doubling the size of the ocean dock and building a large warehouse adjacent to it across the railroad tracks, with an overhead passage and elevator. The great number of American personnel were housed in a camp on the top of Acropolis hill and the administration occupied a large structure erected on First Avenue . . . the water supply . . . was far from adequate. Booster pumps—seven in all— were added to increase the flow and the water was chlorinated much to the chagrin of the local inhabitants.[43]

At Norman Wells, initial construction activity was designed to provide a "minimum in requirements for warehousing, refrigeration, living accommodation, cooking and messing facilities, hospitalization, heating and sanitary requirements." In 1943, when the pace had slackened somewhat, married quarters and accommodations for single women were built, the power plant was expanded, repair and storage facilities improved, and a large dining hall–recreation hall–office complex constructed. In 1944 the camp took on a more permanent look when Cemestos (single-family units) were built for the families of "key personnel" and amenities like a proper fire hall constructed. The transition experienced at Norman Wells—from a frenetic boom town in 1942, with a scattering of hastily constructed buildings, to a small, planned community, completed with a complex of prefabricated buildings and facilities—was typical of the experience in many isolated posts in the Canadian Northwest between 1942 and 1945.

All this new construction, much of which was poorly planned, caused short- and long-term problems for the smaller settlements of the Northwest. Most of them had only the most rudimentary services, and could not meet the demands of their own residents for water and sewage services, let alone respond to the enormous increase in demand that accompanied the American invasion. In communities where residents did not draw their own water from wells and streams, for example, it was often delivered by horse-drawn cart, a system that obviously fell short of meeting the requirements of the new order.

Dawson Creek, for instance, had taken its water from a series of local wells. Soon after the Americans arrived, the increased demand for water caused most of the wells to run dry. The army dealt with the problem by running a 12-inch pipeline from a nearby lake to the camp. This solved the army's difficulty, but since the pipeline bypassed the settlement by two miles, it did nothing for the residents. Eventually Canadian officials applied for and were granted permission to tap into the water line, providing a regular water supply to the civilian population.[44]

In other places throughout the Northwest, water mains, sewage lines, roads, and other community facilities constructed for wartime use eventually became the foundation of postwar municipal services. The U.S. authorities viewed these facilities, which they were compelled in any case to build for their own people, as opportunities to cultivate local goodwill. In several places water, sewer service, and sometimes electricity were provided free to local residents, a generous policy that went a long way to disarm any possible criticism of the invading forces.[45]

To provide these services, and especially to construct the hundreds of buildings needed for headquarters and camp operations, the U.S. authorities had to arrange for the acquisition of the necessary real estate. The Army Corps of Engineers had a number of men who did nothing else but that, real estate officers whose duties were to make formal arrangements with property owners and with municipal, provincial, and national governments. The process was often hampered by technicalities. When Bechtel-Price-Callahan wanted to buy the Jesuit college in Edmonton, for instance, it arranged that the army would buy the property, but then discovered that an act of Congress was required before the military could purchase property in a foreign country. The company then offered to buy it directly, but later backed out when it failed to get financial guarantees from Washington.

In the Dawson Creek–Fort St. John region, the preliminary surveys for the Alaska Highway began without any negotiations with local property owners, generating some understandable resentment. The U.S. authorities were confused by the overlapping federal, provincial, and territorial jurisdictions in Canada. Eventually the Canadian bureaucracy lent a hand; Canadian surveyors from the Land Settlement Branch worked with the Americans to make suitable arrangements in British Columbia, while the Bureau of Northwest Territories and Yukon Affairs helped out in both those places and in northern Alberta. With the threat of expropriation hanging over them, local landowners had little room for haggling, and the policy was to make them offers they could not refuse:

It was decided that our valuations and proposed settlements would be decided before we started to discuss the matter with the farmer concerned, as I did not feel we should allow any bargaining to take place. It is the intention to treat every case in an equitable way and tell them at once what we are going to ask them to accept, so that each man will get the same fair deal, and if any refuse, the figures already set will be our recommendation in any event, and this will be explained to them.[46]

Eventually the responsibility for land acquisitions was transferred to the Land Settlement Branch, a Canadian agency familiar with local laws and regulations. But difficulties continued, particularly when U.S. officials negotiated with Canadian landowners without telling Canadian authorities what they were doing. As with so many aspects of the American advance into the Canadian Northwest, the initial occupation took place without much attention to legalities. However, after the Special Commissioner's Office was set up in 1943 to represent the Canadian government's interest in the region, efforts were made to harmonize and legitimize the Americans' use of land in the various communities of the region.[47] An agreement signed that year called for the Canadian government to buy the land required for the use of the U.S. government, while American civilian contractors were to make their own arrangements. Canada assumed control of leases already signed by Washington, and agreed to make the properties involved available free to the Americans for the duration of the war, subject to six months' notice of cancellation.[48]

The amount of land involved in these arrangements throughout the Northwest was substantial (see table 12). Some was leased for a nominal one-dollar fee, but larger sums were often involved: the Canadian National Railway Company, for instance, leased a block of property in Prince Rupert to the Americans for $24,000 a year, and four of the thirty-six parcels of land in Edmonton were leased for more than $1,000. And this list does not include large blocks of provincial or federal land used by the army of occupation outside the centers of population, or other parcels, such as the White Pass and Yukon Route property in Whitehorse and Skagway, that were part of the army's temporary takeover of a private company.[49] Despite the complex of formal reporting systems and other arrangements that were set up to legalize the American acquisition of land in the Northwest, problems continued to arise, as they were bound to do given the extreme haste in which arrangements were made.[50] American airfields in the Northwest Territories, for example, were built without the completion of proper surveys of the lands on which they stood, making it impossible to secure a proper title to them. The difficulties persisted almost to the end of the war: "In the first place the United States authorities were and seemingly still are unable to produce the leases they have entered into affecting lands in Yukon Territory. In the second place the Special Commissioner has altogether failed to alleviate the situation this is about the only problem we have asked him to undertake." To help out, C. K. LeCapelain, temporarily loaned to the Special Commissioner's Office, was returned to the Bureau of the Northwest Territories and Yukon Affairs with orders to investigate all outstanding property questions in the Yukon Territory.[51]

Table 12   U.S. Land Leases and Assignments, January 31, 1945

Community	Number of Leases
Edmonton, Alberta	36
Fitzgerald, Alberta	2
Grande Prairie, Alberta	1
McMurray, Alberta	1
Onoway, Alberta	3
Peace River, Alberta	2
Dawson Creek, B.C.	9
Fort St. John, B.C.	3
Port Edward, B.C.	9
Prince Rupert, B.C.	37
Regina, Saskatchewan	3
Hudson Bay Junction, Saskatchewan	1
Fort Smith, N.W.T.	2
Whitehorse, Yukon	1

SOURCE: NAC, RG 85, vol. 983, file 15043, W. W. Foster to R. A. Gibson, 9 February 1945.

Another government service that was totally unprepared for the arrival of the army of occupation was the regional educational system. Before the war it had consisted of a small number of day schools that taught Native children when seasonal activities brought their parents in from the bush, a few Native residential schools, and some schools for non-Native children in the larger centers. The influx of the dependents of military and civilian workers overwhelmed these small schools—not in 1942, when the majority of workers arrived without families, but later, when the authorities were trying to establish a more settled workforce:

Canadians are being engaged and quarters have been fixed up for married men in the hope of getting a better class of men who will stay with the job for a reasonable length of time. A considerable portion of the Canadians who have been on the job have been of the type which flit from one job to another. Those who are doing the hiring for the Americans maintain that it would help them get satisfactory personnel if the Canadian Governments would guarantee health, welfare and educational services. [52]

By 1944, the policy of hiring married men with families was proving successful on the British Columbia sections of the highway, where it was reported that "a continuity of labor has been secured resulting in economy and efficiency. It is considered by United States authorities that similar results will follow the provision of educational facilities in the Yukon."[53]

But the addition of even a few hundred children to the tiny regional educational system placed a tremendous burden on it, while at the same time, the lack of a proper school system made it difficult to recruit family men for northern service.[54] There was no problem with the Canol route, which was already in the process of abandonment by 1945, or with the wartime airports, but plans called for 500 families to settle along the Alaska Highway by 1945, and an expansion of services was clearly needed, particularly outside the larger centers. Planning was complicated by the division of authority between the Yukon and British Columbia, which made joint action difficult.[55] One solution suggested by the Americans, who had the responsibility for hiring men for the maintenance camps, was to centralize families with school-age children in a few of them.[56] The alternative was to have a school at every place where there were young children, which would have been very expensive, and which posed the problem of recruiting teachers to serve in such isolated places (see tables 13 and 14). The statistics show that some places had only one or two school-age children, which made a proper school impractical. One proposal was to remove all children on the British Columbia section of the highway to a central location, probably Fort St. John, for schooling.[57] Another was to teach the children by means of a correspondence course, a method favored by bureaucrats because it was cheaper than the alternatives and had been used successfully in remote parts of the Yukon and Northwest Territories for years.[58] That option was given serious consideration by the British Columbia authorities, who commissioned Gordon Shrum, director of university extension at the University of British Columbia, to review the situation. He recommended a correspondence program involving the hiring of two field instructors, at an annual cost of $15,000.[59] George Jeckell, comptroller of the Yukon, warned that such a program should not be free to the parents: "I very much fear that if Government makes the course free," he wrote, "that much less consideration will be given to getting full value out of it by the parents."[60] Another suggestion was a traveling teacher program, in which an instructor would circulate like an itinerant preacher among a number of camps along the highway; Jeckell opposed this idea as well.[61]

Though evidence is scanty, it is likely that a number of children living along the Alaska Highway received a pretty sketchy formal

Table 13   School age Children, Alaska Highway Maintenance Employees, December 1944

	British Columbia	Yukon
Total employees on highway maintenance	450	330
Family apartments available	128	49
Number of children	161	19
Number of children of school age	77	15[a]
Family apartments available, June 30, 1945	142	111

Source: NAC, RG 36/7, vol. 15, file 28-12, Foster to Heeney, 29 December 1944.
[a]Includes 10 at Whitehorse.

Table 14   School-age Children, Alaska Highway Maintenance
Employees, August 1945

Camp	Total Workers	Families	Total Children	School-age Children
Kiskatinaw	7	6	14	11[a]
Blueberry	6	5	14	12[a]
Sikanni	5	5	12	10[a]
Truth	8	7	6	4
Prophet River	6	5	6	4
Fort Nelson Jct.	7	2	2	1
Summit Lake	6	5	1	0
Muncho Lake	6	4	6	3
Coal River	6	4	7	2
Watson Lake Jct.	10	6	9	7[b]
Swift River	8	6	7	5
Teslin	8	6	7	7[b]
Marsh Lake	5	5	5	1
Whitehorse (HQ)	6	2	0	0
Stoney Creek	8	4	5	1
Haines Jct.	9	6	6	4
Destruction Bay	11	5	16	16[a]
Koidern	10	3	5	3
Bridge crew	14	0	0	0
Repair crews	26	0	0	0

SOURCE: NAC RG 22, vol. 109, file 84-32-6, pt. 3, Special Commissioner, 27th
Report, p. 26, 31 August 1945.
[a]Schools recommended for these locations.
[b]Other students in these locations, enough for a shcool.

education during 1944 and 1945. The offerings available through correspondence were meager, and the arrangements made for schooling in some places were fairly rough and ready. In Watson Lake, for example, when a number of workers with families asked for a proper school, Alaska Highway Maintenance offered to provide a school, pay to maintain it, and provide a residence for a teacher. It would supply a female teacher by the expedient of hiring a man married to one. The Yukon territorial government would pay for school supplies and the teacher's salary.[62] Significant improvements in education in the region would come only at the end of the war.

While some aspects of civilian life did improve during the war,

The 18th Engineers band giving a Fourth of July concert for the troops at their camp on Kluane Lake, 1942. The large building is an abandoned roadhouse of gold-rush vintage. (YTA, MM Collection, 3976)

many communities faced major dislocations. Sometimes the disruption of life in the region could be terribly swift, as happened in a notorious incident in Dawson Creek. There, in February 1943, dynamite improperly stored in a downtown livery stable exploded, killing 20 people, injuring over 100, and leveling a city block.[63] The destruction of the local hotel and several restaurants left the community even more pinched for space, and the damage to the local electric plant forced doctors and nurses to attend to the wounded by candlelight. The town, wrote one reporter, "presents a sorrowful sight of boarded windows and injured persons limping around as best they can."[64] A number of communities suffered outbreaks of fire that were associated with the American presence; Whitehorse had at least two serious blazes—one in November 1942 that destroyed the old Mounted Police residence and a private cabin, and another the next month that destroyed the North Star Athletic Association Hall, a private facility leased to the U.S. Army.[65]

Such disasters were not all loss, however. Looking back on the

Dawson Creek explosion, the regional newspaper described it as a "useful disaster," because it resulted in a downtown core of "handsome new modern fireproof buildings." The town, which had a population of about 700 before the war, mushroomed to 10,000, then stabilized at 4,000 by 1945. After the 1943 explosion, the business district of the town was entirely rebuilt:

Many new and modern buildings of brick and stucco construction were erected, and the town now has three modern hotels, five general stores, eight efficient restaurants, five up to date garages, two drug stores, three wholesale houses, and many other retail businesses, including hardware, furniture, lady's ready to wear, electrical, variety and shoe stores, etc., most of them occupying new and modern buildings.[66]

Overall, the war was good for Dawson Creek, despite the great fire. By early 1944 the town's population had increased from a prewar total of about 700 to more than 2,200 in the incorporated area, with 3,000 more in an adjacent subdivision, and this did not include military personnel or the civilian construction camps. In one year, between 1943 and 1944, its assessment on land and improvements had more than doubled, from $425,300 to $942,900. The town had no municipal debt, and was planning to spend $60,000 on permanent improvements. It was also at the starting point of a great international highway.[67]

At the opposite extreme was the slow, lingering deterioration of Dawson City. For the old Yukon capital, which for more than forty years had been the most important town in Canada northwest of Edmonton, the Northwest defense projects were a death sentence. Some early plans for the Alaska Highway had it running through Dawson, but the road as built bypassed the town by more than 200 miles. The bulk of the construction activities also passed it by, with the result that the town, whose population had been stable for years, went into a serious decline, and it was whispered, particularly in the boom town of Whitehorse, that Dawson City was doomed. No one resented the changes more than George Jeckell, whose career in the Yukon Territory went back to his arrival as a young schoolteacher in 1902. He waged a campaign to convince the world that life remained in Dawson City, pointing out that the town still had more than 150 children of school age, and that its residents had not only contributed over $140,000 to a recent War Bond drive, but had bought more than $48,000 worth of liquor between November 1941 and February 1942—apparently a good barometer of civic vitality. "I have observed over a period of years," he wrote, "that Dawson receives many knocks, and even from old-timers, some of whom in their desire to paint a lurid picture of Dawson in the early days, are not averse to creating the impression that Dawson City is now nothing more than a Ghost Town."[68]

But this was whistling in the dark; the Yukon was not big enough to support two urban centers, and when the U.S. Army chose Whitehorse as its regional headquarters, Dawson City's fate was sealed. By 1943, businesses and families were moving from the old city to the new, hoping to capitalize on the opportunities offered by the construction projects. So many people left the Klondike region that its main employer, the Yukon Consolidated Gold Corporation, took the unprecedented step of hiring Native people to work on its dredges. Jeckell refused to visit Whitehorse on any but emergency business, bristled at suggestions that he move his office there, even temporarily, and generally behaved as if the construction projects did not exist. This was foolish, since it made no sense to have the Yukon's administration so far from the center of activity in the Territory, and was also futile, since it did no good to ignore the army of occupation. By 1945 what remained of Dawson City's business community was begging the federal government for a road link to the Alaska Highway—proof, if any was needed, of the new southern orientation of the Territory.[69]

By the end of the war, communities from Edmonton to Fairbanks and down the Mackenzie River valley had been transformed, sometimes almost beyond recognition. The army of occupation had built entire towns, in some places on top of existing settlements. Hundreds of warehouses, administrative headquarters, barracks, quonset huts, garages, and facilities of all sorts had been built to serve the Northwest defense projects. Municipal roads, water and sewage systems, movie theaters, athletic facilities had mushroomed everywhere. Local developers had added to the construction boom by putting up houses, stores, hotels, and other buildings to meet the wartime demand.

Most of these changes were more or less permanent; the communities affected by them would never return to the way they had been in 1940. Some settlements had been completely reoriented; in 1940 they had been clustered around rivers and lakes, serving the fur trade, while by 1944 they looked to the new roads and airfields. The new municipal facilities left behind by the Americans provided the foundation for continued growth in the postwar years. Most important of all, the Northwest defense projects destroyed forever the isolation of the Canadian Northwest, providing easy access by air, road, and telephone to the rest of the continent. Communities once slumbering in the enforced isolation of distance now could anticipate the growth and development of the postwar world.

7. Whitehorse: Creation of a City

"THE ARRIVAL OF the advance party of U.S. Army Engineering Corps on Saturday last presented an unusual sight on the streets of Whitehorse. Never before had such a contingent of uniformed men been seen here. Their advent into the Territory marked a Red Letter Day in the history of the Yukon." Thus the local newspaper, the *Whitehorse Star*, welcomed the arrival of the army of occupation in April 1942. Surely there was good reason to celebrate the event, for it seemed to ensure the future prosperity of the town: "In conjunction with our airport this highway definitely places Whitehorse in an unique position on the map for all time. The town is bound to become a great distributing centre and therefore to all intents and purposes the commercial capital of the Yukon."[1]

Just twelve years later, in 1954, a visitor commented on the appearance of Whitehorse:

The town that now greeted me . . . was a cluttered hodgepodge of wartime jerry building, a wild mélange of tar-paper shacks, outhouses, bunkhouses, Quonset huts, corrugated iron lean-tos, false-fronted frame structures, log cabins from an earlier day, a few trim little bungalows, and a few square blockhouses disguised by imitation brick—all mingled with piles of salvaged lumber and piping, rusted hulks of trucks and bulldozers, and scattered heaps of old oil drums. This was the mess left behind by the army of forty thousand soldiers and construction workers . . . Whitehorse was still cleaning up after them.[2]

Of all the communities in the Canadian Northwest invaded by the American army of occupation, none was affected as profoundly as Whitehorse. Through this once sleepy transportation crossroads passed thousands of men and most of the supplies for the northern sections of the Alaska Highway and the western section of the Canol pipeline and refinery. The U.S. Army Corps of Engineers and the Public Roads Administration both made the community the first headquarters for the northern section of the highway.[3] This administrative importance, and Whitehorse's strategic location at the junction of the highway and pipeline corridors, guaranteed its role as northwest Canada's most important community.[4]

Things had been very different before the war. Whitehorse was originally founded as a small settlement at the head of navigation on the Yukon River, at the foot of Miles Canyon and the White Horse rapids, where a number of gold seekers drowned in 1898. It was given permanent life when it was chosen as the inland terminus of the White Pass and Yukon Railway. The railway, completed in the summer of 1900, ran 110 miles from the Pacific Ocean at Skagway to the Yukon River at Whitehorse and guaranteed the town a permanent existence as an entrepôt for the vast majority of the freight and passenger traffic between the Yukon River valley and the "outside." But it was a highly seasonal existence. Although the railway operated year round, it cut back operations in the winter, since the river steamers with which it connected ran only between May and October. Every spring, several hundred men arrived to work on the railway and the steamers, sparking a seasonal boom that lasted until the end of navigation in the fall. There was a small permanent population—a few businessmen who supplied the travelers hardy or anxious enough to brave a winter sleigh trip from Dawson City to the railhead—but the settlement had few ambitions for growth or expansion. The railway company, which also owned the river steamers, dominated the town; its picturesque log railway station, which still stands, was for many years the community's most impressive structure.

Whitehorse was an unprepossessing place on the eve of World War II. Its population in the census of 1941 was 754, but it fluctuated so wildly with the seasons that it was difficult to tell how many people actually lived there permanently. The town was oriented toward the Yukon River, except for a newly expanded airfield on the bluff that rose behind the town. A number of warehouses, docks, and railway buildings along First Avenue, by the river, provided the focus of economic activity, and a small Main Street business sector ran perpendicular to it. The town's permanent residents lived within a few blocks of the business district, and about thirty squatters and migrant workers, early versions of today's "colourful five percent,"[5] lived in a couple of shanty towns along the riverbank. Some Indians also lived in the town, usually on a seasonal basis, though various official and semi-official policies ensured that they did not live too close to the permanent residential areas.[6] Residents got their water from shallow private wells, or through water delivery, at 6 cents per bucket. Sewage was handled in an equally haphazard fashion; the Whitehorse Inn, for example, discharged its sewage directly into the Yukon River through an open wooden trough.[7] Most homes, however, relied on septic fields, not a satisfactory method in a town with fairly small building lots. The community did have an electric plant, but residential installations were haphazard and not always safe. It also had a telephone system, but it was expensive, and only a few businesses were connected to it. There was no telephone connection to the outside; emergency messages went via telegraph line, and later by radio.[8]

All this began to change when the army of occupation arrived in the spring of 1942.[9] In the summer of that year, Pierrepont Moffat, U.S. ambassador to Canada, reported that the town was bursting at the seams:

After lying dormant, a ghost town, for nearly forty years, it is again enjoying a boom. Prices are fantastic. Accommodation is pitifully inadequate. There are twenty males to each female and beards are coming back in fashion. All night long the airplanes drone overhead, and when in the morning you go out to breakfast—the dining room is in a separate shack—you pass a row of men sleeping in the "parlor." These are the unfortunates who arrived too late to be assigned a bed. The whole development of the town is "frontier."[10]

By June 1942 over 3,000 troops were stationed in the town itself, and more than 6,000 were there by fall, with thousands more close enough to Whitehorse to go there for leave and recreation. One long-time Yukoner was amazed at the transformation:

I was dumfounded with the activity both military and civilian. There seemed to be line ups for everything. If you wanted to eat in a cafe, you lined up; if you went to the theatre, you lined up. As liquor was the only thing rationed line ups were 3 and 4 blocks long. If you went to a dance there were line ups. Gambling houses in tents ran wide open around the clock. Boot leggers had a field day. Moon shiners carried out a thriving business. Every shack in Whitehorse was occupied. . . . Cafes opened in what were once abandoned shacks . . . Every available person was busy.[11]

Even more soldiers and civilian workers passed through the town on their way to the work camps. PRA personnel, civilian and military administrators, air force staff, and even the occasional Canadian added to the diversity of the local population.[12] By April 1943 there were over 10,000 people in Whitehorse, 80 to 85 percent of them Americans.[13]

The spring and summer of 1943 saw the population of Whitehorse at its wartime peak; a year later the number of residents, particularly Americans, had declined. In the first two years of construction, most of the newcomers were American, but after 1943 more Canadians were hired, to work on the refinery and for the Northwest Service Command. By early 1944 there were about 6,000 people in town, 1,800 of them Canadian.[14]

Canadians and Americans generally got along well in Whitehorse, even though the former were at one time outnumbered four to one in their own country. What difficulties did occur as often as not involved the U.S. Military Police, whose officers routinely exceeded their authority and showed indifference to the fact that they were not on American soil. George Black, the Yukon's member of Parliament, who had several run-ins with the MPs on behalf of constituents, referred to them as the "U.S. Army Gestapo" and called them "obnoxious."[15] Other Canadians were upset at what they saw as an aggressive, almost proprietary attitude towards the Canadian North. As C. K. LeCapelain commented in January 1943, "A surprising number of Americans in North Western Canada say that they are here to stay and this very naturally is causing a lot of resentment among Canadians."[16] Canadian officials regularly complained about American "highhandedness" and asked the U.S. au-

Winter view of Whitehorse looking east, with the U.S. Air Force barracks and quonset huts in the foreground and the old town and river behind them. The Yukon and White Pass Railway depot is in the background on the left. (YTA, Cust Collection, 84/64, 21)

thorities to pay greater attention to Canadian regulations and sensibilities.[17] But most incidents that involved Americans treading on the sensitive toes of Canadian nationalism involved the traditional American ignorance about foreign countries (especially Canada, which seemed so unforeign) and unwillingness to realize that there were effective ways of doing things that differed from the "American way."

There were the inevitable brawls and confrontations between individual Americans and Canadians, typically when both parties were drunk, but these were offset to a degree by repeated protestations of friendship on both sides, and by social gatherings and athletic contests. Most observers commented on the positive relations between Canadians and Americans in Whitehorse, and the community, even when full to overflowing, was remarkably peaceful. Ronald McEachern, editor of the *Financial Times,* visited the town in the fall of 1943, and reported that "disappointing though this may be to lovers of high adventure and low rowdy-dow, Whitehorse is today a dull and prosaically well-behaved city—for all of its vigorous history, the loud and determined figures of its storied past, the youthful, adventurous and relatively rich members of its invading army, civilian and military."[18]

Not much was done to prepare Whitehorse for the invasion of the army of occupation; given the urgency of events, there was probably not much that could have been done. The construction workers arrived so soon after the decision was made to build the defense projects—a matter of weeks—that the occupation began almost before the residents of Whitehorse knew it was coming. The town's three hotels could not begin to meet the need for accommodation; the Americans had to press vacant buildings into service, and most of the military workers were housed in a huge tent camp on the bluff overlooking the river valley. Those lucky or important enough to get space in a hotel found it was no Waldorf-Astoria: "The hotel is a wooden structure with two beds per room— you are assigned a bed, not a room—with the walls so thin you hear a symphony of male snores blending together the length of the corridor."[19]

Because the plan was to make the refinery at Whitehorse a permanent facility, the U.S. Army, the PRA, and private contractors leased land in and around the town, and began to build dozens of barrack and other buildings. Within months, a new residential complex had been built to rival the existing community. The construction, which stretched from the staging and supply area at McCrae, a few miles south of town, to the area north of the airport, also drew settlement away from the old center on the riverbank. Many of the buildings, including the army headquarters, were built on the hill overlooking the town.[20] By the time the frenzy of building slowed in 1944, the U.S. government had put over $9 million into local construction projects and the Canadian government had spent $2 million, much of it on the airport.[21] Civilian contractors and the Standard Oil Company, which operated the refinery, put hundreds of thousands of dollars more into the community.

Most local contractors were shut out of this construction bonanza. The Americans had an inexhaustible appetite for building materials, a bottomless purse to pay for them, and no need or desire to give Yukon entrepreneurs a share of the action. The development influenced the town in many ways. Many Yukon residents, attracted to the boom town yet unable to find living accommodations, simply squatted on whatever land was available, throwing up jerry-built dwellings. Some town lots sprouted as many as seven shacks apiece, and other such dwellings encroached on railway or government land.[22] In 1944, about eighty squatters were living along the Yukon riverbank: "[The dwellings] are being added to day by day, and most of them have been erected during the past six months. They comprise all kinds of buildings—mostly dilapidated— from tents and packing box shacks to very nice log cabins."[23] One of the most famous symbols of Whitehorse was built in response to the housing crisis. Martin Berrigan, a local entrepreneur, built several "log skyscrapers"—log houses three stories high—as rental units, one of which survives as a tourist attraction.[24] U.S. agencies and companies built numerous housing units on the hill west of town; a small "colony of new Cemesto huts" went up north of the airport to house refinery employees and their families.[25]

Even during the war, some observers worried that the unregulated and unplanned growth of Whitehorse was breeding trouble for the community. In 1943, C. K. LeCapelain observed,

Concerning local administration in Whitehorse, there is no doubt in my mind that there has been some laissez faire and letting things drift along hoping for the best. But it's building up many future problems which the longer they are left to drift will be the harder to repair and correct. Everyone, both Americans and Canadians, have done what they wished with little control. . . . People build what they like, how they like, where they like almost as long as a private property owner doesn't protest.[26]

The territorial administrator defended himself by pointing out that there was a critical shortage of housing, serviced land, and building supplies, which made squatting and shacks almost a necessity. It was not until much later, in the fall of 1944 when the pressure had eased somewhat, that the Yukon Territorial Council passed a building code, and initiated a building inspection system through the office of the fire chief.[27]

George Jeckell, the Yukon's comptroller, and the one person with the authority to bring some order to the land and housing crisis tht plagued Whitehorse in 1943, was largely indifferent to the community's problems. In the face of much evidence to the contrary, Jeckell was convinced that the growth of Whitehorse was only a temporary phenomenon brought on by the war, and that the Yukon's future remained where it had always been, in Dawson City, the seat of government and his home for forty years. He was therefore reluctant to spend public money on Whitehorse, or even to spend much time in it—this despite the fact that much of the Yukon's revenue in the period came from liquor sales in Whitehorse. [28] Putting money into the town, he argued, was "an unjustifiable procedure at this time . . . in a small urban area like Whitehorse." [29] Whitehorse residents were not pleased by Jeckell's attitude; a visiting journalist "heard the most caustic comment about the remote control government they got from Dawson." [30]

But Jeckell had the imperturbable nature of one who had worked as a civil servant for over four decades, and moreover one who was answerable to a distant federal government rather than to the people he governed. [31] Complaints from Whitehorse were dismissed: "To say that their town is neglected and run down compared with Dawson," he sniffed, "is really laughable." [32] He remained unmoved even when the difficulties extended to territorial public servants, who found it almost impossible to rent housing in Whitehorse, particularly in the midst of wartime inflation. [33] He refused to make any provision for government housing for civil servants, despite a flood of requests, and in the face of urgings from his superior, R. A. Gibson, director of the Bureau of Northwest Territories and Yukon Affairs. [34]

Civil servants working for the federal government were little better off, particularly those in the post office, who were heavily overworked all through 1942, though the postmaster hired a few local residents to help out on a part-time basis. More full-time employees did not arrive until July 1943. [35] Other community services were equally strained. Before the war, the residents of the town had gladly put up with meager services in return for minimal taxes. But within weeks of the arrival of the army of occupation these services broke down. There were shortages of water, not because there was no water around—the Yukon River had plenty—but because the distribution system was so primitive.[36] Sewage was a major problem; one army officer described the town as "one vast cesspool." In an attempt to control dysentery, the Americans were ordered to drink only water that had been treated by army chlorination units. The same water was freely provided to any resident or contractor on request, in an attempt to prevent an epidemic.[37]

Since neither the Yukon nor the Canadian government had either the will or the means to install a proper water and sewer system in Whitehorse, the U.S. Army did the work itself, without asking permission of or notifying either the Canadian or American authorities.[38] When word of this reached Ottawa, action was finally taken, and by the spring of 1943, a plan for a community water and sewage system had been prepared by Canadian and American engineers. The proposal called for a water system that would have provided service for the entire area, including the airport, as well as a sewage collection system, complete with a primary treatment plant. Because both were to be gravity fed, neither system required expensive pumping equipment.[39] The Americans were to lay down the sewer trunk lines essential for their needs, leaving connections in the townsite so that Canadian contractors could hook into the system. It would have been a gift to Whitehorse, largely paid for by the United States and serving its immediate requirements, while promising to meet the needs of the town during the war and for years afterward.

Unfortunately for the town, however, the Americans had second thoughts. In June 1943, in the face of growing uncertainty about the future of the American presence in the region, the U.S. Army Corps of Engineers unilaterally scaled down the plan. The water and particularly the sewage systems, as eventually built, were sufficient for the army but of little use to the private and business residents of Whitehorse. The main sewer line was moved away from Second Avenue, the business district, to Fourth Avenue, which was on higher ground, and this meant that expensive pumping equipment would be required if the townspeople were to use it.[40]

The army solved the problem of local use of the new water supply system by ruling that hotels and restaurants not connected to a

A forest of tents—the U.S. Army camp at Whitehorse in the summer of 1942. (YTA, R. A. Carter Collection, 1548)

supply of chlorinated water were off limits to military personnel. Some businessmen, grumbling, built a small private system, while others paid to link up to the American system.[41] A small sewage system was constructed in the town, a makeshift arrangement of pipes that discharged raw sewage into the Yukon River two blocks upstream from the main business district. It served the commercial core and some of the more prosperous residents, but had little potential for expansion.[42] Later, committees of homeowners and businesspeople were formed to join other sections of the town into this system. But joining the system was voluntary, and the townsite remained "an undeveloped island of cesspits" in the midst of the military area.[43]

Once more Canadian officials failed to offer much support to local residents. George Jeckell feared that the demand for municipal services would put a strain on the territorial treasury and urged Whitehorse to incorporate as a municipality before undertaking any major public works. With the support of federal officials, he advised the town to delay any substantial commitments until after the wartime construction had ended.[44] He did, however, authorize the construction of a water and sewer link between the government building in Whitehorse and the private system that served the business district.[45]

The condition of the streets of Whitehorse was almost as bad as the water and sewer systems. The constant pounding by trucks and heavy equipment damaged the gravel surface and threw a constant dusty haze over the town throughout the summer months. The Americans did maintenance work on the roads they used the most, but the Yukon government did nothing for the rest. What the residents wanted was to have the streets regularly sprayed with oil to lay the dust that choked them, and when the government in Dawson City ignored their request, they organized a petition to the national government in the spring of 1944. Unfortunately, the organizer of the petition was a woman whose father was suspected of communist sympathies, and that was enough to discredit the request in the eyes of the authorities.[46]

The matter of oil for the streets of Whitehorse proved to be somewhat of a cause célèbre, for the dust and potholes were so bad that the residents were stirred from their usual apathy to launch more complaints. C. Rogers, president of the White Pass and Yukon Railway, observed, "The situation in Whitehorse is very bad and the people there are in a very critical, almost ugly mood. They are to a point where good sense may leave them and they may en masse go over to any one who will promise them some relief."[47] A number of groups petitioned the authorities for action. The Whitehorse local of the Hotel and Restaurant Employee's Union sent a list of resolutions to George Jeckell, the last one of which read, "BE IT FURTHER RESOLVED: That failure on your part to take such actions, will be considered on our part a gross negligence of your duties and responsibilities, Therefore, becoming an obstacle in the progress of our community. Hardly, in our estimation a position befitting a public servant."[48] Jeckell had claimed that cheap oil and equipment to spray it were not to be had, but an investigation initiated by Ottawa revealed that the Whitehorse refinery was prepared to supply oil to the town free of charge, and eventually oil was sprayed, and the problem partially alleviated.[49] The affair was a clear indication of the indifference of the territorial administration to the problems of the upstart community of Whitehorse.

In the end it was by default the Americans who provided most of the municipal services to Whitehorse during the war years. They were, for instance, of great help in the area of fire protection and fire fighting. One official remarked that "anybody's fire threatens everybody's property in this windy and wooden town."[50] The U.S. authorities built two fire stations in town and sent their equipment to fight any fire, civilian or military, while the territorial government did its share by purchasing a new fire truck and improving the existing fire station.[51]

Other local amenities were also expanded or built from scratch by the Americans. When the army of occupation first arrived in 1942 it took over the local gymnasium, making it unavailable for community activities.[52] Over the next two years, however, the Americans paid this loan back with interest, building a number of recreational facilities that Whitehorse could hardly have afforded on its own. The U.S. Army and the Royal Canadian Air Force, for instance, built hockey rinks and baseball fields for the numerous teams that sought relaxation in sports.[53] The local movie theater was far too small for the would-be patrons; the U.S. Army built two new ones to handle the demand.[54]

Medical and hospital care also benefited from the presence of the army of occupation. In 1942 the territorial government built an addition to the Whitehorse General Hospital, but there was only one, badly overworked, medical health officer, Dr. Frederick Roth, to keep an eye on local public health concerns.[55] The American military provided for their own health needs, beginning by converting the North Star Athletic Hall into a hospital, and later building a 250-bed hospital for the Northwest Service Command.[56] The military also provided the building material for a further expansion of the Whitehorse Hospital, and gave a surplus building for use as a school in 1944 when the arrival of civilian workers with families to work on the refinery threatened to swamp the local school system.[57]

One sore point, however, was the regional transportation system, particularly the White Pass and Yukon Railway. The enormous demands of the American civilian and military contractors almost overwhelmed this little railway, and the result for the civilian residents of the Yukon was that their needs were put at the bottom of the list of priorities. George Jeckell, whose beloved Dawson City suffered as much as Whitehorse if not more, asked the Americans on a number of occasions to let more civilian goods through on the railroad, but the congestion only grew worse.[58] The railway officials, under pressure from the Americans to carry more supplies, and under attack from Yukoners for ignoring their needs, threw up their hands and recommended that the army lease the line for the duration of the war. The army took over the railway on October 1, 1942, and gradually improved service, but civilian needs still received short shrift.[59] In March 1943 the NWSC ordered the railway to reduce passenger service between Whitehorse and Skagway from daily service to twice a week each way, in order to operate more freight trains.[60] It was not until the fall of 1943, when the frantic pace of construction relaxed somewhat, that the supply of goods for Yukon residents and businesses increased appreciably. But even then Yukon businesses suffered, for the confusion and vastly increased freight load brought on by the construction projects led to serious pilferage from the railroad. The Northern Commercial Co. complained to the railway company:

During the past month we have found that fifty percent of our dry goods and gent's furnishing goods have been broken into and sox, mitts, gloves, shoes, shirts, underwear and dry goods have been taken out of the cases. The same applies to candy in which we lost twenty two boxes of chocolates out of one case and in the case of fresh fruit it is seldom that we get a full case; we have had as much as thirty cantaloupe taken out of a case of forty five.[61]

The president of the railway replied that "pilferage and damage and loss have been terrible, but in rather extensive travel recently I find that to be the situation all over. The moral breakdown all over the country in this regard is appalling." It is noteworthy that in the middle of wartime rationing and desperate shortage of transportation it was still possible to import cantaloupes to Whitehorse.

It was not all loss for Whitehorse business, of course, since local suppliers were able cash in on an undreamed-of demand in 1942. The Americans imported a good deal of their food and almost all

their equipment, but they did purchase some perishable food—
meat, dairy products, vegetables—locally. The result was that
some local businesses, especially Burns and Co. and the Northern
Commercial Co., saw their monthly sales quadruple in 1942 as
compared to the previous year.[62]

Hotels and restaurants also cashed in on the presence of the
Americans. In the early months of the occupation, before the army
could put up its own quarters, officers and senior civilian officials
stayed in the Whitehorse hotels, which as a result were perennially
full. Unfortunately for the proprietors, Canadian wartime price
controls prevented them from charging what the market would
bear, but they responded to the crisis by jamming as many people
as the health regulations would permit into their establishments;
patrons rented sleeping bags and slept on the floor, or rented a bed
for an eight-hour shift.[63] The Yukon and White Pass River steamers
docked at the waterfront were occasionally pressed into service as
floating hotels.[64]

The local restaurants also prospered, since in the early months
of construction, the army messes were restricted to military personnel, leaving the civilians to fend for themselves. By December
1943 Whitehorse had ten restaurants, nine of which had opened
since the arrival of the Americans. One small cafe served 900 meals
a day.[65] Some entrepreneurs tried their hand at price gouging: in
the summer of 1942 the Whitehorse Inn raised the price of its
meals, causing serious problems for Canadians working on government airport construction. Angry customers held a rally at the
theater to voice their complaints. An investigation by the RCMP
revealed that the inn's owner had been "charging in accordance
with the ability of their individual patrons to pay, rather than basing
their rates on any standard of service or quality," but there was no
quick solution to the problem, since the Wartime Prices and Trades
Board did not have a representative in the Yukon.[66] An office was
opened in Whitehorse in the spring of 1943, and prices and wages
in the region were then brought under government control.[67] This
phase of the boom was not long-lived, however, for by 1944, with
most of the American military gone and the maintenance crews
looked after in their own camps, trade fell off considerably, and the
local entrepreneurs had to trim their sails or go out of business.

Lining up for breakfast at Whitehorse in driving snow, 4 May 1942:
"The tall fellow . . . holding plate and cup in left hand is Clemons of
Arkansas, and second to the right of him is Carr of California." (YTA,
Robert Hays Collection, 5699)

Other commercial services in Whitehorse also cashed in on the
presence of the army of occupation. Barbers and taxi drivers, once
marginal or part-time operators, now had all the work they could
handle. Wood dealers cut 10,000 cords for the Whitehorse market
in 1943, delivering to Canadian and American customers. Although
the army had its own facilities, local laundry and dry-cleaning establishments found it worthwhile to move from Dawson City to Whitehorse.[68] The Canadian Bank of Commerce, the only bank in town,
had so much new business that it increased its staff from three to
twelve in 1942.[69] By 1944 the town's commercial and service sectors had expanded considerably, giving it a more prosperous and
permanent business foundation.[70]

The American construction projects put pressure on all parts of
the Whitehorse economy, including the labor force. Before the war,
Whitehorse had attracted most of its seasonal labor force from
outside, particularly the Vancouver region. During the war, how-

ever, regulations restricting the mobility of workers, and the increased job opportunities in the South, made it more difficult to attract seasonal workers north to the Yukon. Employers had to make more attractive offers to locally available workers or endure the bureaucratic procedures of the Labour Board. Demand for workers in the Whitehorse region was so great, however, that many workers throughout the Territory ignored government regulations (which made it an offense to quit a job for a new one without permission) and traveled to the town to get one of the many well-paid jobs available there.[71] One of many examples was a carpenter hired in Dawson by the Yukon government and sent to Whitehorse to work on a new government building; as soon as he got there he quit for a better paying job with a highway subcontractor.[72]

To protect the Canadian labor market, the national government demanded that Canadian workers on the Northwest defense projects, even those employed by American companies, be paid at Canadian wage rates. (American workers, employed by the same companies and doing the same jobs, received substantially higher wages.)[73] But the competition among contractors to secure enough workers often led some of the American ones to ignore the Canadian regulations. When American highway contractors offered Canadian laborers wages a third higher than the rates fixed by the Canadian National War Labour Board, the White Pass and Yukon Railway, suffering under the pressure of increased traffic and prevented by law from paying its Canadian employees similar wages, cried foul.[74] Lengthy negotiations between Ottawa and Washington helped to stabilize the situation, but infractions still continued on many work sites.[75]

The wage disparities between Canadian and American workers do not seem to have caused much tension in Whitehorse. Though the Canadians made less than their American counterparts, most were making much more than they had in the prewar depression.[76] Though most of the really good jobs—in management and in the skilled trades—were taken by people imported from the South, there were plenty of opportunities for local residents, albeit at less skilled and more seasonal tasks. Even the Native people, traditionally at the margin of the labor market, found ready employment in laundry, woodcutting, guiding, cleaning, and making and selling handicrafts.[77]

The demand for labor in Whitehorse became so acute on occasion that it was difficult to find workers for municipal services. George Jeckell observed on one of his infrequent trips to the town, "I found no unemployment in Whitehorse. In fact I had to ask Mr. Wheller to release some of his workmen at the airport so that gravelling of streets in Whitehorse could be done."[78] The Americans helped out here too; in October 1942 U.S. soldiers were authorized to accept work with the town of Whitehorse (at 81½ cents per hour), provided they worked only during off-duty hours.[79]

Second only to the shortage of labor was the shortage of liquor. Yukoners traditionally drank more than the average Canadian, but a small outlet in the mining recorder's office had been enough to supply the demand before the war.[80] Ottawa had originally ruled that the Yukon would be exempt from the strict rationing of liquor that was enforced elsewhere in the country during the war, but the enormous demand, which arose as soon as the Americans arrived in Whitehorse, forced officials to impose quotas on buyers in the Territory.[81] The liquor outlet was moved to larger quarters, but these proved inadequate, and customers had to wait in long, slow lines for stocks that often ran out before their turn came.[82] With the arrival of the first wave of the army of occupation, liquor sales in Whitehorse increased twelvefold, from $7,000 in April 1942 to $86,900 in December, and by March 1944 the territorial liquor account showed a surplus of over $400,000, most of it coming from Whitehorse.[83] Liquor was in demand even among those who did not drink, and it served, like cigarettes in postwar Europe, as a clandestine form of currency. George Jeckell observed that "the patronage of Liquor Stores has greatly increased since the introduction of rationing. Many people who were never known to enter a Liquor Store now have individual permits and appear to get the maximum quantity." The introduction of a permit system only led to the invention of ingenious ways to circumvent it.[84]

It was revealing of the Yukon government's lack of interest in the problems experienced by Whitehorse (or of George Jeckell's lack of interest, which was the same thing) that despite the need for all kinds of municipal improvements during the war, $200,000 of the liquor revenue surplus was put in a reserve fund for postwar use. Jeckell, supported by two other territorial councilors, cited the "shack town" nature of Whitehorse's growth and the uncertainty of its future as the reason for withholding money from the community.[85] He insisted that the town incorporate and begin to raise taxes locally before he would consider spending more territorial money there. A group of Whitehorse businessmen formed the Whitehorse Men's Council to discuss the prospect, and a municipal plebiscite was held on the issue in 1946, but the majority of residents seemed to prefer dusty streets and primitive facilities to higher taxes, and incorporation had to wait until several years after the war ended.[86] Given Jeckell's hostility toward Whitehorse, however, it is unlikely that he would have authorized much expenditure there even if the citizens had done as he wished.[87] Perhaps the best comment on this bureaucrat, a big frog in a very remote pond, came from a Whitehorse banker. Jeckell, he said, "mentally has always remained a school principal: teaching, lecturing, instructing and disciplining his class and never expecting or permitting any talking back."[88] C. K. LeCapelain provided another summary of the Yukon's administrative shortcomings:

It is my firm conviction that there has been a lack of energy, punch and decisiveness in execution in many matters pertaining to the Territorial Government in Whitehorse during the past 20 months or 2 years. Opportunities have been sought for carrying on in the same old peace-time manner, which will no doubt look most convincing on paper, instead of devising ways and means of meeting emergency conditions promptly and expeditiously.[89]

In the final analysis, Whitehorse was left very much on its own to cope with the unprecedented demands and changes of the war. Development proceeded at a breakneck pace, as U.S. military and civilian authorities built housing, warehouses, offices, and other facilities. By 1946 the old river community was all but unrecognizable. Other Northwest communities, particularly Dawson Creek and Fort St. John, faced similar pressures during the boom of 1942, but only in Whitehorse did the boom last so long. The initial invasion of 1942 was followed by waves of civilian contractors, administrators, and pipeline and refinery workers. Together they created a new, if hastily built and poorly planned, community on top of the existing village.

But the boom ended with the war. George Jeckell saw the signs when he visited Whitehorse in May 1945, noting, no doubt with some satisfaction, that the growth had ended and the movement to incorporate had collapsed: "The Town has a deserted appearance compared with the hustle and bustle of former years. . . . There appears now to be a feeling of uncertainty as to the future growth of the town."[90] The rejection of the incorporation plebiscite in 1946 seemed to confirm these doubts. It was not clear if Whitehorse was prepared to capitalize on the economic and political prospects presented by the wartime reconstruction of the southern Yukon.

8. Saying Goodbye to the Yankees

THE ARMY OF occupation, which had arrived in the Northwest with little warning, left before the job it had come to do was finished. But the soldiers did not leave, as they had come, in a massive wave; rather they went in sections and groups, a gradual ebb of men and material that mirrored Washington's slowly waning interest in the Northwest defense projects. The U.S. Army Corps of Engineers, who had been first on the scene, were mostly gone by the end of 1943, leaving behind several transportation units and a skeleton administrative and maintenance staff. When the U.S. government in 1943 made a decision not to proceed with the planned upgrading of the Alaska Highway to civilian standards, the PRA officials and workers soon began to leave.[1] The Canol pipeline workers began to leave as the sections of the line they were responsible for were completed, leaving behind small pumping stations and oil field crews, and what was planned as the foundation of a sizable permanent workforce at the Whitehorse refinery. Even the dead were repatriated when, at the end of 1944, thirty-four Americans buried during the war in the Whitehorse cemetery were disinterred and taken back to the United States for reburial.[2]

The main withdrawal of personnel began in 1943 and continued until in 1946 the U.S. government officially transferred responsibility for the Alaska Highway and remaining facilities to the Canadian government. This withdrawal caused difficulties and dislocations in the Northwest. The wartime boom ended, and the old doubts and misgivings about the economic future of the region were raised again. Hundreds of Canadians left with the Americans, believing that any hope of prosperity would vanish once the projects were wound up. Others, however, stayed, believing that the immense new infrastructure—the airfields, roads, urban development, and communications—was bound to prevent a return to the stagnation of the prewar decades. Canadian government officials stayed too; there were more of them after the war than before, most presiding over a number of new federal welfare programs. The optimists were proved correct: the North experienced unprecedented growth and prosperity in the forty years after the war, due mainly to the continued interest and concern of the Canadian government. But in the short term, the problem lay in coping with the immediate effects of the army of occupation's departure.

The list of facilities to be turned over to the Canadians, or to be scrapped, was a long one, and showed how extensive the American activities in the Northwest had been. The Alaska Highway project included not only the 1,500 miles of more-or-less finished road, but also storage and living quarters in Dawson Creek and Whitehorse; a telephone line from Edmonton to the Alaska boundary; maintenance camps at Fort Nelson, Summit Lake, Liard River, Watson Lake, and Marley River; a large supply station at McCrae; and railhead construction at Dawson Creek. Canol 1 included an oil pipeline from Norman Wells to Whitehorse, ten pumping stations, twenty-three producing wells in the Norman Wells area, refinery and storage facilities in Whitehorse, a service road and telephone line paralleling the pipeline, winter roads in the Mackenzie valley, storage tanks, and living quarters. Canol 2, 3, and 4 had similar facilities. There were weather stations at Fort McMurray, Embarras Portage, Fort Smith, Fort Resolution, Hay River, Providence, Fort Simpson, Fort Wrigley, and Norman Wells; forecasting stations at Whitehorse, Calgary, Edmonton, Fort Nelson, Fort St. John, Prince George, and Watson Lake; and weather observing stations at Brooks Brook, Camp Blueberry, Coal River, Dawson Creek, Devil's Pass, Fawcett, Fish Lake, Muncho Lake, Rancheria, Summit Lake, Swift

River, Trout Lake, Trutch, Wagner, Watson Lake, Whitehorse, and Valley View.[3] Along the Mackenzie waterway, the Americans had built a wharf, rail facilities, storage, housing, and a refrigeration unit at Waterways; a wharf, warehouse, and freight complex at Fitzgerald; freight and gasoline storage facilities and road improvements at Fort Smith; freight transfer facilities at Resdelta; a freight and docking complex at Fort Providence; an airfield at Fort Simpson; and freight facilities at Wrigley. They had also built radio broadcasting stations at Whitehorse, Fort Nelson, Watson Lake, Fort Simpson, and Norman Wells. They had put $16 million into upgrading the port of Prince Rupert. They had built a 250-bed military hospital in Edmonton, as well as warehouse space, a remote receiver station, recreational buildings, and expensive improvements to the Jesuit college (the notorious redwood paneling). There were feeder roads, substantial works in their own right, like the Haines Lateral, the Aishihik road, and Carcross–Jakes Corner road—to say nothing of the airfields constructed for the Northwest Staging Route.[4]

The bureaucratic task of disengaging the Americans from the Canadian Northwest proved much more complicated than the arrangements that had brought them there. There was a great deal to discuss: the future of employees and of all the facilities, equipment, payment for material and services, and the question of future American access to the region.[5] Matters were not helped by the Americans' desire to leave as quickly as possible, and by the Canadians' reluctance to assume any responsibility for the projects except what they had agreed to under the terms of the original documents.

As the projects wound down, the administrators also began to pack up and leave. The Northwest Service Command, left with little to do, negotiated a transfer of its duties to the Alaskan Division of the U.S. Army Air Force. Individual managers were reassigned or left the North for other jobs in civilian life. Major-General W. W. Foster, the special commissioner on defense projects in northwestern Canada, resigned in 1945 to work for the British Columbia Rural Electrification Project.[6] General F. S. Strong, assigned to head the Northwest Service Command at the end of the war, was given the job of closing down operations: "From the start of May in 1944, everything in the Northwest Service Command looked to demobilization, so with authority to write orders sending officers and men back home, we soon began to shrink, especially units not really having much if anything to do."[7] It was not easy to keep up morale under such circumstances. Strong reported, "There has been the feeling here that 'the ship is sinking—let's get out.' However, the War Department does not feel that way. They feel that Northwest Canada is no place for mediocre personnel, and have determined that this is where we should serve."[8]

For Yukoners, one of the most important symbols of the end of the wartime projects was the return of the White Pass and Yukon Railway to its owners. The U.S. Army had taken it over in the fall of 1942, and had run it hard for over two years; critics said that the Americans had run it into the ground. Yukoners had complained bitterly that the army had ignored their need for civilian supplies and were delighted that things could now return to normal. In November 1944 the railway was put under joint military-civilian operation (330 military and 120 civilian employees), although it remained under the army's command.[9] By the summer of 1945 the army had turned it over completely to civilian control.

Not every departure of the army of occupation was greeted with as much enthusiasm: no greater disappointment surrounded the end of the Northwest defense projects than the closing of the Canol pipeline and refinery. Although Canol came to be viewed by American officials as an embarrassment—a horrible example of bad planning and waste—it was not seen that way in the Northwest. Regional promoters saw it instead as the center of their vision of a prosperous and growing economy. The Canol Project promised the Northwest a secure supply of oil, and thus a degree of self-sufficiency and a foundation for economic power that it had never enjoyed before. The revelations of the Truman Commission burst the bubble—Canol was just another unrealized bonanza, and a boondoggle at that. The families who had been recruited and moved north to serve as a permanent workforce on the pipeline felt betrayed; an official from the U.S. Petroleum Administration for War visited Whitehorse at the request of the War Department and recruited many of them for similar employment elsewhere in the

United States.[10] Canadian residents of Whitehorse reacted to the closing with fear and anger, seeing it as a sign of a return to the bad old days of neglect and stagnation.[11]

Still, it was difficult for the Americans to extricate themselves from a project in which they had invested so many millions of dollars, and it took them several months to do so. In May 1944 they announced that they would abandon the oil exploration program in the Northwest. Canadian officials hoped that the private companies would continue their work in the area, but did nothing to ensure that this would happen.[12] In March 1945 Washington announced that the pipeline and the Whitehorse refinery would be closed; crude oil production at Norman Wells stopped on the 8th of that month, while the refinery kept operating until April 5 to use up the crude oil in the system.[13] The Americans offered to sell the system to Canada, an offer Ottawa declined.[14] It was then put up for public sale, but the only buyers were those who wanted to scrap it and move the usable parts to the South.[15] The facilities remained moth-balled for more than two years before Imperial Oil Co. bought the refinery, dismantled it, and moved it to Leduc, Alberta, to service the new discoveries there. In 1947 the L. G. Foster Company of Pittsburgh and the Alberta and Davidson Company of New York bought the abandoned pipeline for a pittance ($70,000) and moved it south.[16] The dismantling exercise sparked another brief mini-boom as workers flooded into the region to cut up and remove the pipe. F. H. R. Jackson, a forest engineer who observed the process, reported that

the pipe is being cut into twenty foot lengths, at the original welds, by six to eight, 3 men, cutting crews. Acetylene torches are used for this work and each crew cut an average of one mile per day. As a quantity of highly inflammable crude oil remains in the line, the pipe is first punctured, on the lower side, with a torch at twenty foot intervals. The escaping oil immediately ignites and is allowed to burn itself out after which the pipe is cut completely. . . . Every reasonable precaution is being taken to prevent the creation of any hazards to our natural resources.[17]

A major problem of the invasion of 1942 had been the difficulty of moving thousands of tons of supplies and equipment into the Northwest; a major problem of the withdrawal was the question of what to do with the enormous amount of surplus. Civilian contractors generally looked after their own equipment. Some were accused, no doubt correctly, of abusing their cost-plus contracts by purchasing unneeded equipment as the projects were closing (new tires for all their trucks, for example), charging the cost to the government, and then immediately shipping the equipment south. The contractors took everything with them that was of any use, leaving piles of junk and equipment damaged beyond repair in scores of abandoned camps.[18] Equipment and supplies owned by the government posed a more difficult problem, since they were subject to bureaucratic regulations, diplomatic discussions, and demands from people who wanted them. Much of this equipment had been damaged, or for some other reason was not worth the expense of shipping south. But Canadian officials worried that leaving it in the North or selling it for a pittance locally would devastate the northern retail trade. There was thus much discussion about what to do with the mountains of war surplus in the Northwest.[19]

The amount of material to be sent south, scrapped, sold, or otherwise disposed of at the end of the war was immense, at least by northern standards. At one point Whitehorse, for instance, had 536 tons of surplus supplies waiting for shipment—mostly kegs of unwanted nails.[20] An estimate of February 1944 identified over 21,000 pieces of equipment in the Northwest, of which 5,400 were still in use and 16,000 marked for removal.[21] On the Canol road alone there were over 1,400 pieces of heavy equipment, including 374 rusting in abandoned camps, of which 100 were dump trucks, 26 cargo trucks, and 10 crawler wagons.[22] Because of the problems associated with returning all this material to the lower forty-eight states, the Americans tried a policy of disposing of much of the material in the Northwest as best they could instead of shipping it home. The army declared that as a general rule "only material critical in the states or items whose resale value exceeds transportation and handling charges will be evacuated."[23] Equipment not needed for military purposes could in some cases be disposed of locally.[24] There was concern about the equipment abandoned in the disused camps: "General Strong feels that Indians, and possibly some prospectors, might do damage, and suggested blocking off the road."[25] Plans called for this equipment to be turned over to the Canadian government, "as is and where is," with the Canadian authorities to remit proceeds from the sale of such goods to the United States.[26] The Americans, however, generally removed all usable equipment and supplies, leaving abandoned camps, nonrepairable machinery, and certain excess supplies for the Canadians to look after.[27]

The Canadian fears that disposal of surplus equipment in the North would upset the local economy proved in some cases true. The U.S. government solicited bids on a variety of items that could not be moved south or would not have paid the cost of doing so, things like abandoned buildings, fuel stores, and piles of coal. Though the sums realized were generally a tiny fraction of the original cost, U.S. officials considered them better than nothing. A huge store of oil, gasoline, and lubricants on the Grimshaw road sold for $7,000, but as one official noted, "if this had not been done it would have resulted in a total loss."[28] But these transactions led, as the Canadians had predicted, to chaos in the Northwest, particularly in the Dawson Creek and Fort St. John areas, where American surplus goods found their way into general commerce. A Dawson Creek entrepreneur received authorization to buy such material and secured large quantities at very low prices, passing them on to friends and business associates.[29] There were also a number of major thefts, and towards the end of the war, speculation in stolen military supplies became common.[30] On several occasions the police discovered large caches of pilfered American equipment in garages and warehouses in the region.[31]

Understandably, many local residents viewed the situation as a unique opportunity to profit by the wartime bonanza, to get while the getting was good—doubtless Uncle Sam would not miss a few bulldozers, and there were more where they came from.

In response to this confusion, the Americans returned to their earlier policy. Some equipment was sold; auctions were held in Dawson Creek, and Whitehorse residents requested that sales be held in their town as well.[32] But most usable equipment was shipped south, and everything else was ordered to be brought to central points and held for disposal through the Canadian authorities. At the collection points, "parties of men, each under the command of an officer, are also sorting out salvage, putting on one side that which is thought to be of value and destroying what has been condemned by U.S. authorities as unfit for use."[33] It was this policy that led to the enduring legend that the Americans, in a colossal fit of dog-in-the-manager selfishness, had decided to destroy what they could not take with them or sell, so that it should not fall into Canadian hands. As with most legends, there is some truth in this one. Unfitness for use exists very much in the eye of the beholder, and as one officer noted,

mattresses or chipped enamel, condemned by a medical officer are destroyed, and some poor settler seeing the action thinks it looks pretty good material and doesn't realize that it is being destroyed under army regulations. A stove is condemned because it is not considered fit for issue to troops, and it is thrown on the dump. Some settler sees it and finds it is not badly damaged and discovers he can make it like new by taking a part from another stove and he starts offering to go and salvage them for his neighbours. The junk business may be a profitable one but we're not in it.[34]

Photographs of dumps along the Alaska Highway, taken by an army intelligence unit, show such items as unused timing chains and gears from engines, an axle in its original packing, unused pieces of sheet steel—things that presumably would be of use to some local resident. Large quantities of perishable and nonperishable goods were burned, buried, or otherwise destroyed by contractors and by the army. Local residents were appalled—here was a cornucopia, and its bounty was being wasted—and they complained to the Canadian authorities.[35] Peter Schroeder, a resident of Dawson Creek, said he had seen barrel heaters, bedding, galvanized piping, steel plates, steel shafting, galvanized iron and tin chimneys, and hams and cabbages thrown onto the Dawson Creek dump, or on other dumps that dotted the Alaska Highway at the larger army or construction camps.[36] A resident of Whitehorse reported seeing "a barracks between two and three city blocks long, packed with winter clothes, parkas, pure wool blankets, comforters, chairs, office desks, and almost everything you could imagine. They stacked them up, poured gasoline over them, set them on fire. Guards stood over them with fixed bayonets so nobody could get anything."[37] Some local residents who tried to scavenge the abandoned material from dumps were threatened with prosecution by American authorities.[38] To a region that had so long been a forgotten

The Peace River bridge, 1944. One of the most famous images of
highway construction, it later collapsed and was replaced by the present
structure. (NA, 111-SC 207151)

have-not part of the continent, such waste seemed not only ob-
scene, but a personal affront. The *Whitehorse Star* commented that
"wanton destruction can never be justified under any conditions or
circumstances," and the *Edmonton Bulletin* predicted that "the
public will be exceeding wroth if Canada does not salvage for civilian
use everything usable but no longer required for the winning of the
war."[39] When these complaints were echoed in southern Canada,
American officials responded by arguing "that certain things which
would have some value in or near urban communities have in fact
no value on the Highway. Materials which are so far from centers
where they can be used would not justify transportation charges to
a possible market"—an explanation that did not come to grips with
the northern complaints.[40]

The Canadian government responded to these complaints in the
summer of 1944 by asking Special Commissioner W. W. Foster

to investigate them. He reported that U.S. officers were under pressure to return as much as was feasible to the lower forty-eight states and recommended that the abandoned maintenance camps be cleaned up and the buildings boarded in, and that they then be turned over to the Canadian government (without compensation, for the facilities had no real value) for disposal.[41] The same, however, could not be done for the Canol camps, which were too isolated to justify systematic removal of surplus materials.[42]

The Americans in their turn, stung by the accusations of waste and miserliness, sent Colonel Curtis Pratt to investigate the situation.[43] His report refuted the criticism, concluding that contrary to rumors, warehouses had not been burned, material that was abandoned was unrepairable (except for some tires, which were subsequently removed), and dumped materials did not justify the costs of transportation. He concluded that the U.S. authorities had made every effort to return salvageable materials, leaving behind only "that not worth the cost of evacuation."[44] And in fact, a thorough postwar investigation by the War Department managed to account for all but 635 of the 30,586 pieces of construction equipment used in the Northwest (see table 15).

Whether Colonel Pratt's evaluation was strictly correct or not is

Table 15   Disposition of Construction Equipment Used in the Northwest

Disposition	Number of Pieces
Transferred to War Department pool in the U.S.	19,339
Worn out and classified as useless	2,749
Sold to the Canadian government	719
Transferred to Alaska Department, War Department	1,690
Transferred to Imperial Oil explorations project	1,136
Transferred to War Department, Prince Rupert	211
Canol Road inventory	1,099
Retained for maintenance and operation of Alaska Highway and other projects	3,008
Unaccounted for	635

SOURCE: United States, *The Alaska Highway: An Interim Report from the Committee on Roads, House of Representatives, Pursuant to H. Res. 255* (Washington, D.C., 1946), p. 39.

difficult to say; certainly there is plenty of eyewitness evidence that directly contradicts the assertion that nothing of value was scrapped. For instance Lake Southwick, who worked as a truck driver for the PRA, remembered

running a Cat, digging big trenches, deep trenches. All the Americans' supplies like motors, tools, what-have-you, everything was taken and buried in those trenches . . . Seemed like a hard thing to do at the time, burying that—you know, big motors, brand new, wrapped in the wax and processed for shipping it overseas in wartime. Complete motors that they could take and slip into a machine, you know, in the battlefields. . . . It seemed hard to bury that stuff.[45]

But whatever the truth of the matter, none of the investigations addressed the main complaint from local residents—that they were not permitted to acquire material deemed useless by the army of occupation and the Canadian authorities (though of course many did manage to acquire large quantities surreptitiously).

This process had political ramifications as well. Harold Winch, leader of the opposition in the British Columbia legislature, visited Fort St. John in 1945 to investigate the continuing rumors of mass destruction. He was particularly disturbed by a conversation he had with a U.S. officer, who told him that the Americans "would be glad to give a lot of useful supplies to farmers and others, or turn it over to the Canadian Government, but the Canadian Government would not accept such surplus, hence the waste." Major-General Foster quickly pointed out that Winch's informant was wrong, and that Canadian authorities were prepared to assume responsibility for American supplies. He did, however, admit that some of the U.S. officials "are not apparently conversant with the arrangement between our two countries regarding disposition of surplus." General Strong suggested that British Columbia was due for a provincial election, and that it was likely that "individuals not in complete sympathy with the present Government might try to make political capital of our handling of salvage property."[46]

The truth of the matter was that the Americans shipped material home when it paid to do so; they looked for buyers for the rest or turned it over to the Canadian government. What no one seemed prepared to do was to give any of it away to local residents; instead, what could be neither shipped nor sold was destroyed. It was this policy that led to the legend of gratuitous destruction and waste. Of course, not everyone was unhappy with the policy. Those entrepreneurs and communities in the Northwest with cash to spend got wonderful bargains from the departing Americans. The huge barrack buildings and warehouses made good office buildings and quarters for the servants of the new welfare state, and for thirty years after the war these "temporary buildings" were a feature of the Canadian landscape.[47] The Whitehorse Baptist Indian School, for example, was housed for years in surplus army buildings. The Canadian government took over the U.S. Army hospital in Edmonton and used it for Native patients. Civic boosters, including the Edmonton municipal government, subsidized local businessmen looking for tenants for the city's many empty war-surplus buildings. Extensive negotiations were carried on with the War Assets Corporation and a number of private companies, including Catelli (spaghetti and pasta) and Prestolite (automobile parts) in an attempt to lure them to Edmonton.[48]

As the army of occupation prepared to leave, there was a public summing up of its work in the Northwest. The Americans were leaving with some of their projects incomplete. The Northwest Staging Route had been completed and fully utilized during the war years. Canol had been finished, then abandoned. But the Alaska Highway had not been upgraded to the promised standard, leaving a large engineering problem to the Canadian Army, which was about to take it over. A Canadian report observed that "the Highway on take-over was found to be generally in fair shape, but it was quite apparent that it had not been completed to the original specifications in many places. Furthermore, weaknesses were beginning to develop, especially in the muskeg area south of Fort Nelson and in the north. Many of the wooden bridges and original culverts required urgent repairs."[49] The Haines Road was little more than a rough trail over the mountains, subject to washouts and other problems, and virtually impassable after mid-October; serious consideration was given to abandoning it.[50] The Canol Road, particularly the part that lay in the Northwest Territories, was in rough shape. When the pipeline was abandoned, maintenance of the road's bridges was stopped, and the route was soon fit only for heavy vehicles.

A major difficulty was that the roads had not fulfilled one the functions intended by their proponents. They were not just for the protection of Alaska; from the beginning of construction, boosters had talked about the long-term benefits that would flow from them and from the airfields that supported them. Years before Pearl Harbor, the Alaska Highway had been touted as a tourist route to the Northwest, an artery through which the blood of commerce would flow to an impoverished region. Thus at war's end there were believed to be thousands of Americans and Canadians waiting to drive over the new highway, and others impatient to capitalize on the supposedly unlimited commercial possibilities of the newly opened frontier.[51] As a result, there was great disappointment with the actual state of the Alaska Highway, unfit as it was for tourist travel, and unhappiness with the rules that severely restricted public access to the road, even after the war was over.[52]

This problem had its roots partly in the prewar expectations, and partly in the publicity that began with the official opening of the highway in 1942 and continued throughout the war. The press releases that accompanied the building of the road did not dwell on its actual condition (it was a rough-hewn trail subject to washouts and frequent closures, fit mostly for use, except in perfect weather, by heavy military vehicles travelling in convoy). It suited the war effort to paint a rosier picture of a usable supply route connecting Edmonton and Fairbanks, destined to become a great commercial link to the Northwest. A committee from the National Park Service described the highway, not as it was, but as it would eventually become twenty-five years after the war:

The Canadian-Alaska Military Highway is the first overland route connecting Alaska with the rest of the North American continent and it opens up a vast new wilderness country. After the war, it is likely that the Highway will be gradually improved and used extensively by tourists traveling to the Canadian wilderness country and to Alaska. It will introduce new problems and means for development of natural resources. It will encourage and make more feasible the harvesting of timber, the development of mining, the hunting of game, and to some extent farming and other related types of development. All of this in turn, will stimulate the development of communities and recreational facilities.[53]

Because articles on the Alaska Highway and the other Northwest projects were subject to military censorship, few reports about the road's actual condition appeared in the press before the end of the war. There was a virtual ban on civilian traffic, except for local residents making short trips, and requests for access to the road usually received a curt reply: "no civilian traffic over this highway will be permitted unless of a nature definitely to the interest of the war effort."[54] A few civilians who had some official reason to drive through to Alaska were given permits to do so, but there was to be no general travel along the road—a reasonable policy, given the fact that it was periodically impassable and ran through a region with almost no tourist facilities. Limiting traffic had the added benefit, from the American perspective, of reducing maintenance costs (a claim made by Canadian officials).[55] George Black, member of Parliament for the Yukon, who was one of few civilians with a permit to travel anywhere on the highway, agreed with the restrictions on its use:

Some people are inclined to complain at the restricted use of the highway. I always remember that it is an American Army road, built in a fit of hysteria brought on in the "home of the brave and the land of the free" by the Japs at Pearl Harbour, built at enormous cost and with shocking waste and until after the war it is not a Canadian possession, and our dear cousins have the exclusive privilege of using and paying for it.[56]

The basic reason that the road was closed to civilian travel, and one the Americans were reluctant to dwell upon, was that it had not been finished, as promised, to a proper civilian standard. Instead, the authorities gave the impression that it was the dreadful perils of the far Northwest, rather than a half-finished job, that made it difficult to keep the road open. This impression prompted a number of responses from helpful citizens, who sent the government suggestions on how to overcome the highway's problems. Fourteen-year-old Clifford Stephenson of Winterset, Iowa, whose father had worked on the highway, suggested the installation of electrically heated grids across the road in places where "glaciers" blocked it.[57] J. B. Caldwell of Paris, Texas, put his finger on a basic contradiction of American policy: "the army refused to allow private cars over the highway because there were no facilities, and at the same time they refused to permit installation of the facilities."[58]

Most of the correspondence from the public on the subject of the highway, however, was in the nature of requests for information, either about tourism or about the possibilities of establishing businesses in the region to capitalize on what many assumed would be a postwar boom.[59] The American policy on such requests was to direct the writers to the Canadian authorities, who would take over the road six months after the war's end.[60]

By the end of the war, complaints were beginning to mount, especially from the Canadian public, about the rigid restrictions on highway travel and their inability to take advantage of the business opportunities they imagined lay along it. Canadian officials fretted that the Americans were skimping on maintenance work, "resulting in a steady deterioration of the military highway which was accepted by Canada in lieu of the type of highway promised by the Americans."[61] These complaints, however, like many emanating from Ottawa, were somewhat hypocritical; the Americans responded to them by offering on several occasions to turn the highway over to Canada immediately, but Ottawa refused to accept responsibility for the road a day before it was legally obliged to do so—six months after the final Axis surrender.[62] Ironically, it was the Canadian Army, not the Americans, that received the lion's share of the criticism about the condition of the highway, no doubt because such complaints, muted before 1945 for the sake of the war effort, were given free expression in peacetime.[63]

By then the Americans had relaxed the regulations somewhat. The British and Yukon Navigation Company, a subsidiary of the White Pass and Yukon Railway, which had a contract with the U.S. Army to carry mail and express packages, was given permission to run passenger buses along the highway twice a week.[64] An Alaska Highway Traffic Control Board was set up in Edmonton to handle civilian requests for access to the road.[65] Everyone except people "under the jurisdiction of the U.S. Military authorities," had to apply for a permit to travel. Applicants had to prove that their vehicles were roadworthy, were refused access to camp facilities, and were compelled to carry all their supplies with them.[66]

When Canada took over the Alaska Highway in April 1946, many assumed the road would soon be open and upgraded for regular commercial and private travel. But the highway was in worse shape than ever in the spring of 1946, having been maintained at a minimal level for the previous two years. Paul Seddicum, the U.S. consul in Edmonton, remarked in 1947, "I may be prejudiced but I feel strongly that there is no attraction connected with the Highway great enough to make the discomfort and possible danger worth the effort." Because of the highway's condition, the Canadian government felt compelled to continue the American policy of limiting access to it. The permit system remained in effect, though it was transferred in 1947 from the office of the special commissioner for defense projects to the RCMP.[67] A control gate at Blueberry, British Columbia, controlled access at the southern end of the road; only cars in good mechanical condition and with sufficient supplies were permitted to pass the gate. The required supplies included extra tires and repair kits; a first-aid kit; 15 gallons of gasoline; extra sparkplugs, fan belt, generator brushes, distributor points, and light fuses; a tow rope; an axe, rifle, and fishing tackle; and food and bedding.[68] Only residents, people on business, or those with some other acceptable purpose for travel were allowed on the road; tourism was still banned, since Canadian authorities regarded the highway as "unsafe for ordinary traffic."[69]

These restrictions naturally put a damper on commercial development along the highway. As with the question of traffic, debate about the opening of the Northwest's highway corridors to business began in the middle of the war and continued through the U.S. withdrawal. A 1943 request for permission to establish a general store and post office at Muskwa, near Fort Nelson, was denied for fear that it would contribute to "Black Market" problems.[70] Even along the American part of the corridor, free enterprise was discouraged. Lands along the highway in Alaska were withdrawn from the possibility of private purchase in order, wrote Brigadier General C. L. Sturdevant, to "prevent unregulated encroachments by filling stations, hot dog stands, tourist cabins and other unsightly adjuncts of civilization."[71] Once the Canadians took over, the policy began to change, and at least on the Canadian part of the highway, officials recommended that it was now "unnecessary to continue the limitation on the development of civilian enterprise;" Acting Special Commissioner L. H. Phinney hoped that private businesses would move in and create a network of services and facilities that would make civilian traffic along the highway feasible.[72]

As the Americans left the region, either en masse or in small groups, the residents of the Northwest often held celebrations to thank them for the efforts and bid them farewell. Banquets were held, speeches made, and protestations of eternal international friendship offered. Whitehorse, which had earlier celebrated the arrival of the troops (see chapter 7), hosted a whole series of such celebrations—when the PRA closed its local office in December 1943, when Standard Oil moved out of the community, and notably when Brigadier General J. A. O'Connor, one of the key commanders of the army of occupation, left the town in February 1944.[73] In Prince Rupert the citizens also celebrated the end of the American occupation of their community. The town had been swamped by the army of invasion to a degree second only to the overwhelming wave that had descended upon Whitehorse. Several thousand men had been stationed there during the war, and the substantial upgrading of its port facilities had transformed the community and given it renewed confidence in its future. In September 1945 the *Prince Rupert Daily News* published a special issue to mark the Americans' departure, selling 4,000 copies to U.S. servicemen. The paper reported that "Prince Rupert people are confident that, after the readjustment to the times of peace, the strategic position of their port will lead to its extensive use in the friendly travel and commerce of the Pacific theatre."[74]

The final stage of the army of occupation's withdrawal was signaled by the arrival of Canadians in the fall of 1945 to arrange for the transfer of control over the Alaska Highway.[75] Much to the disappointment of regional promoters, who hoped to see control of the road put under a civilian agency, the Canadian government decided to give control to the Canadian armed forces, though most of the actual maintenance work continued to be done by civilians. The future of the highway was complicated by the perennial Canadian constitutional bugaboo of federal-provincial relations. A good part of the highway ran through British Columbia, and in Canada, highways are a provincial responsibility. From the beginning, how-

Table 16 Manpower, Department of National Defence Northwest
Highway System, September 1946

Unit	Officers	Other Ranks
Headquarters	13	62
Highway Maint. Est.	5	178
1 Road maintenance company, RCE	4	110
17 work companies, RCE	2	76
19 companies, RCASC	6	114
16 companies, RCEME	3	94
16 detachments, RCAMC	11	29
14 companies, RCOC	2	32

SOURCE: NAC, RG 22, vol. 252, file 40-7-4, pt. 9, Short Report on Northwest
Highway System, 1 April 1946–31 March 1947.

ever, the British Columbia government, reluctant to be saddled
with maintenance or upgrading costs, refused to discuss the future
of the highway or take any responsibility for it.[76]

In November 1945 advance parties of Canadian armed forces
personnel arrived in the Northwest, followed by a larger transition
team in January 1946. The transfer of materials, facilities, and
information was negotiated and arranged throughout that winter.
The Royal Canadian Air Force also arrived to assume control of the
Northwest Staging Route (see table 16). On April 3, 1946, the
official ceremony transferring the Alaska Highway to Canada took
place in Whitehorse, with General A. G. L. MacNaughton representing Canada and Major-General Hoge the United States.[77] By this
time most of the army of occupation was gone; fewer than 1,800
Americans remained in the Northwest, 800 of them in Edmonton—
only a small fraction of the 30,000 who had been in the region three
years earlier. A few stayed to assist with the final transfer of the
highway and airfields and with the disposal of the Canol facilities,
but the American occupation of the Northwest was effectively over.

The leavetaking was friendly; the Americans were glad to be
going, and the Canadians were glad to see them go and to get on with
the job of creating a new North around the wartime infrastructure. It
would be a long and difficult job, for many of the facilities were in
bad shape. The region, dependent on the goodwill and interest of
the Canadian government, faced an uncertain future.

9. The North at War's End

By 1946 the army of occupation was gone, leaving the Northwest transformed. Where riverboats had once been the primary means of travel, there was now an extensive, though rough, network of roads. Where once communications in the Yukon had centered on a single antiquated telegraph line, the army had built a modern telephone system connecting the region with the outside world. Communities that had been small fur-trading centers pursuing a nineteenth-century way of life now boasted substantial administrative and maintenance facilities. Whitehorse had mushroomed from a seasonal village into the largest town in Canada northwest of Edmonton.

All this was not the end but the beginning of dramatic change for the region. The American army of occupation, by its very presence in the Northwest, had posed a challenge to Canadian sovereignty and a reproach to the national government for its decades of neglect. Never again would a Canadian government ignore the North as it had done before 1940. After World War II, Ottawa reversed its old policy of indifference and launched a series of programs to integrate the North socially and economically into the life of the nation.

There was a second factor leading to the integration, which had nothing to do with the army of occupation. The end of the war saw the advent in Canada of the modern welfare state, in which the government increasingly accepted responsibility for the lives of its citizens, particularly the poorer ones—and the Northwest had plenty of these. The first program, and the one that had the greatest initial effect on the region, was the Family Allowance, popularly called the "baby bonus," which was introduced in 1944. The baby bonus as it operated in the North was a fascinating microcosm of the welfare state, for it offered evidence to uphold the arguments of both those who supported and those who opposed it. The government believed that Native parents in the North were not capable of spending this money in proper, government-approved ways. Afraid that the cash would be squandered, the government decreed that for Natives north of the sixtieth parallel (and only them; the policy did not apply to Natives in southern Canada), the allowances were to be distributed in kind—in supplies of powdered milk, approved foods, and the like.[1] The government subsequently continued along the path of paternalistic social control, using the payments to compel Native people to send their children to school—no schooling, no payment—a policy that was to have a dramatic effect on their lives. In the short term, however, the plan was of material benefit, for a serious collapse of the fur trade after 1945 made the baby bonus an important part of the Native economy in the Northwest.[2]

The big loser in the new order was Dawson City. The old gold-rush town, still suffering from the social and economic decline that had occurred when it was bypassed by the Alaska Highway, repeatedly begged the federal government to build a road linking it to the new road. Dawson City's few remaining boosters hoped that such a link would permit the town to challenge the upstart Whitehorse for regional supremacy.[3] But it was not until nearly ten years after the war's end that the road was finally built, and by that time Dawson's fate had been sealed. The tilt towards the southern town that began during the war continued after it, as even more government offices were moved out of Dawson City. By the end of 1946, the population of Whitehorse was five times its rival's—3,680 to 688—and over half of the Yukon's 6,992 residents.[4]

By war's end it seemed inevitable that the Yukon's capital would be moved to Whitehorse, and the speculation was that Dawson City might well decline to the vanishing point. Residents of Whitehorse did not seem in a particularly boosterish mood, however. Hundreds of Canadians left the town in 1945–46, showing a marked lack of confidence in its future. When a few enthusiasts circulated a petition for incorporation as a city, a plebiscite was held on the question in June 1946—but only 130 voters showed up at the polls, and 123 of those voted against the idea. Clearly the residents were not keen on the higher taxes that would accompany municipal status; one government official observed that "the more substantial residents prefer the present system of local administration with low taxation to elected City Council and higher municipal taxation."[5] But the work of the army of occupation had made growth and higher taxes inevitable for Whitehorse, a fact recognized when in 1953 the federal government officially transferred the territorial capital there from Dawson City. Fortunately for the loser in this contest, one aspect of the postwar federal cornucopia was an interest in historical preservation and reconstruction, and no place north of the sixtieth parallel had more to preserve than Dawson City. Beginning in the mid-1960s, millions of dollars of federal money began to flow from Parks Canada into the town, giving it new vitality in the short summer season as a popular tourist destination.

The modernization of the North also raised the question of the political representation of the Yukon and Northwest Territories at the federal level. Though sparsely populated, the two territories were enormous—over 1.5 million square miles—yet the Yukon had only one member of Parliament and the Northwest Territories none at all. The Yukon had a limited amount of self-government; though its commissioner, who had a veto over bills passed by the Territorial Council, was appointed by Ottawa, the Yukon at least was able to elect representatives to the council. The Northwest Territories had no self-government at all; the commissioner was appointed, and so were all the members of the council. Even more astonishing was the fact that the Northwest Territories Council was not based in the Territory; its offices were in Ottawa, which, until 1964 when the seat of government was moved to Fort Smith (and then to Yellowknife), was the capital of the region. Residents of the Northwest Territories, especially those few non-Natives who had lived there for many years and were committed to the region, were anxious to end their political subordination and gain some measure of representative government.

In April 1944, Major-General W. Foster, special commissioner for Northwest defense projects, suggested that it was time to take up the matter of the constitutional evolution of the North.[6] Some felt that the Northwest Territories was not ready for any measure of self-government; Charles Camsell, deputy minister of mines and resources, and commissioner of the Northwest Territories, wrote that "with only a few hundred voters and many of them with little more than the educational status of an Indian, parliamentary representation has not appeared to be warranted."[7] A memorandum prepared for the federal government in March 1946 suggested two options: that the Mackenzie District, where most non-Natives in the Northwest Territories lived, be joined to the Yukon, or that the Mackenzie District be made a territory like the Yukon, with the two to share a single member of Parliament—an idea that found no favor in the Yukon.[8] Nonetheless, it was adopted in 1947, and for several years the Yukon had to share its member of Parliament with the Mackenzie valley region, an arrangement that pleased no one in the North. In the early 1950s the federal government decided to permit the election of some representatives to the Council of the Northwest Territories.

The Northwest defense projects were also in a state of flux after the war, with the exception of the Canol Project, which had been abandoned, mothballed, then dismantled. The Northwest Staging Route appeared to have a future, and the Canadian government, when taking it over, planned to spend money updating and expanding it.[9] But soon the airfields began to decline in importance as technological advances in military and civilian aviation rendered them redundant. The major bases—Watson Lake, Whitehorse, Fairbanks—continued to operate, but within a few years the rest were shut down.

The Alaska Highway, on the other hand, had been perceived as the key to the postwar development of the far Northwest. Despite the fact that the road went the wrong way from the local point of view, bypassing Dawson City and running through hundreds of miles of virtually uninhabited and resource-poor country, it did provide regional access to the South. As early as 1942, postwar concerns figured largely in the planning process for the road. In January of that year, before the project had even been approved, the U.S. Department of the Interior was expressing an interest in preserving the scenic values of the highway, and in developing the route with a view to long-term benefits.[10]

But it was to be a long time before many of these dreams came true, and in the short run, most of the highway's promoters were to be sorely disappointed. In 1943 Charles Camsell had dismissed rosy forecasts for regional development as "pure tommyrot," and predicted (correctly) that there would be no important mineral discoveries on the first 700 miles of the highway.[11] An observer who toured the Northwest in 1944, reported, "The splendid road called the Alaska Highway brings up the question of the possibility of important tourist traffic. I do not see clearly what is to justify keeping this in running order after the military necessity has passed away."[12] Even the U.S. Army stated that the high cost of driving the highway limited their use of the road.[13] Though most insiders realized that there was much more to be done to make the road generally usable, there was a reluctance to point this out, since its corollary was that the Americans had not lived up to their 1942 agreement with Canada to build a finished road. As one observer put it, "We may look for increasing pressure that Canada should build and maintain the kind of a road that the United States promised but did not construct."[14]

When the Canadians took over the highway at the beginning of April 1946, they were compelled to keep in force most of the U.S. restrictions on its use.[15] Traffic was still strictly regulated: civilians required permits to drive along the highway and had to report at control stations along the route.[16] There were only three gas stations on the first 300 miles of the road, and only two in the nearly 300 miles between Whitehorse and Watson Lake. Outside a few centers, there were no hotels and few repair shops. The permit system, imposed under the War Measures Act, was unpopular with the public, particularly American travelers, who naturally expected to be able to drive to and from Alaska as soon as the war was over.[17] Angry letters arrived in Ottawa from J. A. Krug, U.S. secretary of the interior, but the Canadian government was reluctant to change its policy.[18] The complaints increased when in May 1946 the Alaskan authorities, who had jurisdiction over that section of the road, removed all restrictions on civilian travel, despite the fact that there were no more facilities for motorists west of the 141st meridian than east of it. Canada then had to admit Americans from Alaska to the Canadian section of the road without restriction, even though many of them were quite unprepared for the journey, while still requiring permits of all those wanting to drive over the highway from the South.[19]

It was not until Valentine's Day 1948 that the Canadian government lifted its restrictions on civilian travel on the Alaska Highway, and then it was done for a typically Canadian reason: since roads were a provincial responsibility under the Canadian constitution, Ottawa had no right to control traffic on the British Columbia part of the road. By 1948, "sufficient accommodations were already established to permit unrestricted travel next summer for those provided with camping equipment," and the authorities hoped that "the removal of restrictions would encourage the establishment of additional facilities."[20]

With the road opened to civilian traffic at last, northerners braced for another invasion, this time of tourists, their hopes fueled by the publication of a number of newspaper and magazine articles about the great road of adventure.[21] But to their surprise and dismay, the flood of tourists was a trickle; when it came to actually tackling the route, few Canadians and Americans were keen on driving over more than a thousand miles of rough, dusty, car-destroying road (Americans have long been said to have a particular aversion to unpaved highways).[22] One writer commented in 1947, "The Alaska Highway is the most publicized and the least used road in the entire world."[23] Also contrary to expectations, businessmen did not rush to invest in tourist facilities; as late as 1947 there was only one private garage between Fort St. John and Whitehorse.[24]

Many of those who wanted to experience the Northwest at first hand used the two bus systems that served the region—the British and Yukon Navigation Company's buses, which ran from Dawson Creek to Whitehorse, and O'Hara Bus Lines, which operated on the Whitehorse to Fairbanks route, with service to Haines.[25] Both ran three times a week. Very few people traveled the road by private car; in 1947 (the last complete year when permits were required, and the last one for years for which good statistics were kept) only 2,398 cars carrying 6,394 people used the road, and the numbers increased only very slowly thereafter. Remarkably, fewer than 200 of these were Canadians (see table 17).

The federal Department of Mines and Resources did build seven campgrounds in the Yukon for the use of travelers, but this was only partial compensation for the lack of hotels and restaurants.[26] The accommodations built at Rancheria, for example, could handle only ten people; the O'Hara facilities at Haines Junction and Koidern could handle fifty and seventy-five respectively, but bus passengers had first claim on the rooms. Even Whitehorse, with three hotels, had rooms for only 150 people.[27]

The reluctance of business people to invest in tourism in the region was surprising to officials, given the interest expressed during the war. Most of the inquiries about business opportunities, however, had shown a marked ignorance of the region, and most prospective investors seem to have been indulging in daydreams of wealth on the frontier. As an official of the Bureau of Northwest Territories and Yukon Affairs observed in 1947:

It may be our moral responsibility to advise these people in no uncertain manner of the nature of the country, of its possibilities, and its difficulties, of the types of opportunity afforded and of the necessary qualifications required that will at least give them a possibility of success. In this connection, I feel that settlement should be encouraged to follow a definite sequence only. It would appear that the greatest potential wealth of the Yukon Territory is its mineral resources. If such is the case, then it would appear that encouragement should be given primarily to prospectors, mining companies and miners which will in turn given rise to opportunities for tradesmen, labourers, and professional people, which in turn will give rise to communities, towns, shops, schools, etc. But to permit the latter class of people to act in their misguided beliefs, is to permit them to 'put the cart in front of the mule' and may result in much bitter disappointment and needless hardship.[28]

The adventurous souls who did set up business along the highway were taking a considerable risk, both because traffic was light for years and because any competition tended to ruin business for everyone. Bell and Bartholet of Fort Nelson invested over $20,000

Table 17   Alaska Highway Permits Granted, 1947

Reason for Travel	Number of Permits
Returning to homes in Alaska	1,220
Employment	2,497
Homestead or settle	1,257
Business	969
Prospecting and mining	153
Members of U.S. forces and families	241
Attending University of Alaska	34
Hunting in B.C.	23
Total permits	6,394

SOURCE: NAC, RG 85, vol. 1073, file 256-10-1, pt. 1, Alaska Highway During 1947. The U.S. consulate in Edmonton provided slightly different figures, including 2,967 vehicles and 7,594 persons. NA, RG 59, file 842.154, Seattle-Fairbanks Highway/2-1048, Paul Seddicum to Secretary of State, 10 February 1948.

in a store, cafe, repair shop, and gas station in the town, only to hear rumors that the government was encouraging others to open operations in the area. James Bell wrote, "We trust that until other points on the highway have services which are urgently needed and until traffic shows our services inadequate, we will have protection for our pioneering and substantial risk. Then we will take what comes."[29] In British Columbia the provincial government, which refused to take responsibility for its section of the highway, also did little to control the growth of business along it. The government of the Yukon, on the other hand, was more concerned with the precariousness of sub-Arctic commerce, and tried to regulate the number and distribution of highway services.[30] The federal government, which had control over the buildings and other facilities remaining from the construction period, also tried to ensure that suitable rest areas and repair shops were available along the highway.[31]

From the beginning of the defense projects, officials had been concerned to preserve the scenic qualities of the highway corridor. The decision to set aside the Kluane Game Sanctuary was, in part, a reflection of this attitude. Other areas, such as scenic Muncho

Lake and the extensive Liard Hot Springs, both in northern British Columbia, were set aside as provincial parks and thus spared from unregulated commercial development.[32] The fact was, however, that services were few along the highway, and the road a rough and dusty one. A writer for the *Toronto Star Weekly* who traveled the Alaska Highway in 1947 was not charmed by the trip. The 900-mile trip from Dawson Creek to Whitehorse took at least three days, depending on the condition of the road, which remained subject to washouts. Bus travelers, he reported, "have to be two notches above the sissy level, for there are no delightful stops every hour."[33]

The existing rest facilities were a mixed bag: some were attractive, though rustic, while others were unappealing. Two "Welcome Inns," located at Mile 777.7 and Mile 843, were "extremely dirty both inside and out. Meals served are very poor and not too clean. Persons unfortunate in having to stay overnight would be well advised to use their own bedding." Another traveler commented that "it is most difficult to improve an establishment where people operating such places are not clean in themselves."[34] The accommodations at Teslin were somewhat better, though the owner used a water and sewage system that was so defective that it had forced the army to abandon the site.

Reports on tourist facilities in the Northwest also reflected the racism that continued to flourish in the years after the war. A forest engineer reported of one location that "the tourist accommodation recently established at mile . . . is reasonably clean and tidy at present, but, —— being a squaw man, it is likely this accommodation will attract the local Indians and breeds more than the actual tourists and, in time, will fall below the present standard."[35] A sanitary inspector wrote of ——'s roadhouse, "The people are of native origin and it is somewhat difficult to instruct them satisfactorily in the theories of good restaurant and hotel sanitation and food safety."[36] As time passed this situation improved as government engineers kept a close eye on the highway facilities. The unsatisfactory ones were excluded from the promotional literature and eventually went out of business. Gradually a network of sanitary and attractive, if basic, tourist facilities began to take shape along the Alaska Highway.[37]

One apprehension that lingered in the United States for some years after the end of the war was that Canada would eventually decide to abandon the Alaska Highway. As the months passed, American public opinion forgot (if it had ever known) that the highway had been in poor shape when it was turned over to the Canadians, and instead dwelt on the millions of dollars that the U.S. government had poured into the project. In February 1948 Wisconsin representative Charles Kersten demanded that the State Department ask Canada to guarantee by treaty permanent American access to and use of the road. An official "reminded Mr. Kersten as tactfully as possible that Canada was a sovereign and independent state and that the Canadian people were very sensitive about their sovereignty and independence."[38] Though nothing came of this, the Canadian government had been reminded that Americans expected the road to remain open in usable condition.

The postwar period also saw a revival of the old struggle between the West Coast and the prairies for control of the route to the far Northwest. In 1945 the Americans floated a proposal, backed by President Truman, to build a new road, to cost $15 million, from Fort St. James, British Columbia, to Whitehorse, thus cutting off hundreds of miles of the rough southern section of the Alaska Highway.[39] Since the result would have been to funnel traffic from the region south towards the Pacific Northwest of the United States rather than southeast towards the prairies and Great Plains, the idea was enthusiastically adopted by regional promoters, particularly Senator Warren Magnuson of Washington state.[40] Magnuson went to Ottawa along with Governor Gruening of Alaska to drum up support for the idea, but found the Canadian government strongly opposed to it.[41] Nor was the government of British Columbia interested.[42] Before the war, British Columbia had backed such an idea, but the province had committed too much money to roads connecting with the Alaska Highway to consider supporting an alternate route.[43] At the same time, the United States–Canada–Alaska Prairie Highway Association called for 6,700 new miles of highway construction, to cost $167 million, but this did not materialize either.[44]

The residents of Alaska were interested not only in the future of the Alaska Highway, but also in the Haines Lateral, or Cut-off, which provided a road connection between the interior and the coast. The Canadian government, which controlled the northern end of this road, discovered to its dismay when it took over that it was in much worse shape than the main highway. In response to requests from the United States, the Canadian authorities agreed to keep the road open from June to mid-October, but held out little hope for year-round travel.[45] This was not good enough for Alaskans. Their interest in keeping the road open resulted in a strange proposal, backed by Delegate Anthony Dimond of Alaska and Governor Gruening, to exchange the corridor around the Canadian part of the Haines Road for Point Roberts, Washington, or access to a highway south of Trail, British Columbia.[46] American diplomats pointed out that such an arrangement was not necessary; the Canadians had agreed to maintain the Haines Road and to permit tariff-free transit for Americans traveling from Haines through Canada to other Alaskan points.[47] Alaska replied in March 1947 by passing a memorial through the Territorial Legislature asking Washington to approach the Canadian government with a request for such a transfer. The Haines Road, it was argued, went through an area that "is virtually unpopulated and is not known to be of any special or considerable value or importance," and would thus be no loss to Canada.[48] Governor Gruening offered "a segment of Alaska north of the 66th parallel" in compensation. "If it were necessary to throw up something for British Columbia," the proposal continued, "he would favour giving up Skagway and the land along the route of the White Pass and Yukon railway to the British Columbia border. Possibly, however, it would be enough to offer to make Skagway a free port."[49] This startling suggestion, which would have reversed the verdict of the 1903 Alaskan boundary settlement, giving the Whitehorse-Skagway corridor to Canada, went no further than talk, but the Americans continued to put pressure on Canada to keep the Haines Road open and in good shape. When rumors began to circulate that Ottawa, which saw little benefit in honoring the commitment to the road, was planning to close it, the U.S. Department of the Interior offered to pay half the cost of maintaining it.[50]

Yukoners also wanted the road kept open, since it provided a second gateway into the Territory. Commercial firms that served the region claimed that shipping costs could be substantially reduced if the road were kept open all year; British Columbia Steamships Ltd. estimated that supplies could be delivered to the Yukon by truck over the road at a 40 percent saving over the White Pass and Yukon Railway.[51] Other firms, including the Port Chilkoot Co. of Haines, made similar claims.[52] But the road was not used much in the immediate postwar years, probably because it was in such bad shape; in the summer of 1947 fewer than 7 vehicles per day used it, and only 50 cars and 201 trucks in September, the busiest month of the year.[53]

In the postwar years, the Alaska Highway proved to be a powerful stimulus to the development of a regional transportation network. British Columbia, though refusing to take responsibility for its section of the road, authorized work on a highway connecting the Alaska Highway at Fort St. John with the provincial road network at Prince George. Businessmen in the Mayo and Dawson City regions of the Yukon lobbied hard for a highway connection to Whitehorse, hoping to reverse the southward economic shift in the Territory.[54] Alberta promoters pressed the provincial government for improvements to the Edmonton–Grande Prairie road so that business could better capitalize on opportunities in the province's Northwest.[55] Both Alberta and British Columbia boosters got their wish, and a road network eventually developed around the Alaska Highway. The Edmonton–Grande Prairie road was gradually upgraded, and construction proceeded on the Hart Highway in northern British Columbia. The Haines Road remained open, though seasonally. Dawson City, the greatest loser in the wartime bonanza, eventually got a link to the Alaska Highway via Mayo, but not until 1955, when the shift of power to the South was irreversible.[56] Dawson's first road link to the rest of the continent actually came a few years earlier through the construction by the Alaska Road Commission of a minor road northeast from Tok Junction; the summer road that linked it to Dawson, now known as the "Top of the World" highway, is one of Canada's most remote and spectacular roads.[57] Another road, linking Atlin, British Columbia, to the Alaska Highway at Jakes Corner in the Yukon, was opened in the same period.[58]

Residents of the Mackenzie District hoped that the construction of the Canol Project would bring them a share of postwar prosperity and expansion, but they were to be disappointed. Although stories of the oil riches of the Mackenzie valley still circulated, the bad publicity about waste and overspending on the project had given the whole region a bad name.[59] Even the road that had been built at such great cost and effort along the pipeline route from Norman Wells to Whitehorse, providing a land link between the Yukon and Northwest Territories, was left to decay. In 1945 the Americans ceased road maintenance, and two years later the Canadians still had not decided what to do with it.[60] Over the years the condition of the road deteriorated, and the bridges that washed out were not replaced. It was possible to travel on the southern part of the Canol Road as far as Ross River, though jerry-built bridges were sometimes required, but from Ross River northeast to Norman Wells the road was already impassable in some places by regular vehicles by the end of the war. The Canol Project had disappeared, with little benefit to the land it had crossed.[61]

The defense construction projects in the far Northwest during World War II generated considerable debate about the future of the region. As Charles Camsell noted in 1943, the wartime cooperation demonstrated

that it is not necessary for a nation to exercise sovereignty over a country in order to carry on enterprises therein. Had it been recognized that it is not necessary for a nation to "own" an area in order to participate in its development and to reap its share of the advantages from that development there might have been no war today. Herein the United States and Canada have been carrying out a great experiment. Let us all hope it will meet with a success which will recommend it to the policy-makers of the world.[62]

This comment suggested a breathtaking surrender of national responsibility and economic sovereignty over a huge area of Canada, but in the early 1940s this was what often passed for a policy of northern development.

Questions of sovereignty did not worry the Northwest's American promoters. Declaring that the region might well be at the forefront of North America's economic future, Lawrence Drake wrote in *Collier's* magazine, "No land of milk and honey this: no prodigal paradise. Land of mountains and timber it is; storied land of nineteenth-century wealth in gold; land of unfathomed twentieth-century riches in copper, zinc, iron, tungsten and petroleum; land of prodigiously falling waters ready to drive giant power turbines; land for industry; land for labour."[63]

From the early days of the war, planners had been considering how best to capitalize on the construction projects. The North Pacific Planning Project, sponsored by the Joint Economic Committees of the United States and Canada, was established in February 1943 under the joint chairmanship of Charles Camsell for Canada and James Rettie for the United States. It was designed to reduce "the probable post-war economic dislocation consequent upon the changes which the economy in each country is presently undergoing."[64] Canadian officials were at pains to point out that the commission's work was a study plan, not a program of development, but its conclusions suggested the expectation of a common economic future for the Yukon, northern British Columbia, and Alaska.[65] It was the first stage of an effort to chart a common destiny for the Northwest, built on the highway and pipeline projects.[66]

As final victory approached in Europe and the Pacific, interest in the Northwest waned; with the military urgency gone, the need to proceed in lockstep with American, and particularly Alaskan, interests faded. Proposals for joint action continued to surface— for airfield maintenance, highway reconstruction, construction of a connecting road through British Columbia, a railway from the lower forty-eight states to Alaska—but Canadians were increasingly wary of the implications of such ideas.[67] Canada hardly knew how to deal with the financial and logistical responsibility of 1,200 miles of rough, unfinished road, let alone some chimerical railroad scheme. And as one American official realized, "another less tangible, but perhaps more vital, reason for the Canadian attitude is anxiety lest improved communications with the U.S. orient the people of British Columbia further toward the U.S. and away from the Dominion as a whole."[68]

The war years left the far Northwest with an uncertain legacy. It seemed ungrateful for Canada to complain about the state of unfinished roads and dozens of decaying construction camps, when these had been built at no initial cost to Canada and then turned over by the Americans. But Canadians did complain, mostly because the projects had not been built with Canadian needs in mind and had imposed a massive financial burden on the federal, provincial, and territorial governments—and Canada, moreover, sensitive to the implications for sovereignty, had paid the Americans for these facilities at war's end. Canada could not avoid its obligations to the United States and thus grudgingly accepted the necessity of maintaining the Alaska Highway and, after a fashion, the Haines Road—though both would likely have been abandoned but for the 1942 agreement. Other projects, like those associated with the Canol Project, were discarded as the white elephants they were. Very slowly, smaller projects were grafted onto the existing structure, particularly a series of shorter roads that extended the highway network and eventually linked most of the region's communities.

The region would never return to its prewar state. Native communities from northern Alberta to Norman Wells and from Fort Nelson to Kluane Lake had been seriously disrupted. Some of the small trading posts of the 1930s were now substantial highway communities, and would grow even more. The region was no longer isolated from the rest of the continent; it was instead tied to a complex communications network that linked it by road, air, and electronics to the outside world.

The transformation of the region accelerated in the 1950s and 1960s. Many of these changes—the transfer of the Yukon's capital from Dawson City to Whitehorse; the relocation of the administration of the Northwest Territories; the extension of health care and other services to Native communities; a much larger, better financed, and more active federal civil service; expanded communications; and many other changes—could be traced to wartime beginnings. Not all of them, however, resulted from the war. Much social change was a reflection of larger developments in Canada as a whole, though the exposure of regional conditions during the war did give impetus to new experiments in social engineering. In particular, northern Native people found themselves the clients of the postwar welfare state, facing a newly interventionist and assimilationist Department of Indian Affairs, and their communities and lives became increasingly disrupted.

There was widespread disappointment that the wartime projects did not stimulate a great postwar economic boom, partly because some of the early critics were right: the highway did not traverse a rich territory, nor was much of the route particularly scenic. This, combined with the poor quality of the road, deterred tourists from venturing north in the numbers that promoters had predicted. Only the most adventurous came, their cars fitted with windshield and headlight protectors, their roofs loaded with extra tires and gasoline—but there were not enough of these to make a tourist boom. Instead, the highway remained a financial burden to the federal government.

Perhaps the most disappointing denouement of the projects was the fact that very few of the men and women who came north during the war to work on the projects stayed in the region after their work was over. While many of them went home with memories of a great adventure in a beautiful land, only a handful returned to settle there—a great blow to those who had counted on the wartime workers to remain and form the nucleus of the region's economic expansion. By 1946, the non-Native population of the Northwest was in rapid decline, particularly in northern Alberta and the Mackenzie River district, where projects were shut down entirely. Along the Alaska Highway, a much smaller workforce under the direction of the Canadian Army remained, and the Northwest Staging Route's airfields continued to be operated, on a much reduced scale, by the Royal Canadian Air Force. The population of Whitehorse dropped by two-thirds, from more than 10,000 in 1943 to about 3,600 in 1946. But the region never declined to its prewar state. After the surplus population of wartime left, there were still many more people in the region in 1946 than in 1940, and as businesses began to take advantage of new opportunities and the federal government launched the welfare state, the region slowly began to grow.

The agent of this wartime growth was the American army of occupation; changes in the region between 1942 and 1946, and the new pattern of settlement and development that evolved in the postoccupation era were overwhelmingly the result of the American intervention. Canada had stood idly by while the United States had defended and developed its northland; only gradually after 1946 did

Canada assume its obligations to the region. As the North faced the future, and as the different levels of government struggled to come to grips with the reality of the new North, they did so largely on the foundation laid by the United States; to a much greater degree than most Canadians realize, they are still doing so.

Conclusion: Historiographical Reflections on the Army of Occupation

IN MANY WAYS, World War II was the pivotal event of the twentieth century. Just as World War I had sweeping effects on everything from cultural values to sexual expectations to political and diplomatic structures, so too did the second global conflict recast the basic foundations of the human community. This war, even more than the first, engulfed huge parts of the world; while major battles raged in Europe and the Pacific, minor campaigns took place in some of the world's most remote regions—Alaska, Greenland, northern Australia, the Canadian Northwest. This was in every way a world war.

Until recently—reflecting the historical profession's continued reluctance to deal directly with the recent past—historians have shied away from considerations of the social and economic impacts of the war, especially on peripheral regions. Instead, they have focused attention on military questions and on those areas most directly affected by the battles. This situation in part reflects the fact that much of the initial history of wars is written by state-sponsored military historians, whose accounts rarely stray from the battlefields, the command centers, and the embassies. And there was much to tell: the impact of the bombing of England and Germany, the devastation of western Russia, the systematic plunder of Italy and Norway, the great battles for supremacy over the air and seas, and the complexities of combat in Europe and the Pacific theaters.

Over the past decade, however, as time has dulled the immediacy of the events, and as a full range of historical sources have become available, historians have begun to shift their emphasis from military questions (though these continue to receive considerable attention) to broader social, cultural, economic, and political considerations, and have begun to cast a wider geographical net. To put it simply, mainstream historical attention has shifted from the front lines to the home front.

As research expands to new and fertile ground, the range of the impact of World War II is becoming clearer. Research has shown that the turmoil and disruption of World War II had sweeping implications for racial and national stereotypes, the role of blacks in American society, the expansion of an American-based global economy, the role of women in Allied and Axis countries, indigenous populations in areas affected by battles or military occupation. If this research has a weakness, it is that most of the work has been undertaken with the blinkers of national boundaries firmly in place. To the extent that major societal changes are discussed, they are described within the context of a single country, and often with little recognition of their global significance and similarities.[1]

This study of the impact of the American occupation of the Canadian Northwest is, we hope, informed by an awareness that it was an important example of an extremely extensive process. In the first place, the region shared (though with important differences) in many of the societal changes that swept North America during the period. Wartime spending, for instance, sparked a major remobilization and expansion of the continent's industrial capacity, ending a decade of depression and despair, reinvigorating the Canadian and U.S. economies. Yet not all regions were equally affected by the spending boom. The American Northeast flourished, but its wartime prosperity was built on an existing industrial and urban capacity, using labor and factories that had been stilled by the Depression. The American West, however, was another matter, as Gary Nash has documented in his masterful study.[2] The war reshaped the West's economic, social, and urban landscape, ushering in an era of prosperity and continued change. The relationship between the war and the postwar ascendancy of the western states is a vital and now well-known one. Similarly the Canadian West, though on a much smaller scale, experienced major disruptions and underwent considerable reorganization. Historians of the region, however, have almost ignored World War II (in sharp contrast to their handling of World War I) and have made no attempt at a regional analysis of its impact. Gerald Friesen, in his superb history of the prairie West, simply ignores the war as a specific event.[3]

Changes associated with war were not only regional. Major groups in North American society, particularly blacks and women, saw important shifts in their role and status. As a number of historians have shown, in the war years women assumed a more equal role in society. Encouraged by government propaganda and programs to work outside the home, they became integrated into many new areas of the workforce. Many expected that their gains would outlive the war, but they were to be disappointed, for though they had proven their abilities, a widely promoted cult of domesticity pushed them back into the kitchen at war's end, thus setting the stage for the resurgence of women's power through the liberation movements of the 1960s.[4]

American blacks also experienced new opportunities and raised expectations during the war. The rapid industrial expansion to meet wartime demands created thousands of new factory openings for black workers, who migrated to the cities of the industrial Northeast and the West Coast in such numbers as to alter the racial balance in those places. Blacks also served in large numbers in the armed forces. There, as everywhere, they found their opportunities circumscribed by racism. Few blacks were permitted to join combat units until late in the war; the vast majority served well behind the lines in engineering, transport, or supply companies, or in remote regions like the Canadian Northwest. The war experiences of blacks highlighted the contradictions of the American dream, and helped to politicize and radicalize a generation of American blacks. At the same time, the military service and evident ability of black troops undercut one of the foundations of American racism—the idea that blacks were untrustworthy and unreliable—thus helping to make possible the liberalization of American views on race in the postwar era.[5]

While North American historians have begun to identify the national and regional implications of World War II, there has been much less recognition of the global nature of societal change associated with the war. Nor has there been a systematic recognition of America's role in spreading this change throughout the Allied world. The peaceful armies of occupation, of which the U.S. force in the Canadian Northwest was only a small part, carried America's culture, its racial tensions, economic system, political agenda, and military values into the farthest corners of the world.

The impact of these occupations varied from place to place. The arrival of thousands of American troops in Britain seems not to have Americanized the country in any lasting way, but on the contrary to have reinforced its essential Britishness.[6] In Australia, by contrast, the tension between American and Australian values resulted in a serious challenge to the male-oriented, frontierist national attitudes.[7] Canada did not experience a widespread invasion; only the Northwest welcomed significant numbers of American soldiers and civilians. But Canadians were already very familiar with American values and traditions and had, sometimes in spite of themselves, adopted many of them.[8] While there were no sweeping changes on the national level associated with these wartime activities, Canadians' direct experience with American military strength, commercial enthusiasm, and racism made those Canadians in authority who were exposed to it even more protective of the vulnerable parts of the Canadian physical and cultural landscape. The federal government's "discovery" of its northern obligations is the best-known example of this process.[9]

It was, however, in the more peripheral areas (characterized by small populations, limited national political control or administration, and restricted capitalist economic development) that the armies of occupation had their greatest impact. Large cities—London, Sydney, Vancouver, Edmonton—could absorb an influx of American personnel and emerge from the war relatively intact, despite some degree of disruption. The same was not true of smaller, poorer, less well-developed areas. The arrival of thousands of soldiers in Tonga and Trinidad, or in northern British Columbia, the Yukon, and Northwest Territories, seriously disrupted the existing economic order, challenged the status quo, and often resulted in a major reorganization of the local social and economic structure. Certain patterns are discernible in these areas. Their indigenous peoples discovered that the Americans placed little value on their culture (beyond the tourist's fascination with souvenirs), preyed on their women, made little effort to share the seemingly endless American wealth, and in many ways disrupted the local order of things. For some of these groups, the Americans' arrival was the first contact with large numbers of foreigners, and it was often not a happy encounter. When American blacks were part of the army of occupation, the local people discovered the extent of American racism, which was often directed at them as well. In the Australian outback, as in the Canadian Northwest, the indigenous people sometimes got along better with American blacks than with whites, perhaps reflecting a shared experience of racism.[10]

Similarly, the exigencies of military planning and the attitude prevailing towards the environment in the 1940s meant that Americans paid as little attention to the natural landscape as to the cultural. The rapid construction of roads, airfields, and other military facilities quickly reordered large areas of previously untouched lands. The Alaska Highway opened up vast inland territories, assisting with wartime defense and setting the stage for postwar developments. Such activities, undertaken with little concern for wildlife, river systems, forest preservation, or other environmental matters, had significant (though as yet little described) impacts in those areas affected by the military occupation. This was particularly true in the small Pacific islands, where occupation could easily ruin a fragile oceanic ecosystem, or in northern areas, where ecological disruptions left scars that will last for generations.[11]

The legacy of wartime occupation can readily be seen in many of the countries and regions penetrated by the U.S. military. Major projects such as the Alaska Highway provided a foundation for postwar development, and towns like Whitehorse came to prominence after 1945. On the other hand, important regional centers bypassed by military activity, like Dawson, could find themselves doomed. Much of this happened by accident, since most of the projects were undertaken with little thought for peacetime conditions. The roads did not always go in the directions that civilian planners would have wished, nor did they always come close to the mineral or other resources coveted by regional developers. In the countries where the host government kept a close eye on construction, or actually participated in it, the deviation from national and regional priorities was kept to a minimum; Australia is the best example. Where the Americans were left to do as they pleased, on the other hand, as in northwest Canada, the disruption could be severe.

In gauging the impact of these armies, it is useful to compare the general conditions of the areas they occupied with those they did not. Throughout the war, the paranoid Stalin regime refused to allow significant numbers of American troops into the USSR. The Soviets feared precisely what did occur in some occupied territories—the rapid Americanization of local cultures and the sweeping intrusion of American values, especially economic values. By such a quarantine the rulers of the Soviet Union were able to keep capitalism at bay for another forty years.

For the United States, the occupation of major portions of the free world during World War II proved to be the beginning rather than the end of a process. The war drew the United States out of its self-imposed isolationism and made it a leading actor on the world stage. Americans came, with real or feigned reluctance, to assist in an international emergency, were welcomed by many countries as saviors and protectors, and stayed throughout the war to keep the Axis at bay. This was a unique form of imperialism, in which the United States worked through its allies rather than through conquest or colonialism, through peaceful occupation rather than military takeover, and it proved to be remarkably successful.[12]

The United States and its people were also transformed by this process. Hundreds of thousands of them experienced a different culture, often for the first time. Those who came as soldiers often came back after the war as investors, settlers, and developers.[13] Having seen the world and the opportunities it offered, the Americans were not prepared to retreat into an isolationist shell. After the war the United States was at the center of the world stage, where it was determined to continue to play the role of peacemaker and defender of liberty. When the Russians replaced the Axis powers in the national demonology, the United States was able to build on the worldwide military infrastructure developed between 1942 and 1945. The Philippines and many other places, once liberated, remained occupied, leading critics of American foreign policy to complain that cold war rhetoric was simply a front for economic imperialism. Though the occupation of the Canadian Northwest ended with the war, the United States remained a presence in northern Canada, notably in such establishments as the Distant Early Warning, or DEW, line, built to forestall an attack from the Soviet Union.

In this respect the war was only the first stage of a global process—the Americanization of the world's economy and society. Whereas before the war a few tentacles of American mass culture— notably movies, popular music, and to a lesser extent the worship of the automobile—were reaching through the English-speaking world, the armies of occupation brought the full force of this culture to many corners of the globe. When in the 1950s the United States turned from military to consumer production, the lines of military alliance became lines of commercial expansion. In the 1990s, as the United States increasingly loses its economic dominance, we can see in a sense the true end of World War II.

The American occupation of the Canadian Northwest might seem only a minor part of these processes. The events described in this book form essentially a regional study, vital to Canada, but of less importance to the United States. Yet this study, along with similar ones that have dealt with the occupations of the other Allied countries, may profitably be used as building blocks for a long-overdue reconceptualization of World War II. While not losing sight of the military aspect of the war, it is important to recognize its wider importance in world history. It played a crucial role in the Americanization of the globe. Many vital forces—the movement toward a global culture, postwar diplomatic and military realities, the growth of multinational corporations, the decline of racism, the death and rebirth of colonialism, the rapid destruction of indigenous cultures, the spread of consumerism and the resulting pressure on the environment—all can be traced to a greater or lesser degree to the American occupation of Allied nations during the war.

The research agenda flowing from a broad consideration of the army of occupation is a full one. Comparative research in the field remains in its infancy; perhaps the impending fiftieth anniversary of the U.S. entry into the war will spark reconsideration of these issues. It is also to be hoped that the present national barriers between historiographical traditions will, like the once impenetrable Berlin Wall, come tumbling down in the interest of a global understanding of the past. There are so many topics to consider, many of which can be properly studied only from an international perspective: the degree to which American postwar investment followed the path of the armies of occupation; the number of military personnel who returned as settlers or investors to the countries they once occupied; the impact on the United States of the thousands of foreign war brides brought home after the war; cultural changes in areas occupied by Americans; the impact of American contact with indigenous cultures; postwar American designs on the facilities and strategic sites developed during the war years; and the lasting effects of the overseas experience on hundreds of thousands of Americans. Anyone familiar with the subject could add to this list.

Few Canadians or Americans paid much attention to the Canadian Northwest before the war. With the exception of the gold rush of 1897–98 it was to many a region without a past or much of a future. For a brief period in the early 1940s, when the fate of a democratic and free North America seemed to hang in the balance, a spotlight shone on the region as attention was focused on the massive defense projects. When the threat abated, so did interest in the region, at least until the energy crisis of the 1970s turned attention to it once again.

But the wartime invasion left many marks on the region and determined much of its pattern of development in the postwar years. Many changes, and continued development, would follow the path blazed in 1942 by the U.S. Army Corps of Engineers. The Northwest would not return to its prewar somnolence, just as the Allied world would not retreat into the national isolationism and cultural distance of the 1930s. World War II had truly transformed the world, taking a giant step towards the creation of a more global society. The Canadian Northwest was a significant and representative element in a broad and sweeping process that, just as surely as military combat and victory, determined the shape of the postwar world.

Notes

Introduction

1. Susan Mann Trofimenkoff, *The Dream of Nation: A Social and Intellectual History of Quebec* (Toronto: Macmillan, 1982).

2. On Canadians in Britain, see C. P. Stacey and Barbara Wilson, *The Half Million: The Canadians in Britain, 1939–1946* (Toronto: University of Toronto Press, 1987); also Gordon Beckles, *Canada Comes to England* (London: Hodder and Stoughton, 1941); and Jean-Pierre Gagnon, "Canadian Soldiers in Bermuda During World War One," *Histoire Sociale/Social History* 23, no. 45 (May 1990). For a brief description of the impact of the war on Iceland, see S. A. Magnusson, *Northern Sphinx: Iceland and Icelanders from the Settlement to the Present* (Montreal: McGill-Queen's University Press, 1977), pp. 142–44. For Britain in Iceland, see Donald Bittner, *The Lion and the White Falcon: Britain and Iceland in the World War II Era* (Hamden: Archon Books, 1983).

3. Peace-keeping forces, like the troops in Cyprus, operate under quite a different dynamic; they are of course aware of the intensely international and political nature of their duties.

4. For a brief consideration of the diplomatic background to this expansion, with an emphasis on British colonies and Iceland, see George Stambuk, *American Military Forces Abroad: Their Impact on the Western State System* (Columbus: Ohio State University Press, 1963), pp. 15–46. For Australia, see Roger Bell, *Unequal Allies: Australian-American Relations in the Pacific War* (Melbourne: Melbourne University Press, 1977). For

Canada, see Stanley W. Dziuban, *Military Relations Between the United States and Canada 1939–1945* (Washington, D.C.: Department of the Army, 1959).

5. And even before: it is noteworthy that the Atlantic Charter, the basic blueprint for the postwar world, was signed in August 1941, four months before the attack on Pearl Harbor.

6. Monthly Strength of the Army, January 31, 1943 (AGO, MRB, 1943) and Strength of the Army, 1 April 1945 (AGO, MRB, 1945).

7. On black troops in Britain, see Norman Longmate, *The G.I.s: The Americans in Britain, 1942–1945* (London: Hutchinson, 1975); and David Reynold, "The Churchill Government and the Black American Troops in Britain During World War II," *Transactions of the Royal Historical Society* 35 (1985): 113–33. On black troops in Australia, see Kay Saunders, "Conflict Between the American and Australian Governments over the Introduction of Black American Servicemen into Australia During World War Two," *Australian Journal of Politics and History* 33, no. 2 (1987); Kay Saunders and Helen Taylor, "The Reception of American Servicemen in Australia During World War 2: The Resilience of 'White Australia,' " *Journal of Black Studies* (June 1988). See also Jane Fidock, "The Effect of the American 'Invasion' of Australia, 1942–1945," *Flinders Journal of History and Politics* 11 (1985).

8. As of 1945, black soldiers made up 7.63 percent of total enlistment in the army air forces, 4.22 percent of the army ground forces, 11.44 percent of army service forces, and 9.78 percent of War Department groups.

9. Richard Dalfiuma, *Desegregation of the United States Armed Forces: Fighting on Two Fronts, 1939–1953* (Columbia, Mo.: University of Missouri Press, 1989); A. Russell Buchanan, *Black Americans in World War II* (Santa Barbara: ABC-Clio, 1977); Neil Wynn, *The Afro-American and the Second World War* (New York: Holmes and Meier, 1976); B. Nalty, *Strength for the Fight: A History of Black Americans in the Military* (New York: Free Press, 1988).

10. T. Hachey, "Jim Crow with a British Accent: Attitudes of London Government Officials Toward American Negro Soldiers in England During World War II," *Journal of Negro History* 59, no. 1 (January 1974). See also Graham Smith, *When Jim Crow Met John Bull: Black American Soldiers in World War II Britain* (London, 1967).

11. Saunders, "Conflict Between the American and Australian Governments"; K. S. Coates and W. R. Morrison, "The American Rampant: Reflections on the Impact of the U.S. Armed Forces Overseas during World War II," *Journal of World History* 2, no. 2 (1991).

12. A. Palmer, "The Politics of Race and War: Black American Soldiers in the Caribbean Theatre During the Second World War," *Military Affairs*

47, no. 2 (April 1983). On the Caribbean, see also H. Johnston, "The Anglo-American Caribbean Commission and the Extension of American Influence in the British Caribbean, 1942–1945," *The Journal of Commonwealth and Comparative Politics* 22, no. 2 (July 1984).

13. For Greenland, see Herbert Schuurman, *Canada's Eastern Neighbour: A View on Change in Greenland* (Ottawa: Supply and Services Canada, 1976).

14. M. Sturma, "Public Health and Sexual Morality: Venereal Disease in World War II Australia," *Signs* 13, no. 4 (1988).

15. L. Cleveland, "When They Sent the Last Yank Home: Wartime Images of Popular Culture," *Journal of Popular Culture* 18, no. 3 (Winter 1984); M. Sturma, "Loving the Alien: The Underside of Relations Between American Servicemen and Australian Women in Queensland, 1942–1945," *Journal of Australian Studies* 24 (1989).

16. John Costello, *Love, Sex and War: Changing Values, 1939–1945* (London: Collins, 1985).

17. The process has been called "Coca-colonization." For the American impact on Australia, see "The American Invasion, 1942–45," in John H. Moore, ed., *The American Alliance: Australia, New Zealand and the United States, 1940–1970* (Melbourne: Cassell Australia, 1970); Rosemary Campbell, *Heroes and Lovers* (Sydney: Allen and Unwin, 1989); and Fidock, "The Effect of the American 'Invasion' of Australia." For an American perspective on activities in Britain, see Diana Forbes-Robertson and Roger Straus Jr., eds., *War Letters from Britain* (New York: G.P. Putnam, 1941). For Britain, see Longmate, *The G.I.'s.*

18. G. White and L. Lindstrom, eds., *The Pacific Theatre: Island Representation of World War II* (Melbourne: Melbourne University Press, 1990).

19. Akira Iriye, "Contemporary History as History: American Expansion into the Pacific since 1941," *Pacific Historical Review* 53 (1984); W. Roger Louis, *Imperialism at Bay: The United States and the Decolonization of the British Empire, 1941–1945* (New York, Oxford University Press, 1978); G. R. Hess, *The United States' Emergence as a Southeast Asia Power, 1940–1950* (New York: Columbia University Press, 1987).

20. For an examination of one aspect of this transition in the postwar world, see Stambuk, *American Military Forces Abroad.*

21. For Britain, see Longmate, *The G.I.'s.* For Australia, see E. D. Potts and A. Potts, *Yanks Down Under, 1941–45* (Melbourne: Oxford University Press, 1985). See also John Hammond Moore, *Over-Sexed, Over-Paid, and Over Here* (St. Lucia: University of Queensland Press, 1981); M. McKernan, *All In! Australia During the Second World War* (Melbourne: Thomas Nelson, 1983); Russell Ward, *The History of Australia: The Twentieth Century, 1901–1975* (London: Heinemann, 1978); Bell, *Unequal Allies.*

22. Colonial armies, including French forces in New France and British troops in the American colonies and in British North America, played a major role in the social, cultural, economic, and even the political development of these regions. See William J. Eccles, *Canada under Louis XIV, 1663–1701* (Toronto: McClelland and Stewart, 1964); William J. Eccles, *The Canadian Frontier, 1534–1760* (New York: Holt, Rinehart, and Winston, 1969); and Eleanor Senior, *Redcoats and Patriotes: The Rebellions in Lower Canada, 1837–38* (Stittsville, Ont.: Canadian War Museum, 1985).

23. Newfoundland, still a British colony at this time, also played host to thousands of foreign military personnel during the war. See David Mackenzie, *Inside the North Atlantic Triangle* (Toronto: University of Toronto Press, 1988); and John Cardoulis, *A Friendly Invasion* (St. Johns: Bridgewater, 1990).

24. These aspects of the occupation are well covered elsewhere. See Shelagh Grant, *Sovereignty or Security?: Government Policy in the Canadian North, 1939–1950* (Vancouver: University of British Columbia Press, 1988); Morris Zaslow, *The Northward Expansion of Canada* (Toronto: McClelland and Stewart, 1988); and Richard Diubaldo, "The Canol Project in Canadian-American Relations," Canadian Historical Association *Historical Papers* (1977).

1. Prelude to Occupation

1. J. D. MacGregor, *The Klondike Rush Through Edmonton, 1897–98* (Toronto: McClelland and Stewart, 1970). James Michener has written about the episode in *The Journey* (Toronto: McClelland and Stewart, 1989).

2. The Palliser Triangle comprises southeast Alberta, southern Saskatchewan, and the southwest tip of Manitoba. A Bennett buggy, derisively named after R. B. Bennett, prime minister from 1930 to 1935, was a car or a truck pulled by a horse.

3. W. A. C. Bennett, later premier of British Columbia, came to the Peace River country in this period. His experiences convinced him of the potential of the north and demonstrated the difficulties that inland areas had promoting their interests against Vancouver and Vancouver Island. Much of his later political life was influenced by this period. See David Mitchell, *W.A.C. Bennett* (Vancouver: Douglas and McIntyre, 1983).

4. Peter Usher, *Fur Trade Posts of the Northwest Territories, 1870–1910* (Ottawa: Department of Indian Affairs and Northern Development, 1971).

5. A. J. Ray, "Periodic Shortages, Native Welfare and the Hudson's Bay Company," in K. S. Coates and W. R. Morrison, *Interpreting Canada's North: Selected Readings* (Toronto: Copp Clark, 1989). Ottawa used the

Hudson's Bay Company as a cheap means of distributing relief in the Northwest Territories.

6. Ken Coates and W. R. Morrison, *Treaty Report: Treaty 11* (Ottawa: Treaties and Historical Research Centre, 1986). See also Rene Fumoleau, *As Long as This Land Shall Last* (Toronto: McClelland and Stewart, 1973).

7. On the police, see W. R. Morrison, *Showing the Flag: The Mounted Police and Canadian Sovereignty in the North, 1894–1925* (Vancouver: University of British Columbia Press, 1985).

8. K. Coates, "Best Left as Indians: The Federal Government and the Indians of the Yukon, 1894–1950," *Canadian Journal of Native Studies* 4, no. 2 (Fall 1984).

9. D. J. Murdoff, quoted in Ken Coates, *Canada's Colonies*, p. 113. For additional examples of this competition, see NAC, RG 85, vol. 852, file 7869, pt. 1, Grant Savage to Buffalo Park Department, 5 June 1935, Director to Wardler, 11 June 1936, Memorandum re: Grant Savage, white trapper, 1 April 1938; ibid., pt. 2, Savage to Gibson, 10 March 1942.

10. Ken Coates and W. R. Morrison, "More Than a Matter of Blood: The Churches, the Government and the Mixed Blood Populations of the Yukon and Mackenzie River Valley, 1890–1950," in F. L. Barron and J. Waldrum, eds., *1885 and After* (Regina: Canadian Plains Research Centre, 1986).

11. On the life of a prospector in this era, see F. B. Watt, *Great Bear: A Journey Remembered* (Yellowknife: Outcrop Press, 1980); and Fred Peet, *Miners and Moonshiners: A Personal Account of Adventure and Survival in a Difficult Era* (Victoria: Sono Nis Press, 1983).

12. Robert Bothwell, *Eldorado: Canada's National Uranium Company* (Toronto: University of Toronto Press, 1984).

13. Grant, *Sovereignty or Security?*, 41.

14. NAC, RG 85, vol. 925, file 11836, pt. 1, R. A. Gibson to Commissioner, RCMP, 2 September 1941.

15. Lewis Green, *The Gold Hustlers* (Anchorage: Alaskan Northwest, 1977); K. S. Coates and W. R. Morrison, *Land of the Midnight Sun: A History of the Yukon* (Edmonton: Hurtig, 1988), chap. 5.

16. The name preferred in Canada for these people is "Inuit."

17. Robert McCandless, *Yukon Wildlife: A Social History* (Edmonton: University of Alberta Press, 1986).

18. For a discussion of social conditions in Yellowknife c. 1942, see NAC, RG 85, file 7391, Memorandum of Meeting on Local Conditions— Yellowknife Settlement, 19 July 1939.

19. K. S. Coates and W. R. Morrison, "War Comes to the Yukon," *The Beaver* (October/November 1989).

20. *Regina Leader Post,* 14 September 1939.

21. YTA, YRG 1, ser. 1, vol. 60, file 35193, PC 3065, 11 October 1939.

22. McConachie's northern airline grew into Canadian Pacific Airlines. Grant McConachie, *Bush Pilot with a Briefcase: The Happy-go-lucky Story of Grant McConachie* (Toronto: Doubleday, 1972). See also *Edmonton Journal*, 17 July 1941; and NA, RG 85, vol. 306, file 1009-9(1). For information on air travel in the far Northwest before World War II, see NA, RG 85, vol. 1190, file 352-2/204, vol. 1; ibid., file 352-2/201, vol. 1; ibid., vol. 658, file 3318-3; YTA, YRG 1, ser. 1, vol. 57, file 33909A2, file 1.

It was a sign of the importance of this new technology to the region that airplane service to the far Northwest was exempted from wartime restrictions on air travel. NAC, RG 85, vol. 306, file 1009-9(1), R. A. Gibson to J. A. Wilson, 13 September 1939; *Northern Miner*, 28 September 1939.

23. Morris Zaslow, "The Development of the Mackenzie Basin, 1922–1940," Ph.D. dissertation, University of Toronto, 1957.

24. Gordon Bennett, *Yukon Transportation: A History*, Canadian Historic Sites Occasional Papers in Archaeology and History 19 (Ottawa, 1978).

25. Alaska had a somewhat better transportation network. Fairbanks, the gold-mining community in the center of the Territory, was connected by rail to Seward and by the Richardson Highway to Valdez, both coastal ports. In addition, there were numerous roads and trails to mining camps and settlements. Claus-M. Naske, *Paving Alaska's Trails: The Work of the Alaska Road Commission* (New York: University Press of America, 1986).

26. Terrence Cole, "Klondike Contraptions," *The Northern Review*, no. 314 (Summer-Winter 1989). Considerable effort and money were expended on developing a regional wireless communication system. See the correspondence in NAC, RG 85, vol. 601, file 2401, particularly Extracts, Exchanges of Correspondence, Memoranda, Etc. . . . , 2 January 1935.

27. David Hall, *Clifford Sifton*, 2 vols. (Vancouver: University of British Columbia Press, 1982 and 1984), 2:176–88.

28. NAC, RG 85, vol. 880, file 8975, Dawson Board of Trade to T. A. Crerar, 14 May 1937, Jeckell to Sec. of State, 30 April 1937, Jeckell to R. A. Gibson, 31 May 1937.

29. Roman Catholic schools in the Yukon received government support, while those in British Columbia did not. A union between province and Territory would have meant bringing the two systems in line with each other. For Prime Minister W. L. M. King, a cautious man always anxious to avoid sectarian conflict, the potential for trouble was too great, and the annexation of the Yukon was called off. Richard Stuart, "The Yukon Schools Question, 1937," *Canadian Historical Review* 64, no. 1 (1983).

30. NAC, RG 85, vol. 880, file 8975, Peace River Chamber of Commerce, Petition for Reorganization of Territory, 19 April 1939.

31. Ibid., M. Meikle Memo: Request by the Province of Alberta for the Annexation of Part of the Northwest Territories, 24 January 1941.

32. YTA, YRG 1, ser. 1-A, vol. 9, file 466iv, G. I. MacLean to W. W. Cory, 4 June 1929. This issue can be followed in Robin Fisher, "T. D. Pattullo and The British Columbia to Alaska Highway," and David Remley, "The Latent Fear: Canadian-American Relations and Early Proposals for a Highway to Alaska," both in Ken Coates, ed., *The Alaska Highway: Papers of the 40th Anniversary Symposium* (Vancouver: University of British Columbia Press, 1985). See also Grant, *Sovereignty or Security?*, pp. 46–47.

33. His comments were read to the visiting commission by W. D. MacBride. NAC, RG 14, D2, vol. 416, file 137A, British Columbia–Yukon–Alaska Highway Commission, Preliminary Report (Ottawa, 1940), 50–51.

34. NA, RG 59, Decimal File 842.154, Seattle/Fairbanks Highway/341, Memorandum of Conversation, 6 August 1941.

35. Ibid.

36. This was assumed by regional promoters. NAC, RG 22, vol. 250, file 40-7-4, vol. 2, J. H. McNeill to G. A. Jeckell, 3 March 1939.

37. ACE, 72-A-3173, box 15, file 50-15, Stimson to Wilbrun Cartwright, 2 August 1940.

38. YTA, YRG 1, ser. 1-A, vol. 9, file 466iv, Jeckell to R. A. Gibson, 7 March 1939.

39. *Report of the Alaskan International Highway Commission* (Washington: Government Printing Office, 1940).

40. *Dawson Daily News,* 25 June 1937. This was not an original thought, nor was this the last time it was raised. American interest in the highway to Alaska had always had a great deal to do with military considerations. *Dawson Daily News,* 23 October 1941.

41. British Columbia–Yukon–Alaska Highway Commission, *Preliminary Report on Proposed Highway Through British Columbia and the Yukon Territory to Alaska* (Ottawa: Kings Printer, 1940); British Columbia–Yukon–Alaska Highway Commission, *Preliminary Report on Proposed Highway Through B.C. and the Yukon Territory to Alaska* (Ottawa: Kings Printer, 1941), p. 32.

42. *Dawson Daily News,* 12 July 1941, 1; NAC, RG 126, vol. 37.

43. EMA, RG 11, Class 90, file 23, F. S. Wright to Mayor and Aldermen, City of Edmonton, 25 November 1937; *Stewart News and Northern B.C. Miner,* 3 December 1937; EMA, RG 11, Class 90, file 23, F. S. Wright to City Clerk, Edmonton, 30 May 1938, F. S. Wright to Herbert Putnam, Library of Congress, 30 May 1938.

44. EMA, RG 11, Class 90, file 23, J. A. MacKinnon to R. J. Gibb, 8 November 1936, J. A. MacKinnon to R. J. Gibb, 8 November 1936.

45. Wahpeton is a small town in North Dakota, with a population in 1940 of 3,747; Portal is a customs post on the 49th parallel, whose population in that year was 499.

46. EMA, RG 11, Class 2, file 15, F. S. Wright to Commissioner J. A. Hodgson, 23 April 1941.

47. Literature distributed by the United States–Canada–Alaska Prairie Highway Association showed a map with a trunk highway running diagonally from Chicago to Edmonton through Fargo and Minot, North Dakota, with feeder roads from Bismarck, Billings, Great Falls, and Helena. EMA, RG 11, Class 90, file 33, "Post War Highway Program Proposed by United States–Canada–Alaska Prairie Highway Association."

48. EMA, RG 11, Class 90, file 31, F. S. Wright to J. A. Hodgson, 18 December 1941; *Edmonton Journal,* 17 December 1941.

49. EMA, RG 11, Class 90, file 29, Aitken to Hodgson, 2 May 1941.

50. Ibid., United States–Alaska Highway Conference, Directors' Meeting, 22 May 1941, Minutes of the United States–Alaska Highway Conference, 22 May 1941.

51. Ibid., Minutes of the United States–Alaska Highway Conference, 22 May 1941, Resolution 1: To the President of the United States of America and the Honorable Members of His Majesty's Privy Council of Canada.

52. Ibid., Copy of Resolution, Edmonton Municipal Council, 26 May 1941, and J. A. Mackenzie to J. H. Ogilvie, 14 June 1941.

53. EMA, RG 11, Class 90, file 30, Memorandum re: Alaska Highway, 2 July 1941 (by F. S. Wright), Memorandum re: United States–Canada–Alaska Prairie Highway Association, 29 July 1941 (by C. Grant and J. A. MacKenzie).

54. EMA, RG 11, Class 90, file 29, T. A. Crerar to Mayor John W. Fry, 23 June 1941, and Report of Canadian Delegation to Ottawa re: Alaska Highway (J. A. MacKenzie and C. Grant), 31 July 1941.

55. Grant, *Sovereignty or Security?,* p. 60.

56. Ibid., pp. 60-61.

57. Quoted in ibid., p. 75.

58. These negotiations can be traced in detail in M. Bezeau, "The Realities of Strategic Planning: The Decision to Build the Alaska Highway," in Coates, ed., *The Alaska Highway,* and Grant, *Sovereignty or Security?,* pp. 74-78.

59. NA, RG 59, Decimal File 842.154, Seattle/Fairbanks Highway/354, J. D. Hickerson to Mr. Berle, 31 January 1942.

60. LC, Harold Ickes Papers, box 93, file Alaska 2, Ickes to Bliven, 19 May 1942.

61. ACE, 72-A-3173, box 16, file 50-14, H. R. 3095, which is dated, seemingly incorrectly, 5 February 1941.

62. EMA, RG 11, Class 90, file 32, Report of Halvor Halvorson, president of United States–Canada–Alaska Prairie Highway Association, 23 October 1942.

63. Ibid. The Appian Way was designed in part to make it easier for Roman legions to subdue the Italian provinces; one wonders if Halvorson was aware of the fact.

64. NA, RG 165, OPD611, Alaska (section 1), Sherburne to Murray,

23 February 1942; ACE, 72-A-3173, box 15, file 50-15, A. Breitenstein to Chief of Engineers, 8 May 1943, J. S. Lamb to General G. Marshall, 21 May 1942.

65. NA, RG 30, box 188, Basis for Estimates—Alaska Highway Project, Pierrepont Moffat to Secretary of State for External Affairs, 17 March 1942, Mackenzie King to U.S. Minister to Canada, 18 March 1942.

66. Ibid., Basis for Estimates—Alaska Highway Project, 18 March 1942.

67. ACE, X-1-16, Memorandum re: Alaska Highway surveys, 4 February 1942.

68. ACE, 72-A03173, box 15, file 52-1, C. L. Sturdevant to Colonel W. Hoge, 3 March 1942.

69. NAC, RG 22, vol. 251, file 40-7-4, pt. 3, Cabinet War Committee, Document Number 101, Military Highway to Alaska, n.d.

70. NA, RG 30, box 188, Basis for Estimates—Alaska Highway Project, Thomas MacDonald to Brig. Gen. Sturdevant, 4 March 1942, Sturdevant to MacDonald, 16 March 1942. Sturdevant accepted MacDonald's terms with only a few amendments.

71. ACE, X-1-16, Memorandum re: Alaska Highway by C. L. Sturdevant, 4 February 1942.

72. ACE, 72-A-3173, box 18, J. L. Clark to Chief of Engineers, 14 February 1942.

73. Stefansson was a regular contributor, often unsolicited, of ideas and opinions to the American and Canadian governments. ACE, 419, Early Data on Canol Project, 22-30, V. Stefansson to General Pyron, 10 May 1942; *Calgary Albertan,* 31 December 1941. See also Richard Diubaldo, *Stefansson and the Canadian Arctic* (Montreal: McGill-Queen's University Press, 1978).

74. NAC, RG 85, vol. 944, file 12725A, Ministerial Regulations Governing Importations and Domestic Purchases in Connection with the Construction of the United States–Alaska Highway. This circular provided a list of duty-free (construction-related) and dutiable (personal use and selected additional items) goods.

75. Official documents on the Canol Project were not signed until late June 1942. Grant, *Sovereignty or Security?,* pp. 80-82. See also Diubaldo, "The Canol Project."

76. Diubaldo, "The Canol Project."

77. ACE, 419, Early Data on Canol Project, 22-30, J. K. Cornwall to William Clarke, 28 April 1942.

2. Invasion of the Bulldozers

1. *The Alaska Highway: Interim Report from the Committee on Roads, House of Representatives.* Anxious American companies were assured

that virtually all this heavy equipment was purchased in the United States. ACE, RG 338, box 29, 52A 434, Carl J. Lomen to Senator Tom Connolly, 28 April 1943; Maj.-Gen. E. Reybold to Senator Connolly, 14 May 1943.

2. In February 1947, Snag had the doubtful honor of registering the lowest temperature ever recorded in Canada, −81.4°F, or −63°C.

3. See newspaper accounts in ACE, 72-A-173-3. The United States also sent shiploads of supplies to the Soviet port of Vladivostok. The ships passed within easy striking range of Japan, but were not attacked by the Japanese, who did not want to offend the USSR.

4. ACE, A52-A34, box 31, 686.61, "Site Board Report Covering Locations of Flight Strips along the Alcan Highway," prepared by Maj. L. B. McCloud, c. September 1942.

5. ACE, X-1-11, *Summary Northern Route, Air Transport Command*, 3. A proposal for facilities construction called for Class II Sub-Depots to have a hangar, airplane repair and supply sheds, and 17 huts (each 20 × 48 feet).

6. The buildings included one hangar (130 × 160 feet), two 40 × 80-foot structures (repair and supply), and 18 huts (20 × 48 feet), which included everything from administration offices to a crash truck station and guardhouse.

7. ACE, X-1-11, Commanding General, Army Air Force to Commanding General, Air Transport Command, 21 April 1943.

8. NAC, RG 22, vol. 107, file 84-32-6, 2nd Report of the Special Commissioner for Defence Projects in Northwest Canada, Part 4, Northwest Staging Route (Air).

9. Material on this protest is widely available. The criticism was led by those who, like Donald MacDonald, Thomas Riggs, and Charles Stewart, had worked on the different Alaska Highway commissions and had come out in favor of one of the British Columbia routes. See NA, RG 59, D.F. 842.154, Seattle/Fairbanks Highway/364, Lewis Clark to Secretary of State, 14 March 1942 re: Alaska Highway, press and other reaction; ACE, 72-A-3173, box 15, file 50-15, Secretary of War to Wilburn Cartwright, n.d., Alaskan International Highway Commission to Senator H.T. Bone and M.C. Wallgren, 2 March 1942, Charles Stewart to Thomas Riggs, 20 February 1942, Cowper Rochfort to Charles Stewart, 12 March 1942; ibid., file 52-2, Frederic Delano to President, 13 April 1942 (which advocated immediate construction of a railway), Secretary of War to William Cartwright, n.d., S. 579 (bill to authorize the construction of a military supply highway to Alaska), 28 January 1943; NAC, RG 22, vol. 251, file 40-7-4, pt. 3, Report of Subcommittee of Foreign Relations Committee Having under Consideration Senate Resolution 253; ACE, 72-A-3173, box 16, 50-39, John Holzworth to Senator J. Murray, 12 June 1942; *Pic*, 19 August 1942, "Scandal of This War Is the Alaska Highway."

10. Surveys: ACE, X-1-14, War Department, "Report on Survey: Trans Canadian Alaska Railway Location"; ACE, X-1-12, Press Release, 10 December 1942. The announcement concluded, "The War Department does not consider that a military necessity exists for its construction at the present time."

Cost-accounting: ACE, X-1-14, "Certain Economic Factors Relating to the Location, Construction and Future Usefulness of the Trans Canada Alaska Railway," National Resources Planning Board, 2 October 1942.

NA, RG 338, box 2, Fort St. John, General Pierrepont Moffat to Secretary of State, 24 April 1942; ACE, 72-A-3173, box 15, 52-8, Delano to Somervell, 25 May 1943, J.A. O'Connor to Commanding General, Services of Supply, 12 October 1942. The debate came complete with yet another dispute between proponents of the B.C. connection and those favoring a prairie route. See ACE, 72-A-3173, box 15, 52-8, A. J. Breitenstein to Reybold, 19 November 1942.

11. ACE, 72-A-3173, box 15, Alcan Highway Publicity, Press Release: Entire Alcan Highway Opened for Army Supply Trucks, 29 October 1942; ibid., 16/20, History, Organization and Progress of the Military Road to Alaska. See also Stan Cohen, *The Trail of '42* (Missoula: Pictorial Histories, 1988). See also David Remley, *Crooked Road: The Story of the Alaska Highway* (New York: McGraw Hill, 1976).

12. ACE, 72-A-3173, 16/20, History, Organization and Progress of the Military Road to Alaska. *Ponton* is the way the Army Corps of Engineers spells *pontoon*. The ponton equipage was the pontoon bridge that preceded the more permanent trestle bridge.

13. ACE, X-2-10, H. W. Richardson, "From a War Correspondent's Notebook—I," Whitehorse, 25 June 1943.

14. Roy Minter, *White Pass: Gateway to the Klondike* (Toronto: McClelland and Stewart, 1987).

15. ACE, X-1-12, Press Release, Army Leases Alaska-Canadian Railroad, 19 October 1942; NAC, RG 36/7, vol. 48, Privy Council file, P.C. 10067, Order in Council authorizing the lease of the White Pass and Yukon Railway to the Government of the United States of America, 6 November 1942.

16. YTA, YRG 1, ser. 1, vol. 61, file 35402, Gibson to J. W. Gibben, 8 October 1942, C. K. LeCapelain to R. A. Gibson, 25 February 1943.

17. Interview with Archie MacEachern.

18. Churchill was speaking about the battle of El Alamein, which took place a month before the highway opened.

19. *Whitehorse Star*, 20 November 1942, 27 November 1942. The paper had planned to publish large numbers of the commemorative issue for sale to the thousands of workers in the area, but mechanical problems prevented it from cashing in on the opportunity. ACE, 72-A-3173, box 18, Alaska-Canada Highway Dedication (program); *Vancouver Daily Province,*

24 April 1943; *Whitehorse Star*, 6 November 1942; *Dawson Daily News*, 28 November 1942; Congressional Record-House, 21 January 1943, speech by Warren Magnuson.

20. Heath Twichell, "Cut, Fill and Straighten: The Role of the Public Roads Administration in the Building of the Alaska Highway," in Coates, ed., *The Alaska Highway*.

21. R. Melville Smith was able to capitalize on a massive reduction on highway construction in Ontario—where the budget was reduced from $35 million or $40 million to $9 million, thus freeing many workers and contractors for northern service. ACE, 72-A-3173, box 15, 52-1, Memorandum for the Under-Secretary of State for External Affairs, 14 April 1942. This situation led to the odd speculation that the Ontario Highways Department would be called on to build the Alaska Highway.

22. This event was captured on film by Richard Finnie and was included in his documentary, *The Alaska Highway*.

23. ACE, 72-A-3173, box 15, 50-15, J. S. O'Connor to Commanding General, Army Services Forces, 14 July 1943.

24. Ibid., B. Somervell to Commanding General, North West Service Command, 7 July 1943.

25. NA, RG 30, box 188, Basis for Estimates—Alaska Highway Project, Changing of Standards and Confusion of Instructions.

26. Ibid., Canadian Alaska Highway Contractors, Sections D and F, Management—R. Melville Smith Co., Ltd.

27. NA, RG 165, O.P.D. 463.7, section I-A, case 28, Memorandum, 19 January 1944.

28. Interview with John Mueller, Denver, Colorado (Victoria, B.C., April 1989).

29. ACE, 72-A-3173, box 15, 50-16, W. B. Poland to Col. F. Delano, 6 March 1943.

30. Ibid., Secretary of War to Secretary of State, 13 November 1942; NAC, RG 22, vol. 104, 84-32-1A, vol. 2, Pierrepont Moffat to Secretary of State, 28 November 1942.

31. Naske, *Paving Alaska's Trails*.

32. P. S. Barry has suggested that *Canol* stands for Canadian American Norman Oil Line. P. S. Barry, *The Canol Project: An Adventure of the U.S. War Department in Canada's Northwest* (Edmonton: published by the author, 1985). See Standard Oil Company (N.J.) report, ACE, 425-Canol Project, Misc. Papers, Pamphlets, "Power to Strike from Alaska."

33. Geologic surveys were conducted throughout the Mackenzie River valley. See the Final Geological Reports, completed for numerous areas, in ACE, Misc. 422, G.C.-44.21.

34. ACE, 72-A-3173, box 18, Report on Canol Project, Bk. 1, Roosevelt to Harold Ickes, 10 June 1942.

35. Barry, *The Canol Project*, p. 5.

36. Even Prince Rupert, a seemingly minor adjunct to the project, had almost 2,900 men working on the facilities there in January 1943. NA, RG 338, box 53, Narrative Reports—Imperial Oil Limited, Gerald Tyler, Report of Progress, Prince Rupert District, 25 January 1943.

37. 388th Engineer Construction, 89th and 90th Engineer Heavy Ponton Battalions, communications teams, and auxiliary personnel. NA, RG 407, box 23193, SGCD-838-0.2, "A Brief History of the 838th Signal Service Company," April 1943.

38. *Whitehorse Star*, 28 April 1944, 5 May 1944.

39. ACE, 72-A-3173-1, "Draft of Report on the Canol Project," 17 December 1943.

40. The committee that reported on the Canol Project was harshly critical of it. Its conclusion was *"The committee is definitely of the opinion that the Canol project should never have been undertaken, and that it should have been abandoned when the difficulties were called to the attention of the War Department"* (italics in original). *Additional Report of the Special Committee Investigating the National Defense Program,* 78th Cong., 1st Sess., Report No. 10, Pt. 14 (Washington, Government Printing Office, 1944), p. 7.

41. L. Woodman, "CANOL: Pipeline of Brief Glory," *The Northern Engineer* 9, no. 2 (Summer 1977): 27.

42. Barry, *The Canol Project,* pp. 344-45.

3. The Native People and the Environment

1. *Edmonton Journal,* 12 July 1941.

2. NAC, RG 27, vol. 676, file 6-5-75-5-1, L. E. Drummond to R. A. Gibson, 3 July 1942.

3. *Edmonton Journal,* 12 July 1941.

4. "Indians Puzzled by Rush on Road," *Edmonton Journal,* 20 March 1942.

5. "Road 'Swell Idea,' Says North Indian," *Edmonton Journal,* 23 November 1942.

6. *Edmonton Journal,* August 15 1942.

7. Knox F. McCusker, "The Alaska Highway," *The Canadian Surveyor* 8 (July 1943).

8. Barbara Bardie and Ken Coates, "The Gravel Magnet" (television program produced for Northern Native Broadcasting Yukon, 1988).

9. NAC, RG 27, vol. 676, file 6-5-75-5-1, T.R.L. MacInnes to L. E. Drummond, 23 June 1943.

10. Questionnaire answered by Hampton Primeaux, Rayne, Louisiana, 1989.

11. NAC, RG 85, vol. 1872, file 550-2-1, J. E. Gibben to Mr. Gibson, 31 May 1946.

12. Ibid.

786

13. Questionnaire answered by A. Forgie, Edmonton, Alberta, 1989.

14. Questionnaire answered by Joe Garbus, Westhaven, Conn., 1989.

15. McCandless, *Yukon Wildlife*.

16. This issue, particularly as it relates to the Yukon, is described in Ken Coates, "The Sinews of Their Lives: Aboriginal Resource Use and the Law in the Yukon Territory, 1894–1950," in K. Abel and J. Friesen, eds., *Aboriginal Resource Use and the Law* (forthcoming).

17. YTA, YRG 1, ser. 3, vol. 10, file 12-20C, R. Sampson to D. M. MacKay, 20 May 1944, G. Jeckell to R. A. Gibson, 20 July 1944.

18. John Marchand, "Tribal Epidemics in the Yukon," *Journal of the American Medical Association* 123 (1943): 1019–20. See also YTA, Anglican Church, Champagne file, S. Webb to Bishop, 9 July 1943.

19. Interview with Daniel Johnson, January 1988.

20. YTA, YRG 1, ser. 1, vol. 9, file 149B, pt. J, C. K. LeCapelain to R. A. Gibson, 17 July 1943.

21. *Northern Lights* (newsletter of the Anglican Diocese of Yukon) 32, no. 1 (February 1943): 2. Bessie Johnston received a citation from Dr. P. E. Moore, superintendent of medical services, Indian Affairs Department, for her work during the epidemic.

22. J. Honigman, letter to the editor, *Journal of the American Medical Association* 124 (1944): 386.

23. NAC, RG 85, vol. 1872, file 550-2-1, D. J. Martin to Constable, RCMP, Watson Lake, 19 April 1943.

24. NAC, RG 85, vol. 916, file 11032, J. P. Harvey to Secretary, Indian Affairs Branch, 31 October 1942.

25. Interview with Kitty Grant, January 1988.

26. NAC, RG 85, vol. 1872, file 550-2-1, Const. J. D. Waring to O. C., RCMP, Whitehorse, 21 April 1943.

27. NA, RG 338, NWSC, box 26, file 314.7, Organization Histories, Annual Report, Post Surgeon, Post of Whitehorse, 1943, 26.

28. See Ken Coates, "The Alaska Highway and the Indians of the Southern Yukon," and Julie Cruikshank, "The Gravel Magnet," in Coates, ed., *The Alaska Highway*.

29. *Edmonton Journal*, 11 April 1944.

30. NA, RG 338, box 47, Field Memo Book, General Orders No. 50, 23 August 1943, Section III: Limits (such orders were occasionally extended to entire Indian settlements); ibid., NWSC, box 9, General Orders, 1944, General Orders No. 50: Off-Limits, 14 September 1943 (relating to the community of Tanacross, Alaska).

31. NAC, RG 85, vol. 1872, file 550-2-1, Inspector W. Grennan to N.C.O. in Charge, RCMP, Selkirk, 20 October 1942.

32. John and I. Honigman, "Drinking in an Indian-White Community," *Quarterly Journal of Studies on Alcohol* 5 (March 1945): 575–619.

33. See Ken Coates and Judith Powell, *The Modern North* (Toronto: James Lorimer, 1989).

34. These were formally known as the Mackenzie Valley Pipeline Inquiry and the Alaska Highway Pipeline Inquiry, respectively.

35. NWSC, microfilm reel 16, United States Defense Construction Projects in Canada, Minutes of Meeting, c. 1944.

36. NAC, RG 36/7, vol. 1, file 3-3, W. J. Taylor to Dr. J. A. Urquhart, 23 July 1943.

37. NAC, RG 85, vol. 608, file 2614, R. A. Gibson to J. M. Wardle, 19 June 1946.

38. Ibid., R. A. Gibson to R. M. Brown, 22 July 1946.

39. YTA, YRG 1, ser. 1, vol. 69, file 21, RCMP Report: Forest Fires—Kluane Lake District, 5 October 1943; Jeckell to R. A. Gibson, 4 September 1943.

40. NAC, RG 85, vol. 944, file 12725A, Dave Wilson to George Black, 9 September 1943; ibid., vol. 1512, file 1000/200, pt. 1, C. K. LeCapelain to R. A. Gibson, 15 October 1943. A cord is 8 feet long, thus 18,000 cords are 144,000 feet or 27.43 miles long—an impressive pile.

41. YTA, YRG 1, ser. 1, vol. 6, file 466i, R. A. Gibson to C. K. LeCapelain, 10 March 1943.

42. Ibid., R. A. Gibson to C. K. LeCapelain, 22 March 1943.

43. YTA, YRG 1, ser. 8, file 466-3a, F.H.R. Jackson to R. A. Gibson, 6 August 1945.

44. YTA, YRG 1, ser. 1, vol. 6, file 466i, C. K. LeCapelain to R. A. Gibson, 1 April 1943.

45. YTA, YRG 1, ser. 1, vol. 6, file 466iii, George Black to Jeckell, 23 March 1942; ibid., ser. 3, vol. 10, pt. 2 of 2, file 12-20A, G. A. Jeckell to R. A. Gibson, 22 September 1942.

46. NAC, RG 126, vol. 37, Testimony by Joe Jacquot before the Berger Commission, 21 April 1976. Jacquot also spoke of rumors that fighter planes had shot caribou and moose in open areas. McCandless, *Yukon Wildlife*, argues for a limited loss of game. For the Native perspective, see "The Gravel Magnet."

47. YTA, YRG 1, ser. 1, vol. 6, file 4661, LeCapelain to R. A. Gibson, 1 September 1942.

48. YTA, YRG 1, ser. 3, vol. 10, file 12-20, RCMP Patrol—Kluane to Yukon-Alaska Border and Rtd., 30 November 1943.

49. Ibid., Jeckell to Cronkite, 24 December 1943, 5 January 1944; Harrison Lewis to Mr. Smart, 2 November 1945.

50. NAC, RG 85, vol. 1390, file 406-11, vol. 1-A, Indians of Burwash Landing to J. E. Gibben, 23 June 1946.

51. YTA, YRG 1, ser. 1, vol. 6, file 466i, LeCapelain to Gibson, 1 September 1942.

52. NAC, RG 85, vol. 944, file 12743, pt. 2, J. A. Phillips to Mountie, 17 August 1944.

53. YTA, YRG 1, ser. 1, vol. 6, file 466i, LeCapelain to Gibson, 1 September 1942.

54. Interview with Charlie Taylor, Whitehorse, January 1988.

55. McCandless, *Yukon Wildlife.*

56. YTA, YRG 1, ser. 3, vol. 10, file 12-20B, pt. 2 of 3, L. A. Pierre to Prentiss Brown, 16 April 1943, C. K. LeCapelain to J. S. Bright, 12 June 1943.

57. Interview with Leslie H. (Bud) Schnurstein, May 1988.

58. Interview with Jim and Iris Sutton, June 1988. The incident described took place near Dawson Creek.

59. NAC, RG 85, vol. 944, file 12743, pt. 1, C. K. LeCapelain to R. A. Gibson, 3 January 1943.

60. YTA, Miscellaneous Manuscripts 37-38, Heath Twichell to "My Dear Ones," 3 June 1942.

61. YTA, YRG 1, ser. 3, vol. 17, pt. 2 of 2, file 28798, S. H. Rosen of Saskatoon Tannery Co. to George Black, 10 September 1943.

62. Ibid., Cronkite to O. C., "G" Division, 29 October 1943. The fact that the RCMP should concern itself with a matter so far from its jurisdiction shows how wide-ranging its influence over the lives of the Native people was.

63. NAC, RG 126, vol. 37, Testimony of Joe Jacquot before the Berger Commission.

64. YTA, YRG 1, ser. 3, vol. 17, pt. 2 of 2, Alleged Unlawful Pollution of Streams—Complaint of Mrs. D. Mackintosh, 20 August 1943.

65. YTA, YRG 1, ser. 3, vol. 10, file 12-20B, G. A. Jeckell to R. A. Gibson, 15 June 1943.

66. YTA, YRG 1, ser. 3, vol. 10, file 12-20A, pt. 2 of 2, Ira Gabrielson to Hoyes Lloyd, Supt. of Wildlife Protection, 31 October 1942.

67. NAC, RG 85, vol. 944, file 12743, pt. 1, R. A. Gibson to Ira Gabrielson, 15 January 1943.

68. YTA, YRG 1, ser. 3, vol. 10, file 12-20B, W. E. Crouch to R. A. Gibson, 3 February 1943.

69. Ibid., Gibson to Jeckell, 3 June 1943.

70. YTA, YRG 1, ser. 3, vol. 10, file 12-20, Advance Release AMS of Wednesday, 20 October 1943.

71. YTA, YRG 1, ser. 3, vol. 10, file 12-20B, pt. 2 of 3, Hoffmaster to Gibson, 23 August 1943, Gibson to Hoffmaster, 27 August 1943. See also NAC, RG 85, vol. 1160, file 331-2/200-1, G.E.B.S. to Mr. Gibson, 13 April 1943.

72. Morris Zaslow, *Reading the Rocks: The Story of the Geological Survey of Canada, 1842–1872* (Toronto: Macmillan, 1975).

73. YTA, YRG 1, ser. 3, vol. 10, file 12-20A, pt. 1 of 2, F. R. Butler to Jeckell, 9 March 1942.

74. YTA, YRG 1, ser. 3, vol. 10, file 12-20B, F. C. Lynch to R. A. Gibson, 8 June 1943, Memorandum by R. M. Anderson, 8 June 1943, Gibson to Jeckell, 10 June 1943.

75. NA, RG 30, vol. 187, file 003.12-Canada, H. Raup to W. E. Thorne, 24 September 1943.

76. YTA, YRG 1, ser. 3, vol. 14, file 241-5, R. A. Gibson to G. A. Jeckell, 18 May 1944; ibid., vol. 17, file 28798, pt. 2 of 2, D. H. Sutherland to Commissioner, RCMP, 28 March 1944.

77. YTA, YRG 1, ser. 3, vol. 14, file 241-5, R. A. Gibson to Jeckell, 31 May 1944.

78. McCandless, *Yukon Wildlife*, examines this process.

79. As this relates to the Yukon Territory, see Ken Coates, "Upsetting the Rhythms: The Federal Government and Native Communities in the Yukon Territory, 1945 to 1973," in Gurston Dacks and Ken Coates, eds., *Northern Communities: The Prospects for Empowerment* (Edmonton: Boreal Institute for Northern Studies, 1988).

4. Law and Order in the Occupied Northwest

1. On this, see Morrison, *Showing the Flag.*

2. NA, RG 338, box 1, 010.6, Military Laws, Memo: Military Jurisdiction over Civilian Employees, 30 1943.

3. There are unfortunately no records extant for the military police relating to the Northwest Service Command. According to American archivists, very few military police records of any type from World War II have been preserved.

4. NA, RG 165, OPD 320.2, Canada, Section I, Case 28, Bush to Commanding General, 9 February 1943.

5. NA, RG 338, Box 4, 5-2, Intelligence Reports, Intelligence Report, 1 April–15 April 1945, Issue No. 5.

6. The tangled history of American extraterritorial rights in Canada is summarized in Dziuban, *Military Relations.*

7. Ibid., p. 297.

8. Privy Council 5484, cited in ibid., p. 297.

9. Privy Council 9694, cited in ibid., p. 300.

10. NA, RG 338, box 1, 010.6, Military Laws, C. B. Peck to Commanding Office, Dawson Creek, 29 May 1943.

11. NA, RG 338, NWSC Roll 2, General Orders, "Courts-Martial Procedure for Trial of Civilians in Northwest Service Command," General Order No. 34, 31 July 1943.

12. NA, RG 338, box 1, 010.6, Military Laws, Hayes to Division Engineer, 20 May 1943.

13. NAC, RG 22, vol. 107, file 84-32-6, pt. 1, Alaska Highway Survey, 21 December 1943.

14. NAC, RG 85, vol. 959, file 13517, Circular Memorandum to All Detachments of "G" Division, Royal Canadian Mounted Police, 28 June 1943.

15. NA, RG 338, box 1, 010.6, Military Laws, Administrative Memorandum, No. 63: Jurisdiction over Civilian Personnel, 5 May 1943.

16. Ibid., Military Laws, District Engineer to Commanding General, 8 June 1943.

17. NA, RG 338, NWSC, box 9, General Orders, 1944, General Orders, No. 34: Courts-Martial Procedure for Trial of Civilians in Northwest Service Command, 31 July 1943.

18. NA, RG 338, NWSC, box 18, Staff Meetings, 1943–1944, Staff Conference, 17 August 1944.

19. NA, RG 59, 811.203/352, PS/ATB, American Consul to J. Graham Parsons, 12 November 1943.

20. NA, RG 338, box 2, Fort St. John, General, Deputy Attorney General to Brig. Gen. J. A. O'Connor, 10 November 1943.

21. NA, RG 59, file 811.203/365, Robert English to Secretary of State, 11 December 1943.

22. NA, RG 338, box 1, NWSC, 0.92, Foreign Affairs and Relations, NOSIG to CG NWSC, 12 December 1943.

23. Ibid., NOSIG to CG NWSC, 20 April 1943.

24. NA, RG 59, file 811.203/365, Robert English to Secretary of State, 11 December 1943. See also NA, RG 338, box 2, Fort St. John, General, Conference on Civil-Military Legal Jurisdiction, 11 December 1943, for notes of the meeting.

25. Dziuban, *Military Relations*, p. 299, states that "the opinions are contained in *Reference re Exemption of U.S. Forces From Canadian Criminal Law* (1943), Canadian S.C.R. 483." For a synthesis of these opinions, he refers readers to Archibald King, "Further Developments Concerning Jurisdiction over Friendly Foreign Armed Forces," *American Journal of International Law* 40 (1946): 272–74.

26. *Edmonton Bulletin*, 30 December 1943.

27. NA, RG 59, file 811.203/376, Robert English to Secretary of State, 31 December 1943.

28. NA, RG 59, file 811.203/389, American Consular Service, Edmonton to J. Graham Parsons, 18 January 1944.

29. YTA, NWSC, roll 2, "U.S. Agreements, Military Personnel," 6 April 1944.

30. NAC, RG 85, vol. 960, file 13528, Inspector Sault to Commissioner, RCMP, 16 July 1943. Dr. Harvey had the powers of a magistrate and could hear such cases.

31. *Whitehorse Star,* 20 October 1944.

32. NA, RG 36/7, vol. 40, file 28-23, pt. 2, T. H. Callahan to A.D.P. Heeney, 17 November 1943.

33. Questionnaire answered by Hampton Primeaux, Indian Bayou, Louisiana, 1989.

34. NAC, RG 85, vol. 958, file 13439, LeCapelain to Col. K. B. Bush, Chief of Staff, NWSC, Whitehorse, 18 August 1943.

35. NAC, RG 36/7, vol. 40, file 28-23, pt. 1, George Black to Brig. Gen. F. S. Strong, 5 January 1945, Strong to Black, 25 January 1945, Black to Strong, 27 January 1945.

36. NAC, RG 85, vol. 960, file 13560, Re: Chester Neff: Failure to keep right of road when meeting another motor vehicle, March 1944.

37. NAC, RG 85, vol. 958, file 13439, W. W. Foster to R. A. Gibson, 24 August 1943.

38. NA, RG 338, box 2, Fort St. John, General, Conference on Civil-Military Legal Jurisdiction, 11 December 1943.

39. NAC, RG 22, vol. 107, file 84-32-6, pt. 1, Alaska Highway Survey 1943, 21 December 1943.

40. NA, RG 338, box 4, file 5-2, Intelligence Reports, Intelligence Report, 11 February–28 February 1945, Issue No. 2.

41. NAC, RG 36/7, vol. 36, file 11-23, F. Whiffin: Service Investigation Criminal, 30 July 1946; Conclusion of Case Report, Criminal-Theft (Major) U.S. and Canadian Gov't Equipment, 24 October 1946. The investigations were inconclusive.

42. Special allocations were made for Norman Wells and Eldorado Mines, and residents could also order a certain amount of liquor through the mail.

43. YTA, YRG 1, ser. 1, vol. 61, file 35404, pt. 1, Liquor Regulations Amendment, 17 May 1943; ibid., pt. 2, Jeckell to Gibson, 13 November 1943.

44. During the Depression, people applying for welfare assistance in some Canadian jurisdictions were compelled to surrender their liquor permits.

45. YTA, YRG 1, ser. 1, vol. 61, file 35405, pt. 2, Jeckell to Gibson, 26 February 1944.

46. NAC, RG 36/7, vol. 40, file 28-23, pt. 2, W. E. Sanderson to Division Engineer, Northwest Division, 23 September 1943.

47. Interview with Cale Roberts, New Westminster, B.C., June 1988.

48. NAC, RG 85, vol. 945, file 12806, F—— R——, Fort Smith, NWT, Interdiction Of: Territorial Liquor Ordinance, 15 August 1942.

49. NA, RG 338, NWSC, box 9, Numbered Memorandum, 1943, Memorandum No. 143, II: Liquor Control, 21 July 1943; ibid., box 44, Office Memoranda, District Circular Letter No. 39, Liquor Permits, 28 February 1944.

50. YTA, YRG 1, ser. 1, vol. 61, file 35405, pt. 1, Liquor Restrictions in Canada, 31 March 1943.

51. NAC, RG 85, vol. 948, file 13076, Liquor Conditions—Watson Lake, YT, 22 June 1943. See also *Whitehorse Star,* 3 September 1943.

52. The word *hooch* comes from the region; the coastal Indians made a liquor they called *hoo-chin-oo.*

53. NA, RG 338, box 42, Monthly Historical Reports, Historical Report for February 1943, describes the loss of forty-two cases of liquor at Skagway. See also NA, RG 338, NWSC, box 18, Staff Meetings, 1943–1944, Conference Notes on Meeting, 10 June 1943, and Staff Meeting, 24 November 1944.

54. NAC, RG 85, vol. 949, file 13094, Re: Liquor Conditions, Watson Lake, Y.T., 18 November 1942.

55. Questionnaire answered by Alex Forgie, Edmonton, 1989.

56. Questionnaire answered by Cyril Griffith, Naicam, Saskatchewan, 1989.

57. McEachern questionnaire.

58. He later denied making the statement, although a number of witnesses reported hearing him voice his displeasure with the inconsistent punishments. NAC, RG 85, vol. 949, file 13094, Re: F—— M——, Fort Smith, N.W.T., Infrac, Section 99, N.W.T. Act, 8 December 1942; ibid., file 13097, F—— M——, Fort Smith, N.W.T. Infra. Sec. 99, N.W.T. Act, December 1942.

59. YTA, YRG 1, ser. 1, vol. 61, file 35405, pt. 1, Jeckell to Bush, 13 April 1943.

60. YTA, YRG 1, ser. 1, vol. 61, file 55405, pt. 1, 1 April 1943.

61. Ibid., file 35405, pt. 1, Bush to Jeckell, 21 April 1943.

5. Men, Women, and the Northwest Defense Projects

1. Stacey and Wilson, *The Half Million.*

2. The classic study of rape is Susan Brownmiller, *Against Our Will: Men, Women and Rape* (New York: Simon and Schuster, 1973), especially chap. 3, "War."

3. See Costello, *Love, Sex and War.*

4. See Cleveland, "When They Send the Last Yank Home"; Albert Guererard, Jr., "Novitiate," *Virginia Quarterly Review* 21, no. 1 (1945); Sturma, "Loving the Alien."

5. The phrase comes from the end of World War I; it was Lloyd George's promise for a better life for veterans, cruelly unfulfilled. See Ruth Pierson, *They're Still Women After All: The Second World War and Canadian Womanhood* (Toronto: McClelland and Stewart, 1986).

6. See Nalty, *Strength for the Fight;* Neill Wynn, "War and Social Change: The Black American in Two World Wars," in B. Bond and I. Roy, eds., *War*

and Society, vol. 2 (London: Crown Holm, 1977); Wynn, *Afro-American;* H. Sitkoff, "Racial Militancy and Interracial Violence in the Second World War," *Journal of American History* 58 (December 1971); Dalfiuma, *Desegregation;* Phillip McGuire, "Desegregation of the Armed Forces: Black Leadership, Protest and World War II, " *The Journal of Negro History* 68, no. 2 (spring 1983); A. Russell Buchanan, *Black Americans in World War II* (Santa Barbara: ABC-Clio Press, 1977); Marvin Fletcher, *The Black Soldier and Officer in the United States Army, 1891–1917* (Columbia: University of Missouri Press, 1974).

7. Over 2,400 black American troops were sent to Trinidad in 1942, and even there they were resented because they had so much more spending money than the local population. Palmer, "Politics of Race and War."

8. See Hachey, "Jim Crow"; and Thomas E. Hachey, "Walter White and the American Negro Soldier in World War II: A Diplomatic Dilemma for Britain," *Phylon: The Atlanta University Review of Race and Culture* 39, no. 3, (fall 1978).

9. YTA, 82/48, pt. 2, Gudrun Sparling file.

10. See Wendy Chapkis, "Sexuality and Militarism," in E. Isaksson, *Women and the Military System* (New York: Harvester-Wheatsheaf, 1988); Judith Stiehm, ed. *Women and Men's Wars* (Oxford: Pergamon Press, 1983); Bob Connell, "Masculinity, Violence and War," and Adam Farrar, "War: Machining Male Desire," both in *War/Masculinity* (Sydney, Australia: Intervention Press, 1985); C. Bryant, *Khaki-Collar Crime* (New York: Free Press, 1979).

11. The *Edmonton Journal* reported weddings between American servicemen and local women at the rate of about one per month in 1942 and 1943.

12. Judith Hicks Stiehm, "The Man Question," in Stiehm, ed., *Women's View of the Political World of Men* (New York: Transnational Publishers, 1984).

13. There is the occasional record of homosexuality. In the summer of 1943 a medical officer reported that "at least two cases of Lymphogranuloma inguinale were beyond doubt contracted through sodomy practiced by Negro troops at Fort Smith." NAC, RG 338, NWSC, box 30, 314.7, Military Histories, Major J. F. Lubben to Commanding General HQ, Force 2600, 24 July 1943.

14. There are no statistics to support this assertion, but a number of people interviewed commented that most of the civilian workers were between thirty-five and fifty years old. The military workers were the same age as other servicemen; the average age of the American soldier in 1944 was twenty-six. Lee Kennett, *G.I.: The American Soldier in World War II* (New York: Charles Scribner's Sons, 1987), p. 22.

15. For example, Robert Macdonald and Benjamin Totty, Anglican missionaries in the region, had married Native women. See Coates, "Best Left as Indians."

16. "Life in Sub-Arctic Is Far from Dull," *Edmonton Journal,* 15 December 1943.

17. NA, RG 59, decimal file 842.502/43, John Randolph to Secretary of State, 15 January 1943.

18. NA, RG 338, box 1, Foreign Affairs, Major General J. A. Ulio memorandum re: Policy in regard to dependents of Officers, etc., 15 December 1942, Major General L. Lutes to Commanding General, Northwest Service Command, 18 December 1942, Major General Lutes Memo re: Authority and expenses incident to moving dependents, 18 January 1943, Memo: Evacuation of Dependents of members and employees in the Northwest Service Command, 29 December 1942, Major T. L. Ferguson to Commanding Officers, 31 January 1943.

19. NA, RG 338, NWSC, box 35, 370.05, N. W. Division, All Dependents of American Employees Who are Living in Edmonton, c. January 1942; RG 59, decimal file 842.502/43, Randolph to Secretary of State, 14 January 1943.

20. NA, RG 338, NWSC, box 35, 310.05, List of Dependents of Employees of J. Gordon Turnbull . . . , c. 1942, Memorandum to Mr. Epps, 31 December 1942.

21. NA, RG 338, NWSC, box 35, file 370.05, NW Division, Lt. Col. Hayes to Division Engineer, 21 February 1943.

22. NA, RG 338, box 62, file 300.64, vol. 1, Lt. Col. P. Michener to All Contractors, 9 February 1943.

23. NAC, RG 36/7, vol. 36, file 28/1, Ada Smith to F. Harrington, 15 March 1945. Ada Smith had worked for a time in Edmonton and was appealing for release from a $27.50 overpayment of wages during her service.

24. NA, RG 338, box 2, Fort St. John, General, Edmonton Chamber of Commerce review of Edmonton Housing Situation, 11 January 1943. See also NA, RG 59, decimal file 842.502/43, Randolph to Secretary of State, 14 January 1943.

25. NA, RG 338, box 1, Foreign Affairs, R. W. Hitchcock to Hon. Henrik Shipstead, 12 February 1943.

26. NA, RG 338, box 2, Fort St. John, General, W. P. Jones to Brigadier General O'Connor, 3 February 1943.

27. NA, RG 338, NWSC, box 35, file 370.01, John Randolph to Colonel T. Wyman, 11 February 1943.

28. NA, RG 338, box 2, Fort St. John, General, R. G. Rose to Brig. General O'Connor, 11 February 1943, Colonel H. A. Montgomery to Reg. Rose, 17 February 1943.

29. NA, RG 338, NWSC, box 35, unlabeled file, Major J. Collins to Division Engineer, 18 February 1943.

30. NA, RG 338, box 62, file 336, vol. 2, Conference with Colonel Wyman, 22 February 1943. On Standard Oil's general housing policy, see NA, RG 338, box 17, NWSC and District, Staff Meetings, Minutes of Meeting, 12 May 1944 (emphasis in original).

31. ACE, 77-80-0066, box 413, file 113, Housing for Families of Standard Oil Company Employees. The Canol refinery was closed before the housing program was implemented.

32. NA, RG 338, box 1, Foreign Affairs, R. Sheddon to Commanding Officer, 28 July 1943.

33. Ibid., Lt. Col. T. Ferguson to Adjutant General, 11 March 1943, Major General Ulio to Hon. Henrik Shipstead, 22 March 1943, O'Connor to Division Engineer, 8 April 1943.

34. NA, RG 338, NWSC, box 10, Office Memos, Lt. Col. C. M. Clifford to All Concerned, 29 June 1943.

35. NA, RG 338, box 1, Foreign Affairs, Hollingsworth to C. G., NWSC, 15 July 1943.

36. Ibid., B. B. Miller to Division Engineer et al., 11 July 1943.

37. Ibid., Worsham to Commanding General, 22 July 1943.

38. Ibid.

39. Travel restrictions remained in force. Dependents were required to travel to the work camps by bus. NA, RG 338, box 12, NWSC Circular Letter 1944, Circular Letter No. 105, 15 May 1944.

40. NA, RG 338, box 1, file 991.711, Armies and Navies, Brig. General O'Connor to Commanding General, 27 January 1944.

41. NA, RG 338, box 1, file 091.711, Armies and Navies, Glandon to C. G. NWSC, 1 February 1944.

42. NA, RG 338, box 12, NWSC, Circular Letters 1944, Lt. Col. Clifford to All Concerned (Circular Letter No. 21), 23 March 1944.

43. NAC, RG 36/7, vol. 47, file 28-12, L. H. Phinney to Foster, 3 January 1945.

44. Ibid. Another report gave the numbers as 175 families with a total of 114 children. The discrepancy is likely due to the continued transiency of the workforce. NAC, RG 36/7, vol. 47, file 28-12, Lt. Col. R. Tatum to Major General Foster, 21 December 1944.

45. NAC, RG 22, vol. 109, file 84-32-6, pt. 3, 32nd Report, p. 18, 31 January 1946.

46. *Washington Post*, 16 March 1943; ACE, 72-A-3173, Alcan Highway-Publications.

47. NA, RG 407-7, 91-DC1-2.1, Annex No. 3 to G-2 Periodic Report No. 48, 17 April to 24 April 1943.

48. NAC, RG 36/7, vol. 40, file 28-23, pt. 2, Command V. D. Officer to Command Medical Officer, 15 July 1943.

49. NA, RG 85, vol. —, file—(details withheld due to personal nature of contents of file).

50. NA, RG 407, vol. 7, file 91-DC1-2.1, Annex No. 3 to G-2 Periodical Report No. 56, Psychological, 12–19 June 1943.

51. Diamond Jenness, "Canada's Indians Yesterday: What of Today?" in I.A.L. Getty and A. S. Lussier, eds., *As Long as the Sun Shines and Water Flows* (Vancouver: University of British Columbia Press, 1983), p. 160. Jenness confuses the military with the civilian workers; the story sounds like a typical soldiers' tall tale.

52. *North Star Magazine,* November 1944.

53. Questionnaire answered by Connie Bafford, Lusk, Wyoming, 1989.

54. NAC, RG 27, vol. 676, file 6-5-75-3, Ernest Manning to A. MacNamara, 14 January 1943.

55. NAC, RG 27, vol. 676, file 6-5-75-3, Ernest Manning to A. MacNamara, 14 January 1943.

56. NA, RG 338, NWSC, box 35, file 337, Staff Meetings, Staff Directors Meeting, 22 February 1944.

57. NA, RG 338, NWSC, box 44, file 300.6, Memos, Memorandum: Policy on Recreational Facilities, 17 June 1943.

58. NA, RG 338, NWSC, box 44, file 300.6, Memos, Memo: Information on Use of District Engineer Camp Facilities, c. July 1943.

59. "With the arrival in Edmonton of so many American soldiers there has been a marked increase in number in international marriages." NA, RG 59, file 123 R 15/365 1/2, John Randolph to Secretary of State, 31 March 1943.

60. NA, RG 338, NWSC, box 9, Numbered Memoranda, 1943, Memorandum, 22 July 1943.

61. "The act is alleged to have occurred in a wood where the accused is alleged to have met a local school teacher accompanied by her school children . . . concern as to what the local and possibly international reaction may be if the findings of the new and legal court martial indicate that the case against Private James may have been due more to misunderstanding and hysteria on the part of the witnesses and public than to any guilty intent on the part of the accused." NA, RG 59, decimal file 811.203/134, John Randolph to Secretary of State, 15 June 1942; ibid., file 811.203/144, John Randolph to Secretary of State, 2 July 1942.

62. NAC, RG 85, vol. 865, file 8327, Report of Constable G. W. Allen, Fort Smith, 21 June 1942.

63. NA, RG 338, box 1, file 092, Foreign Affairs and Relations, Memorandum, Colonel C. R. Hazelton, 26 April 1943.

64. Ibid., 20 April 1943.

65. *Dawson Daily News,* 5 November 1942.

66. A sample: "Parson: 'Miss Epsom, I'se gwine to lead you out inter dis heah stream and wash out every spot o' sin you's got!' 'Lawsy pahson,' giggled the erstwhile frolicsome damsel, 'in dat li'l ole shallow creek?'" *Dawson Daily News,* 13 October 1942.

67. Interview with Stacia Gallop, July 1989.

68. NAC, RG 36/7, vol. 40, file 28-23, pt. 2, Command V. D. Officer to Command Medical Officer, 15 July 1943, gives an excellent statement of this preoccupation.

69. NAC, RG 85, vol. 658, file 3418, Report re: Alleged Houses of Prostitution, Dawson, Y.T., 24 October 1940.

70. NA, RG 338, NWCS, box 26, file 314.7, Organization Histories, Annual Report, Post Surgeon, Post of Whitehorse, 1943.

71. ACE, A52-434, box 31, file 726.1, Monthly Report of Venereal Disease in the Units of Medical Detachment, 35th Engineers Regiment, April 1942.

72. NA, RG 59, vol. 407-7, file 91-DC1-2.1, Annex No. 3 to G-2 Periodic Report No. 43, 13 March 1943 to 20 March 1943. The VD rate among the U.S. troops occupying Germany in 1945 rose from fifty cases per thousand at the beginning of the year to five times that by the end of the year. Kennett, *G.I.,* p. 216.

73. NA, RG 338, NWSC, box 32, file 319.1 (Staff Meetings), Staff Meeting, Dawson Creek, 26 April 1944; ACE, 77-80-0066, box 416, file 7010.2, Captain M. Gajewski to District Engineer, 6 July 1943.

74. Fred J. Peet, *Miners and Moonshiners: A Personal Account of Adventure and Survival in a Difficult Era* (Victoria: Sono Nis Press, 1983).

75. NAC, RG 85, vol. 658, file 3418, H. H. Hansen to Commissioner, RCMP, 29 June 1940, Report re: Alleged House of Prostitution, Dawson, Y.T., 24 October 1940.

76. NAC, RG 85, vol. 1512, file 1000/200, pt. 1, Conditions at Whitehorse, 16 August 1944.

77. Ibid.

78. YTA, YRG 1, ser. 1, vol. 62, file 35410, Unorganized Territory: Report by L. E. Faryon, 22 November 1944.

79. NA, RG 338, box 47, Activation New Detachments, General Orders No. 2, 2 February 1943.

80. Men at the meeting included: Col. Lane, C.O., U.S. Army Post, Dawson Creek; Lt. Col. Laurion; Lt. Col. W. Draper, Intelligence and Internal Security; Major G. Penny, G2 Intelligence; Capt. E. Bussey, Protective Security Officer, U.S. Army Engineer; Capt. C. Allen, Adjutant, U.S. Army Post, Dawson Creek; Capt. W. Emslie, GIII Intelligence, Canadian Army; Major Sinclair, Assistant Commissioner; J. Shirras, B.C. Police; Inspector Mansell, B.C. Police, Pouce Coupe.

81. NAC, RG 36/7, vol. 40, file 28-23, pt. 2, Command V.D. Control Officer to Command Medical Officer, 15 July 1943.

82. NA, RG 407, vol. 7, file 91-DC1-2.1, Annex No. 3 to G-2 Periodical Report No. 56, Psychological, 12–19 June 1943.

83. NAC, RG 85, vol. 941, file 12618, Cpl. Allen Report, 7 May 1942.

84. Sylvia Van Kirk, *Many Tender Ties: Women in Fur Trade Society, 1670–1870* (Winnipeg: Watson and Dwyer, 1980); Jennifer Brown, *Strangers in Blood: Families in Fur Trade Country* (Vancouver: University of British Columbia Press, 1980).

85. NAC, RG 85, vol. —, file —. In this and subsequent instances where the names of the women involved in rape or assault cases are included in the files, the specific citations have been omitted. A number of different files have been consulted.

86. YTA, YRG 1, vol. 59, file 34362, pt. 2/3, Jeckell to R. A. Gibson, 22 December 1943.

87. NA, RG 407-7, file 91-DC1-2.1, Annex No. 3 to G-2 Periodic Report No. 43, 13 March–20 March 1943.

88. The police report stated that the men got into the school dormitory "with the assistance and connivance" of three girls, aged twelve, ten, and eight; "the girls were not seduced, no penetration in the slightest degree having taken place. Nevertheless, the offences committed by these two men amount to indecent assaults upon females." NAC, RG 85, vol. —, file —.

89. NAC, RG 85, vol. 7391, A. Cumming, Chief Mining Inspector to H. E. Hume, 3 November 1932.

90. NAC, RG 85, vols. —, files —.

91. Ibid.

92. Ibid.

93. Ibid. This particular file contains a number of police reports and correspondence concerning the case, May 1943–July 1943.

94. Ibid.

95. Ibid.

96. Ibid.

97. A very similar case occurred in Fort Smith in April 1943. That charge also was dropped when police decided that the woman reported the "rape" to protect herself from a jealous common-law husband.

98. NAC, RG 85, vol. —, file —.

99. YTA, YRG 1, ser. 1, vol. —, file —.

100. Coates and Morrison, "More than a Matter of Blood."

6. The Transformation of Northern Communities

1. F. Rainey, "Alaskan Highway: An Engineering Epic," *National Geographic Magazine* 83, no. 2 (February–March 1943): 155.

2. John Herd Thompson, *The Harvests of War: The Prairie West, 1914–1918* (Toronto: McClelland and Stewart, 1978) is a good example of this.

3. G. Nash, *The Transformation of the American West*.

4. Rocanville now displays the "world's largest oil can" as a town symbol. On the program in Alberta, see H. and T. J. Palmer, *Alberta: A New History* (Edmonton: Hurtig, 1990).

5. Frobisher Bay, now Iqaluit, did not exist as a community before the war. It was called into being as a weather station for the Crimson Route. See Quinn Duffy, *The Road to Nunavut: The Progress of the Eastern Arctic Inuit since the Second World War* (Montreal: McGill-Queen's University Press, 1988).

6. *Vancouver News-Herald,* 19 May 1943.

7. The *Edmonton Journal* gleefully reprinted an article from the Springfield, Massachusetts, *Union* about a resident of that city who had taken a job in a U.S. engineering office in Edmonton, "a village with less than 100 permanent residents . . . the last place to be served by railroad and persons desiring to continue their travel north must resort to dog sleds" (15 December 1942).

8. *Edmonton Journal,* 20 April, 1 April 1943, 28 November 1942. The amounts for building permits were $854,180 in March 1943 and $235,600 in March 1942.

9. Ibid., 2 December 1942.

10. ACE, 72A3173-3, Major Hage to Division Engineer, 26 January 1944.

11. RG 59, decimal file 125.37IHI/54, Randolph to Secretary of State, 5 June 1943. The U.S. authorities were very concerned that the purchase of this stately, historic home would touch off an international "incident." Although the takeover was noted in the local press, it was not commented on unfavorably. *Edmonton Journal,* 9 June 1943; *Edmonton Bulletin,* 10 June 1943.

12. NA, RG 59, decimal file 842.20/209, PS/MEM, Randolph to Secretary of State, 1 July 1942.

13. *Edmonton Journal,* 22 June 1943.

14. Ibid., 28 December 1942.

15. Ibid., 11 November 1943.

16. *North Star Magazine,* November 1944.

17. *Edmonton Journal,* 13 July 1943.

18. *Edmonton Bulletin,* 16 November 1942.

19. *Financial Times,* 23 December 1942.

20. NA, RG 338, box 62, file 300.64, vol. 1, Memorandum: To all persons associated with the Canol Project, 28 September 1942.

21. *Edmonton Journal,* 30 October 1942.

22. NA, RG 59, decimal file 123 R 15/339, Randolph to Secretary of State, 3 September 1942.

23. NA, RG 59, decimal file 123 R 15/355, Randolph to Secretary of State, 18 May 1942.

24. The Rotary Club of Edmonton, *Welcome American,* copy in RG 59, decimal file 842.43/20 PS/RA.

25. NA, RG 165, ODP 336, Canada (Section I) (Case 1-21), Pierrepont Moffat to John D. Hickerson, Assistant Chief, Division of European Affairs, State Department, 23 October 1942.

26. NA, RG 338, box 1, 014.13, Relations, Civil and Military Authorities, Wing Commander C.M.G. Farrell (RCAF) to Col. T. L. Mosley, (USAAF), 14 November 1942, J. W. Fry to Commanding General, Air Transport Command, Washington, 14 November 1942, M. Blackwood to Edmonton City Commissioners, 13 November 1942. The dates of these letters suggest that they were solicited to prove a case; the file contains similar protestations of goodwill from the commanding officer of M Depot, RCAF, from local businessmen, from the provincial attorney general, and from others.

27. NA, RG 338, NWSC, box 10, Office Memos, Office Memorandum No. 176, Community Chest Drive, 16 September 1943.

28. NAC, RG 85, vol. 944, file 12725A, C. K. LeCapelain to R. A. Gibson, 7 August 1942.

29. *Whitehorse Star,* 12 June 1942. The move proved very profitable over the following years. For a report on the company's commercial success in 1943, see *Whitehorse Star,* 7 January 1944, pp. 1, 3.

30. *Edmonton Bulletin,* 21 November 1942.

31. Interview with Chuck Baxter, Surrey, B.C., June 1988.

32. McCusker, "Alaska Highway," 9.

33. NA, RG 338, NWSC, box 44, Office Memorandum, District Circular Letter No. 5, 1 July 1943; ibid., box 9, NWSC Memorandum (1944), Memorandum No. 57, 3 April 1944.

34. NA, RG 338, NWSC, box 9, Numbered Memoranda, 1943, Memorandum No. 185, 4 September 1943.

35. ACE, 72A3173, box 18A, Alcan Highway-Publicity, Memorandum for the Press, November 1942.

36. ACE, 600.1, vol. 1, Canol Project, Construction and Installation, Wyman to Adcock, 2 November 1942. See also ibid., Adcock to Major Michener, 29 October 1942, which complains of the problems of log construction in the area and a general shortage of space and usable logs.

37. NAC, RG 85, vol. 865, file 8327, Cpl. W. Stewart to Officer Commanding, Fort Smith Sub-Division, 16 October 1942.

38. ACE, 52A434, box 29, Major K. McCausland to Chief of Transportation, 5 December 1942.

39. ACE, 72A3173-1, Telephone Conversation Between Major Wild and Colonel Worsham, 19 April 1943.

40. NA, RG 338, box 10, NWSC, Office Memoranda, 1944, Office Memorandum, 15 November 1944.

41. NAC, RG 24, vol. 6475, NWHS, 5315W90, vol. 2, Major General Penhale to Army Headquarters, 23 May 1949.

42. ACE, A-52-434, box 30, file 611, "The Alaska Highway: Report of First Year Construction," Camp Facilities and Workers, p. 70.

43. R. G. Large, *Prince Rupert: A Gateway to Alaska and the Pacific* (Vancouver: Mitchell Press, 1960), p. 68.

44. NA, RG 59, D.F. 842-154, Seattle/Fairbanks Highway/550, Canadian Legation Memorandum, 18 May 1943, Department of State Memorandum, 14 June 1943. The Canadian government contributed $125,000 toward the construction of the line. NAC, RG 85, vol. 958, file 13439, Order in Council authorizing construction of a water supply system for the village of Dawson Creek, B.C., P.C. 5226, 29 July 1943.

45. NAC, RG 85, vol. 658, file 3318-3, George Jeckell to R. A. Gibson, 6 August 1945. The request from Matthew Watson, a store owner in Carcross, for access to the army water and electric light services is in YRG 1, ser. 1, vol. 8, file 466I, Matthew Watson to Mr. Jeckell, July 1945. Jeckell observed, "I know it is the general policy of the United States authorities not to accept payment for such service."

46. NAC, RG 22, vol. 251, file 40-7-4, vol. 6, Macdonald to Director, 7 May 1943 (two letters).

47. NAC, RG 22, vol. 107, file 84-32-6, pt. 1, Special Commissioner on Defence Projects, 5th Report, Recommendations, pp. 16–17.

48. The agreement also called for the Canadian Department of Transport to purchase the Jesuit college in Edmonton and lease it back to the United States. ACE, vol. 419, Jesuit College, 22-31, W. W. Foster to Division Engineer, 13 July 1943.

49. YTA, YRG 1, ser. 1A, vol. 7, file 466bii, Leases held by Public Roads Administration and Its Contractors, 15 April 1942. This document lists five major blocks of land in Whitehorse leased from the White Pass and Yukon Route.

50. As this relates to the Yukon Territory, see YTA, YRG 1, ser. 1A, vol. 7, file 466bii, R. A. Gibson to G. A. Jeckell, 16 September 1943. For a diplomatic description of the procedures, see ibid., N. A. Robertson to United States Minister to Canada, 7 September 1943.

51. NAC, RG 85, vol. 1870, file 540-1-1, pt. 1, A. L. Cumming to R. A. Gibson, 21 March 1944.

52. NAC, RG 85, vol. 957, file 13417, pt. 1, R. A. Gibson to Jeckell, 20 September 1944.

53. NAC, RG 36/7, vol. 15, file 28-12, Foster to Heeney, 29 December 1944.

54. YTA, YRG 1, ser. 1, vol. 70, file 21, pt. 3, pt. 1, G. W. Epton to

T. A. Crerar, 26 August 1944; NAC, RG 36/7, vol. 47, file 28-12, Charles Weddington to Captain Bruce Kent, 2 December 1944.

55. NAC, RG 36/7, vol. 15, file 28-12, W. W. Foster to Dean Buchanan, 11 December 1944.

56. YTA, YRG 1, ser. 1, vol. 70, file 21, pt. 4, file 2, Jeckell to Gibson, 1 February 1945.

57. NAC, RG 36/7, vol. 42, file 11-15, Foster to Hart, 26 August 1944.

58. NAC, RG 85, vol. 957, file 13417, pt. 1, Gibson to Jeckell, 20 September 1944.

59. NAC, RG 36/7, vol. 15, file 28-12, "An Educational Programme for the Families of the Maintenance Staff of the Alaska Highway," c. 1944.

60. YTA, YRG 1, ser. 1, vol. 70, file 21, pt. 4, file 4, Jeckell to Gibson, 17 October 1944. See also ibid., file 3, Health and Education—Alaska Highway, November 1944.

61. NAC, RG 36/7, vol. 47, file 28-12, Charles Weddington to Bruce Kent, 2 December 1944.

62. YTA, YRG 1, ser. 1, vol. 70, file 21, pt. 4, file 3, Higgins to Jeckell, 23 December 1944.

63. *Fort St. John Alaska Highway News,* 4 January 1945.

64. *Whitehorse Star,* 17 February 1943.

65. *Whitehorse Star,* 13 November 1942, p. 1, 18 December 1942, p. 1.

66. *Fort St. John Alaska Highway News,* 4 January 1945.

67. *Edmonton Journal,* 17 February 1944.

68. YTA, YRG 1, ser. 1-A, vol. 9, file 466iv, Jeckell to Thomas Riggs, 26 March 1942.

69. Richard Stuart, "The Impact of the Alaska Highway on Dawson City," in Coates, ed., *The Alaska Highway,* 188–204.

7. Whitehorse: Creation of a City

1. *Whitehorse Star,* 10 April 1942, p. 2.

2. Pierre Berton, *The Mysterious North* (Toronto: McClelland and Stewart, 1956), p. 99.

3. The PRA moved its administrative staff from the town in the winter of 1943. The Northwest Service Command also moved its headquarters to Edmonton in 1943, when work on the highway slowed, but moved it back again in the fall of 1944. See the *Whitehorse Star,* 3 December 1943, 1 September 1944.

4. Portions of this chapter are drawn from Ken Coates and Judith Powell, "Whitehorse and the Building of the Alaska Highway, 1942–1946," *Alaska History* (Spring 1989): 1–26. For a summary history of the Whitehorse

sector of the Alaska Highway, see ACE, X-5-4, "History of the Whitehorse Sector of the Alcan Highway," 10 June 1943.

5. The phrase is used half humorously, half scornfully, to describe the drifters, squatters, loners, and eccentrics who are said to make up that proportion of the Yukon's population today.

6. Jim Lotz, *People Outside: Studies of Squatters, Shack Towns, and Shanty Residents and Other Dwellings on the Fringe in Canada* (Ottawa: St. Paul's University, 1971), 113–28.

7. NAC, RG 85, vol. 1160, file 331-2/200-1, Notes on Water Supply, Whitehorse, by A. H. Perry, August 1939.

8. The U.S. Army completed a line to Edmonton in May 1943. *Whitehorse Star*, 24 July 1942, p. 3. The newspaper printed a telephone directory for Whitehorse, which included only nineteen entries. *Dawson Daily News*, 28 May 1943.

9. *Whitehorse Star*, 10 April 1942. The paper issued a "Cordial Welcome" to Brig. Gen. W. Hoge and the incoming troops.

10. NA, RG 59, D.F. 842.154, Seattle Fairbanks Highway/434, Pierrepont Moffat to Adolf Berle, 20 July 1942.

11. NAC, RG 126, exhibit 618, Testimony of Joe Jacquot, 21 April 1976.

12. ACE, Box X-1-16, Public Relations Branch of the Northwest Service Command, The Alaska Highway," undated, pp. 6, 15–18. See also ACE, Box X-5-4, "History of the Whitehorse Sector," 10 June 1943, pp. 4–5.

13. NAC, RG 85, vol. 1160, file 331-2/200-1, H. M. Dilworth to Hugh [Keenleyside], 30 March 1943, Memorandum on Water Supply and Sewage System for Whitehorse, 12 April 1943, Royal Canadian Mounted Police Sub-Division Report, 3 May 1943.

14. YTA, YRG 1, ser. 1, vol. 59, file 34362, pt. 2, Jeckell to Gibson, 14 February 1944; ibid., vol. 61, file 35386, pt. 2, Perry, Memorandum on Sewage Disposal, 10 August 1944.

15. NAC, RG 85, vol. 1512, file 100/200, pt. 1, George Black to R. A. Gibson, 4 January 1944.

16. NAC, RG 85, vol. 1160, file 331-2/200-1, LeCapelain to Gibson, 20 January 1943.

17. NAC, RG 85, vol. 1160, file 331-2/200-1, LeCapelain to Gibson, 7 December 1942.

18. NAC, RG 85, vol. 1512, file 1000/200, pt. 1, McEachern article, *Financial Times*, 2 October 1943 (typescript).

19. NA, RG 59, file 842.154, Moffat to Berle, 20 July 1942; NAC, RG 85, vol. 951, file 13200, RCMP Report, 24 December 1942.

20. YTA, YRG 1, ser. 1, vol. 7, file 466bii, Leases Held by Public Roads Administration and Its Contractors," 15 April 1942; *Whitehorse Star*, 7 January 1944, p. 3.

21. *Whitehorse Star*, 27 October 1944, p. 1.

22. NAC, RG 85, vol. 1512, file 1000/2000, pt. 1, Rogers to Black, 11 July 1944; ibid., vol. 1161, file 331-2/200, pt. 2, LeCapelain to Gibson, 31 July 1944.

23. NAC, RG 85, vol. 1161, file 331-2/200, pt. 2, LeCapelain to Gibson (31 July 1944?).

24. Yukon Historical Museums Association, *Whitehorse Heritage Buildings* (Whitehorse: YHMA, 1983), p. 32.

25. *Whitehorse Star*, 27 January 1944, p. 4.

26. NAC, RG 85, vol. 1512, file 1000/200, pt. 1, LeCapelain to Gibson, 15 October 1943.

27. NAC, RG 85, vol. 1512, file 1000/200, pt. 1, Jeckell to Gibson, 25 October 1944.

28. He spent only five weeks in Whitehorse between March and September 1943. Other territorial officials followed Jeckell's lead and remained in Dawson. The territorial road superintendent, inexplicably, spent "only a few days in Whitehorse" in 1942 and 1943. NAC, RG 85, vol. 1512, file 1000/200, pt. 1, LeCapelain to Gibson, 28 April 1944.

29. YTA, YRG 1, ser. 1, vol. 59, file 34362, pt. 2, Jeckell to Gibson, 27 May 1944; NAC, RG 85, vol. 1160, file 331-2/200, pt. 1, Jeckell to Gibson, 17 February 1944.

30. NAC, RG 85, vol. 1512, file 1000/200, pt. 1, McEachern article, *Financial Times*, 2 October 1943 (typescript).

31. The commissioner of the Yukon was and is appointed by the federal government, not elected locally. In the past decade, however, the position has become mostly a ceremonial one, and the power has passed to the elected Territorial Council.

32. NAC, RG 85, vol. 1512, file 1000/200, pt. 1, Jeckell to Gibson, 18 October 1942.

33. Canadian federal civil servants based in the Yukon also complained that, in the inflated wartime circumstances, their salaries and special northern allowances did not properly compensate for the costs of living in the region. YTA, YRG 1, ser. 1, vol. 59, file 34362, Civil Servants to Captain Black, 20 June 1946.

34. YTA, YRG 1, vol. 59, file 34362, Gibson to Jeckell, 13 May 1944, and Jeckell to Gibson, 27 May 1944.

35. Interview with Louis Cyr, Whitehorse, June 1989; *Whitehorse Star*, 9 July 1943, 1.

36. NA, RG 338, NWSC, Unnumbered Memoranda, 1943, Shortage of Water, 22 February 1943.

37. Dwight Oland, "The Army Medical Department and the Construction of the Alaska Highway," in Coates, ed., *The Alaska Highway*, p. 65. NA, RG 112, file HD314, box 3, "History of the Medical Department of the

Whitehorse Sector Alcan Highway"; NAC, RG 85, vol. 1160, file 331-2/ 200-1, LeCapelain, Memorandum on Water Supply, 12 April 1943, Preliminary Report on Water Supply, 30 November 1942.

38. NAC, RG 85, vol. 1160, file 331-2/200-1, Dilworth to Hugh, 30 March 1943.

39. YTA, YRG 1, ser. 1, vol. 61, file 35386-1, LeCapelain, Water Supply and Sanitation, 13 March 1943; NAC, RG 85, vol. 1160, Memorandum on Water Supply, 12 April 1943.

40. NAC, RG 85, vol. 1160, file 331-2/200-1, Jeckell to Gibson, 18 July 1943.

41. NAC, RG 85, vol. 1160, file 331-2/200-1, LeCapelain to Gibson, 7 December 1943; NA, RG 112, file HD314, box 3, "History of the Medical Department of the Whitehorse Sector Alcan Highway," 1942.

42. NAC, RG 85, vol. 1160, file 331-2/200-1, LeCapelain to Gibson, 29 October 1943; YTA, YRG 1, ser. 1, vol. 61, file 35386, Perry, Memorandum on Sewage Disposal, 10 August 1944.

43. YTA, YRG 1, ser. 1, vol. 61, file 35386-2, Extracts of letter from LeCapelain to Director, Lands, Parks and Forest Branch, 14 October 1944, A. H. Perry, Sanitary Engineer with the Canadian Department of Pensions and National Health, Memorandum on Sewage Disposal, 10 August 1944.

44. YTA, YRG 1, ser. 1, vol. 59, file 34362, pt. 2, Jeckell to Gibson, 27 May 1944; ibid., vol. 61, file 35386, pt. 2, Jeckell to Gibson, 24 October 1944; ibid., vol. 59, file 34362, pt. 2, Gibson to Jeckell, 13 May 1944, Jeckell to Gibson, 27 May 1944.

45. NAC, RG 85, vol. 1160, file 331-2/200-1, LeCapelain to Gibson, 29 October 1943, LeCapelain to Gibson, 7 December 1943.

46. YTA, YRG 1, ser. 1, vol. 61, file 35386, Petition of Citizens of Whitehorse to Prime Minister Mackenzie King, undated (1944). The petition's organizer was Thelma Stevens, whose father allegedly was "definitely a man of limited or moderate ability who has a flair for Marxist theories and acts as a sort of gospel or propaganda distributor for Red activities" (NAC, RG 85, vol. 1512, file 100/200, pt. 1, "The Matter of the Petition of Thelma Stevens"). The RCMP investigated the Stevens family and reported that her husband, George, "has always been of the 'loud-mouthed' type, but will never be of any importance." Inspector Cronkite said, "The petition could not have been signed by 500 residents of Whitehorse without the signature of visiting Americans. The petition was not considered seriously by the permanent residents of the community who are well aware with whom the civic responsibilities lie" (ibid., Cronkite to Black, 14 June 1944).

47. NAC, RG 85, vol. 1512, file 1000/200, pt. 1, C. Rogers to Black, 11 July 1944.

48. YTA, YRG 1, ser. 1, vol. 61, file 35386, pt. 2, Hotel and Restaurant Employees' Union to G. A. Jeckell, 21 July 1944.

49. NAC, RG 85, vol. 1512, file 1000/200, pt. 1, Jeckell to Gibson, 4 April 1945, Gibson to W. W. Foster, 26 July 1944, Unsigned letter to Gibson, 23 June 1944.

50. NAC, RG 85, vol. 1512, file 1000/200, pt. 1, *Financial Times,* report by Ronald McEachern, 2 October 1943 (typescript).

51. NAC, RG 85, vol. 1512, file 1000/200, pt. 1, Jeckell to Gibson, 2 September 1943; ibid., vol. 1161, file 331-2/200, pt. 2, unsigned to Gibson, 23 June 1944.

52. NAC, RG 85, vol. 951, file 13200, RCMP Report, 24 December 1942.

53. NA, RG 407, box 22331, ORCO-3470-0.1, District of Whitehorse Military Softball League, 8 May 1944; "Whitehorse Hockey League Schedule," *Whitehorse Star,* 3 March 1944.

54. NAC, RG 85, vol. 1512, file 1000/200, pt. 1, Jeckell to Gibson, 2 September 1943; "Hollywood Comes to the Yukon," *Whitehorse Star,* 24 September 1943, p. 1. American authorities were concerned about safety in the theaters, and declared one off limits when the owner refused to make renovations. NAC, RG 85, vol. 1512, file 1000/200, pt. 1, Whitney to Mathewson, 5 August 1943, Jeckell to Gibson, 2 September 1943.

55. NAC, RG 85, vol. 1512, file 1000/200, pt. 1, McEachern Report, 2 October 1943.

56. NAC, RG 85, vol. 951, file 13200, RCMP Report, 24 December 1942; NA, RG 112, Entry 54B, box 15A, file HD350.05, Essential Technical Data, 1 August 1943.

57. YTA, YRG 1, ser. 1, vol. 59, file 34362, Jeckell to Gibson, 3 September 1943; ibid., vol. 61, file 35402, Rogers to Lockwood, 21 May 1943; NAC, RG 85, vol. 1512, file 1000/200, pt. 1, LeCapelain to Gibson, 28 April 1944; YTA, YRG 1, ser. 1, vol. 59, file 34362, pt. 2, Jeckell to Gibson, 14 February 1944, Jeckell to Gibson, 27 September 1944.

58. YTA, YRG 1, ser. 1, vol. 6, file 466iii, Black to Mitchell, 4 June 1942.

59. Gordon Bennett, *Yukon Transportation: A History,* Canadian Historic Sites Occasional Papers in Archaeology and History, No. 19 (Ottawa, 1978), pp. 137–38; NA, RG 338, NWSC, box 5, file 333.5, Report on the White Pass and Yukon Route and Subport of Skagway, 15 January 1943.

60. NA, RG 338, NWSC, box 11, Unnumbered memoranda, 1943, 24 February 1943.

61. YTA, YRG 1, ser. 1, vol. 61, file 35402, C. A. Penner to K. B. Hannan, 18 September 1943.

62. NAC, RG 85, vol. 944, file 725A, LeCapelain to Gibson, 24 July 1942. American highway contractors could make local purchases up to

$500 monthly. Orders above that amount had to be placed through the PRA offices in Seattle.

63. Rainey, "Alaskan Highway," p. 148; NAC, RG 85, vol. 944, file 12725A, LeCapelain to Gibson, 24 July 1942.

64. YTA, YRG 1, ser. 1, vol. 61, file 35386, pt. 2, Jeckell to Gibson, 24 October 1944.

65. Rainey, "Alaskan Highway," p. 148; NAC, RG 85, vol. 1160, file 331-2/200-1, LeCapelain to Gibson, 7 December 1943.

66. NAC, RG 85, vol. 945, file 12769, Report re: Whitehorse Inn Hotel-Whitehorse, Yukon, 29 July 1942.

67. *Dawson Daily News,* 9 April 1943. The board was incredibly persistent on price increases. For details on a prosecution of a barber for increasing his rate from 75 cents to $1, see NAC, RG 85, vol. 961, file 13626, RCMP Division file 43G269-12K1, June 1943.

68. NAC, RG 85, vol. 944, file 12725A, Wilson to Black, 9 September 1943; YTA, YRG 1, ser. 1, vol 59, file 34362, Jeckell to Gibson, 14 February 1944.

69. NAC, RG 85, vol. 1512, file 100/200, pt. 1, McEachern report, 2 October 1943. The Canada Bank of Commerce became the Canadian Imperial Bank of Commerce in 1952.

70. In 1944, Controller George Jeckell identified the following licensed business in Whitehorse: Hotels (3), Clubs (1), Unlicensed Clubs (1), Banks (1), Licenses to sell tobacco (4), Restaurants (9), Bakers (2), General Merchants (5), Other Merchants (3), Taxis (8—number of cars), Plumbing and Heating (1), Dentist (1), Physician (1), Barrister (1), Optometrist (1), Wood Dealers (5), Water Service (3), Draying (3), Auctioneer (1), Insurance (3), Barbers (7—number of chairs), Scavenger (1), Light Plant (1), Pool Room (3—number of tables), Jeweler (2), Moving Picture Theatres (2), Transfer and Express (1), Druggist (1), Photographers (3), Wood Saw Machines (1), Broker (1), Bowling Alley (1), Cleaning and Pressing (1), Dressmaker (1). YTA, YRG 1, ser. 1, vol. 59, file 34362, pt. 2, Jeckell to Gibson, 14 February 1944.

71. NAC, RG 27, vol. 676, file 65-75-5-1, Memorandum of meeting, 6 July 1942.

72. NAC, RG 85, vol. 658, file 3318-3, Jeckell to Gibson, 3 September 1943.

73. NA, RG 338, vol. 1, box 62, file 336, Memorandum, 3 June 1942.

74. ACE, Acc. 72-A-3173, box 15, file 50-19, Rogers to Black, 20 May 1942; YTA, YRG 1, vol. 59, file 34362, pt. 2, Jeckell to Gibson, 26 February 1943.

75. YTA, YRG 1, vol. 61, file 35402, Rogers to Mitchell, 3 March 1943.

76. ACE, Acc. 72-A-3173, Report, 18 May 1942; NAC, RG 27, vol.

676, file 65-75-1, Labour Conditions (schedule), 1 June 1942; NA, RG 338, vol. 1, box 62, file 336.6, Labour Conditions, 11 July 1942.

77. K. S. Coates, "The Alaska Highway and the Indians of the Southern Yukon," in Coates, ed., *The Alaska Highway,* pp. 152–57.

78. YTA, YRG 1, ser. 1, vol. 8, file 476A, Jeckell to Simmons, 31 August 1942; NAC, RG 85, vol. 1512, file 1000/200, pt. 1, Jeckell to Gibson, 18 October 1943; NA, RG 338, box 10, Office Memo, 24 October 1942.

79. NA, RG 338, NWSC, box 10, Office Memos, Memorandum, 24 October 1942.

80. There are no private liquor vendors in Canada; in every jurisdiction, liquor is sold through retail outlets controlled by the government.

81. Yukoners were also generally exempt from nationwide rationing of many products. "Remote areas" in Canada were also exempt. NAC, RG 85, vol. 943, file 12725, pt. 2, Bulletin Number 117, REMOTE AREAS, 11 January 1943.

82. NAC, RG 36/7, vol. 658, file 3318-3, Jeckell to Gibson, 16 December 1943.

83. YTA, YRG 1, ser. 1, vol. 61, file 35405, pt. 2, Jeckell to Gibson, 26 February 1944; NAC, RG 85, vol. 1160, file 331-2/200-1. Jeckell to Gibson, 17 February 1944.

84. NAC, RG 85, vol. 658, file 3318-3, Jeckell to Bigson, 3 September 1943.

85. NAC, RG 85, vol. 1160, file 331-2/200-1, Jeckell to Gibson, 17 February 1944.

86. NAC, RG 85, vol. 1512, file 1000/200, pt. 1, McEachern article, *Financial Times,* 2 October 1943 (typescript). George Jeckell argued that there was little support for incorporation in the community. He reported, "I gained the impression that the organization referred to consisted mainly of the younger element who had little at stake in the town so far as property is concerned, and who would not be affected by the higher taxation which would naturally follow with the incorporation of Whitehorse as a town" (NAC, RG 85, vol. 1512, file 1000/200, pt. 1, Jeckell to Gibson, 18 October 1943).

87. Jeckell staunchly defended his record as territorial administrator, pointing out that Whitehorse had received over $70,000 in government expenditures in 1942 and over $100,000 the following year and provided only $7,500 in taxes and business licenses. (He failed, however, to indicate territorial expenditures in Dawson City or to point out that Whitehorse provided the bulk of the Yukon's liquor revenues—over $200,000 in 1943 alone.) NAC, RG 85, vol. 1512, file 1000/200, pt. 1, LeCapelain to Gibson, 28 April 1944, Jeckell to Gibson, 18 October 1943.

88. NAC, RG 85, vol. 1512, file 1000/200, pt. 1, LeCapelain to Gibson, 28 April 1944.

89. NAC, RG 85, vol. 1512, file 1000/200, pt. 1, LeCapelain to Gibson, 28 April 1944.

90. YTA, YRG 1, ser. 1, vol. 59, file 34362, Jeckell to Gibson, 30 May 1945.

8. Saying Goodbye to the Yankees

1. A decision that was greeted with sharp disappointment in the region, and with resignation by Canadian authorities, who agreed that wartime priorities took precedence over local development and the American promises of 1942. ACE, 72A3173, box 15, Alaska Highway Publicity; *Ottawa Citizen*, 11 February 1943.

2. YTA, YRG 1, ser. 1, vol. 70, file 21, pt. 4, file 4, Higgins to Jeckell, 23 October 1944.

3. Fourteen of these stations were closed in the fall of 1945. NAC, RG 85, vol. 954, file 13355, Phinney to Heeney, 4 September 1945.

4. NAC, RG 22, vol. 133, file 84-32-2, pt. 1, United States Defence Projects and Installations in Canada, January 1944.

5. On the transfer of the telephone and telegraph service, see NAC, RG 85, vol. 948, file 13082, Extract from 33rd Report by Special Commissioner, 28 February 1946.

6. NA, RG 84, Foreign Service Posts, Canada-Edmonton, General Records, box 48, Streeper to Atherton, 1 May 1945.

7. F. S. Strong, Jr., *What's It All About?: Thoughts from the Nineties* (privately published, 1985), chap. 12, "Adventures of a Retread," p. 152.

8. NA, RG 338, NWSC, box 18, Staff Meetings, 1943–1944, Staff Conference, Whitehorse, 25 October 1944. Strong himself moved on in 1945. The NWSC was placed under the authority of the 6th Service Command, based in Chicago. NAC, RG 36/7, vol. 2, file 3/5, Foster to Camsell, 14 May 1945.

9. NA, RG 338, box 19, Discontinuance of NWSC, F. S. Strong to Commanding General, Army Service Forces, 21 April 1945.

10. ACE, 72A3173, box 18, BR2, Rep. on Can. Project, Norman Wells Field, Administrative and Clerical, March 1945; NA, RG 338, box 1, 050 Canol Project 1945, Somervell to Davies, 5 March 1945.

11. *Whitehorse Star*, 23 March 1945, p. 5. This is a reprinting of a letter from Tom McEwen of the Labor Progressive Party of British Columbia to Prime Minister W.L.M. King (NAC, RG 85, vol. 978, file 14663, McEwen to King, 12 March 1945).

12. *Whitehorse Star*, 12 May 1944, p. 1.

13. ACE, X-5-2, War Department, Bureau of Public Relations, Canol Project to be Discontinued, 8 March 1945; ACE, box 429, 125A, "Rehabilitation," Clifford to Imperial Oil Limited, 7 March 1945, Disposal of Canol Refinery and Crude Pipe Line, 5 May 1945. Parts of the pipeline remained

in operation. Ironically, it was used to bring in oil from Skagway to White-horse and, from there, to various stations along the Alaska Highway.

14. ACE, box 429, 125A, "Rehabilitation," Memorandum for the War Department Liaison Officer for Petroleum, 13 November 1945.

15. Ibid., Patterson to Gillette, 21 April 1945, Engel to Patterson, 22 March 1945, Patterson to Engel, 26 March 1945, Beckman to Tolan, 18 May 1945, Clifford to Chief of Engineers, 5 June 1945.

16. Barry, *Canol Project,* 344.

17. NAC, RG 85, vol. 941, file 12604A, F.H.R. Jackson to Gibson, 15 November 1947.

18. There were a large number of these. A list prepared in February 1945 identified 133 abandoned camps (5 not visible from the Alaska High-way); an additional 12 maintenance camps were temporarily closed at that time. NAC, RG 36/7, vol. 42, file 11-10, Abandoned Camps along Alaska Highway, 19 February 1945.

19. There was, for example, the question of whether used American goods sold to a Canadian company (such as Imperial Oil's purchase of Canol supplies) were subject to customs duties. NAC, RG 36/7, vol. 2, file 3/5, Phinney to Heeney, 23 August 1945; ACE, 72-A-3173, box 15, Documents 1944, Thirty-Third Recommendations, Approved 20 December 1944.

20. NA, RG 338, NWSC, box 18, Staff Meetings, 1943–1944, Staff Conference, Whitehorse, 25 October 1944.

21. ACE, 72-A-3173, box 3, Burdick to Sloan, 1 February 1944.

22. NA, RG 338, box 21, Summary: Equipment Left at Various Camps along Canol Road, n.d.

23. Resale value was calculated to be 40 percent of commercial wholesale prices. Transportation and handling charges were set at $4.50 per hundred-weight or $2.25 per cubic foot. NA, RG 338, box 19, Discontinuance, NWSC, Criteria to Evacuation of Excesses of Whitehorse Supply Area, n.d.

24. As this relates to Alaska, see ACE, 52-A-40, box 44, file 400.703, A. Anderson to Office of the Chief Engineer, 31 May 1944, E. R. Needles to Division Engineer, 6 June 1944.

25. NAC, RG 36/7, vol. 2, file 3/5, Foster to Camsell, 14 May 1945.

26. *Edmonton Bulletin,* 25 July 1944, "U.S. Equipment is Allotted to Canadian Government."

27. NA, RG 338, NWSC, box 18, Staff Meetings, 1943–1944, Staff Conference, Whitehorse, 16 August 1944.

28. NA, RG 338, box 17, NWSC and District Staff Meetings, 28 March 1944.

29. NAC, RG 36/7, vol. 15, file 28-25, A. Carpenter to Director, Intelligence & Security, 11 March 1945.

30. NAC, RG 36/7, vol. 49, file 10-5, Cst. R. G. Sangster Report Re: Customs Conditions, Whitehorse, Yukon, 22 December 1944.

31. NAC, RG 36/7, vol. 15, file 28-25, Extracts from Report of A. H. Carpenter, 11 March 1945.

32. *Whitehorse Star*, 8 June 1945, p. 3, "U.S. Surplus Supplies."

33. NAC, RG 85, vol. 957, file 13417, pt. 1, Foster to Heeney, 14 July 1944.

34. Col. F. S. Strong, quoted in the *Edmonton Bulletin*, 25 July 1944, "U.S. Equipment Is Allotted to Canadian Government." See also ibid., "U.S. Army Handling Salvage on Alaska Road to Dominion." For a direct editorial response to Strong's statement, see *Edmonton Bulletin*, 26 July 1944, "Northern Salvage Up to Canada." NA, RG 338, box 4, S-2, Intelligence report, n.d.

35. NAC, RG 36/7, vol. 3, file 2-A, Foster to Secretary, Cabinet War Committee, 25 August 1944. ACE, 29-52A434, "Canadian Reporter 'Verified' Alcan Highway Salvage Waste," n.d. Also NAC, RG 36/7, vol. 3, file 2-A, Foster to Heeney, 21 July 1944.

36. NA, RG 59, file 842.154, Seattle Fairbanks Highway/7-2944, "Ten Year Supply of Drugs Tossed over Cliff in North" (newspaper not identified). See also *Ottawa Journal*, "Demand Probe of Destruction," 25 July 1944. American officials investigated the complaint and found it, to their satisfaction, to be unfounded. NAC, RG 36/7, vol. 36, file 11-16, Greenlee to Foster, 3 August 1944.

37. *Edmonton Journal*, 11 July 1944.

38. *Edmonton Bulletin*, 25 July 1944, "Claim Settlers Are Prosecuted over U.S. Goods."

39. *Whitehorse Star*, 4 August 1944, p. 2; *Edmonton Bulletin*, 26 July 1944, "Northern Salvage Up to Canada."

40. ACE, 29-52A434, Major Hurley to General Robins, 18 July 1944; NAC, RG 36/7, vol. 36, file 11-16, Extract from Hansard, 28 July 1944, T. Dauphinee to W. L. M. King, 12 July 1944; NA, RG 59, file 842.154, Seattle Fairbanks Highway/7-2944, Bob (American Embassy, Ottawa) to J. G. Parsons, 26 July 1944.

41. The camps were, for administrative and accounting purposes, considered to be part of the Alaska Highway. See NAC, RG 36/7, vol. 42, file 11-10, Acting Special Commissioner to Chief, Canadian Liaison Section, 6 October 1945.

42. NAC, RG 36/7, vol. 3, file 2-A, Foster to Secretary, Cabinet War Committee, 25 August 1944.

43. *Edmonton Bulletin*, 7 July 1944; *Washington Post*, 3 August 1944, "Army to Probe Destruction of Valued Supplies."

44. NA, RG 59, DF 842.154, Seattle-Fairbanks Highway/8-2944, Memorandum to the Press, 25 August 1944, Department of State, Division of European Affairs to Hickerson, 29 August 1944.

45. Interview with Lake Southwick, Taylor, B.C., July 1988. Mr. Southwick was born and raised at Charlie Lake, seven miles north of Fort St.

John, and was named after the lake—his full name is Charlie Lake South-wick. Charlie Lake was the last place northwest of Fort St. John where a car could be driven in 1942; it was there that the American bulldozers actually had to begin knocking down trees to build the Alaska Highway. The community considers itself the "real" beginning of the highway.

46. NAC, RG 36/7, vol. 36, file 11/16, Foster to Strong, 12 May 1945, Foster to Henney, 12 May 1945, Strong to Foster, 16 May 1945.

47. Most of the "temporary buildings" that remained into the late 1960s—Ottawa had many of them—were built by the Canadians, but the structures left over from the Northwest defense projects served the same functions.

48. EMA, RG11, Class 64, file 12 contains a number of letters on this initiative, undertaken in the summer of 1946.

49. NAC, RG 22, vol. 252, file 40-7-4, pt. 9, Short Report on Northwest Highway System, covering period 1 Apr. 1946–31 March 1947.

50. NAC, RG 85, vol. 1515, file 351-2-21, pt. 1, Walsh to Secretary, National Defence, 14 June 1946. George Black raised questions in the House of Commons about the possible abandonment of the Haines Road. See *Whitehorse Star,* 13 April 1945, p. 6.

51. ACE, 72A3173, 18a, Alcan General, L. Petrigni to Whom It May Concern, 23 October 1944.

52. Major-General T. Robins, who knew better, wrote in October 1945 that "the highway proper is in excellent condition" (ACE, 29-52A434, Robins to Thomas, 10 October 1945).

53. ACE, 29-52A434, Memorandum for the Director: A land plan survey for the Canadian Alaska Military Highway, 23 January 1942 (the date appears to be in error; it is probably 1943).

54. ACE, 72A3173, box 16, 50-26, Jack Mage to Reid, 13 April 1943.

55. NAC, RG 85, vol. 967, file 13876, pt. 1, Gibson to Deputy Minister, 26 July 1945.

56. Ibid., Black to Gibson, 1 February 1945.

57. ACE, 72A3173, 18a, Alcan General, C. Stephenson to President Roosevelt, n.d. The "glaciers" were the frozen outflows of springs and creeks, which made the road impassable in the spring and fall.

58. ACE, 29-52A434, Caldwell to Connally, 18 November 1945.

59. Ibid., Thomas to Reybold, 2 June 1944.

60. ACE, 72A3173, 18a, Alcan General, De Bardeleben to Winsor, 7 September 1944.

61. NAC, RG 85, vol. 967, file 13876, pt. 1, Gibson to Deputy Minister, 26 July 1945.

62. NAC, RG 85, vol.1073, file 256-10-1, pt. 1, Phinney to Heeney, 23 August 1945.

63. NAC, RG 36/7, vol. 45, file 10/10, Hanington to Walsh, 6 December 1946.

64. YTA, YRG 1, ser. 1, vol. 8, file 466-3a, Rogers to Jeckell, 11 October 1945.

65. ACE, 29-52A434, Crawford to Connally, 14 December 1945. The main board consisted of Major A. Foushee, U.S. Army, and Capt. Hogg, Special Commissioner's Office. Deputies were located in Fort. St. John, B.C., and Whitehorse, Yukon.

66. NAC, RG 22, vol. 109, file 84-32-6, pt. 3, 25th Report of the Special Commissioner, 30 June 1945 (copy of bulletin from Joint Traffic Control Board, 1 June 1945).

67. NA, RG 59, 842.154, Seattle-Fairbanks Highway/4-947, P. Seddicum to Foster, 9 April 1947.

68. Winter travelers also had to carry light bulbs, heater, electric tape, copper wire, and alcohol to be used as gas line antifreeze. NAC, RG 85, vol. 967, file 13876, pt. 1, A. S. McDougall to T. S. Mills, 13 January 1947.

69. NA, RG 59, 842.154, Seattle-Fairbanks Highway/4-3047, Acheson to J. A. Krug, 30 April 1947; ibid., Seattle-Fairbanks Highway/4-947, P. Seddicum to Foster, 9 April 1947.

70. NAC, RG 36/7, vol. 41, file 11/5, Worsham to Foster, 3 July 1943.

71. ACE, 72-A-3173, box 15, file 52-1, Sturdevant to Hickerson, 28 August 1942; ibid., file 5015, Ickes to President, 8 January 1943.

72. NAC, RG 36/7, vol. 45, file AH, 1-0-1, Phinney to Heeney, 24 June 1946.

74. *Whitehorse Star,* 3 December 1943, p. 1, 25 February 1944, p. 1.

74. *Prince Rupert Daily News,* 15 September 1945.

75. Details of part of this transfer are provided in *The History of 17 Works COY RCE, 1 April 1946–31 March 1964* (departmental publication, n.d.).

76. NAC, RG 36/7, vol. 42, file 11/5/1, Phinney to Foster, 24 January 1946. See the articles by Stephen Harris and Ken Coates in Coates, ed., *The Alaska Highway.* The attitude of the British Columbia government has not changed towards the question.

77. NAC, RG 22, vol. 109, file 84-32-6, pt. 3, 35th Report of the Special Commissioner, 30 April 1946.

9. The North at War's End

1. NAC, RG 85, vol. 1125, file 163-1, vol. 1, R. A. Gibson to G. A. Jeckell, 1 May 1945; Re: Esquimaux and Residents of North West Territories and Yukon, 9 March 1945. "In the case of all Nomads and Esquimaux, the amounts that are to be paid will be paid direct to your [Lands, Parks and Forests Branch, Department of Mines and Resources] Branch in trust, and arrangements will be made through your Branch for Trade Orders to be issued to the families in question." Ibid., George Davidson to R. A. Gibson, 2 April 1945, A. S. Dewdney, Supplementary Report of the Field Matron, Fort McPherson, July 1947.

2. Ibid., Appreciation Shown by the Indians for Family Allowance (comments recorded from Fort Providence, Fort Good Hope, and Fort McPherson). For a contemporary journalistic description of the Natives' response to the allowance, see "No Losers in This Stork Derby," *American Weekly*, 3 March 1946.

3. YTA, YRG 1, ser. 1, vol. 63, file 35538, folder 2, F. E. Woodside to Hon. J. Allison, 4 February 1947, Woodside to Camsell, 12 March 1945.

4. NAC, RG 85, vol. 655, file 3008, Population of the Yukon Territory, 28 December 1946. Whitehorse's population included 230 members of the RCAF, 240 Indians, and 3,210 other whites; Dawson had 673 whites and 15 Indians. Whitehorse's dominance in the Territory is even more pronounced today; in 1989 the city had more than 20,700 of the Yukon's 29,800 residents, while Dawson's population was 1,790. *Revised Population Estimates of the Yukon* (Whitehorse: Bureau of Statistics, June 1989).

5. NAC, RG 85, vol. 1512, file 1000/200, pt. 1, Gibson to Cumming, 26 June 1946.

6. NAC, RG 22, vol. 107, file 84-32-6, pt. 1, Recommendations Yukon and Northwest Territories, included with a letter, Foster to Camsell, 27 April 1944.

7. NAC, RG 22, vol. 107, file 84-32-6, pt. 1, Camsell to Heeney, 5 May 1944.

8. NAC, RG 36/7, ser. 7, vol. 15, file 2831, J. A. Glen Memorandum to the Cabinet, 1 March 1946; YTA, YRG 1, ser. 1, vol. 54, file 33226, Black to Gibben, 17 February 1947.

9. "Canada Gets Ready-Made System of Bases," *American Aviation* 8, no. 7 (1 September 1944).

10. ACE, 72A3173, box 15, Canadian-Alaska Military Highway, Land Planning Survey, Memorandum for the Director, 23 January 1942.

11. ACE, 29-52A434, Memorandum of Conversation, 29 September 1943.

12. Griffith Taylor, "Arctic Survey, IV: A Yukon Domesday: 1944," *Canadian Journal of Economics and Political Science* 14, no. 3 (August 1945): 438.

13. NA, RG 59, file 842.154 Seattle Fairbanks Highway/3-2649, John Martyn to Secretary of State, 26 March 1949.

14. YTA, YRG 1, ser. 1, vol. 70, pt. 4, file 1, J. A. Glen to A. M. Cameron, 30 April 1946.

15. NAC, RG 85, vol. 967, file 13876, pt. 1, Traffic Control Board, 1 April 1946, outlines the restrictions on highway traffic.

16. Permission was granted "providing that the applicant can prove that he is self-contained and knows fully the conditions for which he must make provision." NAC, RG 36/7, vol. 41, file 11-1, pt. 2, Walsh to Secretary, Department of National Defence, 1 June 1946.

17. The War Measures Act was a Canadian law passed before World War I, which permitted the federal government, in time of war or insurrection (or "apprehended" war or insurrection), to in effect suspend civil liberties and govern by decree. It was the basis of all the wartime regulations, ranging from food rationing to the expulsion of Japanese-Canadians from the West Coast. It could be imposed in peacetime as well, as during the "October Crisis" of 1970 in Quebec.

18. YTA, YRG 1, ser. 1, vol. 70, file 21, pt. 4, Krug to James Byrnes, 5 April 1946; NAC, RG 36/7, vol. 141, file 11-5-2, Heaps to Heeney, 3 July 1946, Cronkite to O. C. "G" Division, 30 July 1946; ibid., file 11-1, pt. 1, Guide to Travellers, 28 November 1946. See also YTA, RG 1, ser. 1, vol. 8, file 466-3b, General Information Concerning the Alaska Highway–Canadian Section (Northwest Highway System), c. 1947.

19. NAC, RG 85, vol. 967, file 13,876, pt. 1, Paul Mansen to (various newspapers), 22 May 1946.

20. NAC, RG 24, vol. 5937, file HQ 186-9-7, vol. 2, Keenleyside to Sharpe, 25 February 1948.

21. Cecil Barger, "It's a Long Road," *Alaskan Sportsman* (November 1945); "The Alaska Highway Pays Off", *Toronto Star Weekly*, 28 June 1952; "Gold Adventure," *Toronto Star Weekly*, 17 December 1955. These are but a few of the dozens of articles and newspaper stories about the highway.

22. For a contemporary expression of this belief, see T. A. Crerar's comment in *Report of the Standing Committee on Tourist Traffic* (Ottawa, 1946), p. 16.

23. "Has the Alcan Got a Future," *Toronto Star Weekly*, 26 April 1947.

24. There were a number of requests for information and inquiries from promoters. Few of these bore fruit. See YTA, YRG 1, ser. 1, vol. 70, file 21, pt. 4, file 1, Robert Campbell to W. L. Mackenzie King, 9 April 1946.

25. NAC, RG 36/7, vol. 43, file 11-17-2, Rogers to Phinney, 29 July 1946, discusses aspects of White Pass and Yukon Route expansion. The company received a franchise to operate on the Yukon portions of the highway, a right that "will not be an exclusive franchise but there will be a provision in the agreement that a second franchise will not be approved until traffic is considered to warrant such action" (YTA, YRG 1, ser. 1, vol. 70, file 21, pt. 4, file 1, Gibson to Phinney, 17 May 1945). Ibid., vol. 64, file 35970, Atherton to Wrong, 1 October 1946, describes O'Hara's service along the northern portion of the Alaska Highway and the Haines Lateral. Some of the bus stops were operated out of tents. NAC, RG 85, vol. 1073, file 256-10-1, part 1, Johnson to Gibson, 26 October 1946.

26. NAC, RG 85, vol. 1073, file 256-10-1, pt. 1, Alaska Highway During 1947.

27. YTA, YRG 1, ser. 1, vol. 64, file 35996-1, Jackson to Gibson, 30 September 1946.

28. NAC, RG 85, vol. 854, file 7929A, G. Esper to Mr. Payton, 6 January 1947.

29. NAC, RG 85, vol. 1073, file 256-1-1, pt. 1, Bell to Commissioner for Northern Projects, 17 February 1947.

30. *Report of the Standing Committee on Tourist Traffic* (Ottawa, 1946), p. 9. Testimony by L. Phinney.

31. YTA, YRG 1, ser. 1, vol. 64, file 35996-1, Development of Government and Tourist Facilities (Alaska Highway), 31 December 1946, List of Recommended Land Reservations for Development of Tourist Camping Facilities, or Scenic Value or of National or Historic Interest along the Alaska Highway in the Yukon Territory, c. 1947.

32. NAC, RG 85, vol. 1010, file 17410, Phinney to Carson, 6 July 1946, Benney to Phinney, 15 July 1946, Certified Copy of a Minute of the Executive Council, #2880, 4 December 1946.

33. "Has the Alcan Got a Future," *Toronto Star Weekly,* 26 April 1947. The highway's supposed dangers came to be one of its primary attractions.

34. NAC, RG 85, vol. 1073, file 256-10-1, pt. 2, Inspections—Mile 918 to 1221, c.1949.

35. NAC, RG 85, vol. 1073, file 256-10-1, pt. 1, F.H.R. Jackson to Gibson, 23 February 1948. Name deleted.

36. NAC, RG 85, vol. 1073, file 256-10-1, pt. 2, J. Locke, Inspections—Mile 918 to 1221, c. 1949.

37. NAC, RG 85, vol. 1073, file 256-10-1, pt. 2, Establishments along the Alaska Highway, c. 1949.

38. NA, RG 59, file 842.154, Seattle Fairbanks Highway/2-1348, Foster re: Demand of Congressman Kersten, 13 February 1948.

39. *Whitehorse Star,* 29 June 1945.

40. NA, RG 59, file 842.154, Seattle Fairbanks Highway/11-1645, Report to Mr. Acheson, 16 November 1945. See also "Let a Survey Determine the Route," *Mining World* (July 1945); *Spokesman-Review,* 27 June 1945.

41. NA, RG 59, file 842.154, Seattle Fairbanks Highway/2-1646, Memorandum of Conversation, 18 February 1946; ibid., 1-2347, Memorandum of Conversation, 23 January 1947.

42. Ibid., 3-2746, Edwin Stanton to Secretary of State, 27 March 1946.

43. Ibid., 3-246, Edwin Stanton to Secretary of State, 2 March 1946; *Victoria Daily Colonist,* 14 July 1945.

44. EMA, RG 11, Class 90, file 34, Mackenzie to Dear Sir, 4 July 1944. See also NAC, RG 22, vol. 252, file 40-7-4, pt. 8, Resolutions: United States–Canada–Alaska Prairie Highway Association, c. 1945.

45. NA, RG 59, file 842.154, Seattle Fairbanks Highway/9-346, Lewis Clark to Secretary of State, 3 September 1946.

46. Ibid., 4-3045, Memorandum for File, 23 June 1945; ibid., 8-2547,

Edwards to Foster, 25 August 1947. Point Roberts is a U.S. community at the tip of a peninsula south of Vancouver. Because the forty-ninth parallel cuts across the middle of the peninsula, the only land access from the community to the rest of the state of Washington is through Canada. It would have made geographic, though not political, sense to transfer the entire peninsula to Canada.

47. Ibid., 4-3045, Memorandum of Conversation, 30 April 1945.

48. Ibid., 10-345, Senate Joint Memorial, 14 March 1947.

49. Ibid., Memorandum of Conversation, 3 October 1945.

50. Ibid., 2-2647, A. B. Foster: Maintenance of the Haines Cut-off, 26 February 1947; ibid., 2-1347, Chapman to Marshall, 13 February 1947.

51. YTA, YRG 1, ser. 1, vol. 64, file 35970, H.J.C. Terry to Hon. J. A. Glen, 1 November 1947; NA, RG 59, file 842.154, Seattle Fairbanks Highway/12-347, C. Heinmiller to Foster, 28 September 1948. The latter suggests that the White Pass and Yukon Route was leading the opposition to keeping the road open.

52. NA, RG 59, file 842.154, Seattle Fairbanks Highway/12-347, C. Heinmiller to Foster, 3 December 1947. See also the attached report, "The Haines Cutoff, Overland Freightway to the Interior Alaska and the Yukon."

53. NAC, RG 85, vol. 1515, file 351-2-21, pt. 1, Memorandum re: Haines Highway, 3 December 1947.

54. YTA, YRG 1, ser. 1, vol. 63, file 35538, folder 2, Jeckell to Gibson, 15 April 1946, Submission in Support of Petition for Construction of a Highway Between Whitehorse, Mayo and Dawson, Yukon Territory, 9 December 1946.

55. EMA, RG 11, Class 90, file 37, A. Christiansen, Alaska Highway Committee to Mayor and Commissioners, 6 July 1946; ibid., file 35, Caton to Mayor Ainlay, 20 November 1945.

56. YTA, YRG 1, ser. 1. vol. 63, file 35538, folder 1, Connell to Gibson, 19 July 1949, Hume to Gibson, 22 July 1949.

57. YTA, YRG 1, ser. 1, vol. 63, file 35538, folder 2, P. C. Hitt to Heeney, 12 December 1946, discusses early plans for the Tok to Dawson road. See also ibid., White and Firth, B.C.–Yukon Chamber of Mines to Gibben, 21 May 1947, which asked the government to shift funds from the Whitehorse-Mayo winter road to the Dawson-Tok road.

58. Ibid., Gibson to Jackson, 22 May 1947. The Atlin project was "pretty well down on the list of the roads that the Yukon Administration wishes to have built," and suffered the additional complication of requiring Yukon, federal, and British Columbia government cooperation. Getting the support of the latter was particularly problematic.

59. J. P. de Wet, "Exploration for Oil in the Northwest Territories," *Canadian Mining Journal* (September 1944).

60. YTA, YRG 1, ser. 1, vol. 63, file 35538, folder 1, Gibson to Gibben, 4 November 1947.

61. What is left today of the road is described in S. R. Gage, *A Walk on the Canol Road* (Oakville, Ont.: Mosaic Press, 1990).

62. NAC, RG 22, vol. 106, file 84-32-5A, pt. 1, "The Opening of the New Northwest," an address by Dr. Charles Camsell, c. 1943.

63. *Colliers,* 20 November 1943, p. 58.

64. NAC, RG 22, vol. 106, file 84-32-5A, pt. 1, Crerar to Rose, 10 February 1943.

65. NAC, RG 22, vol. 106, file 84-32-5A, pt. 1, Memorandum, 17 February 1943.

66. *The North Pacific Planning Project, Report of Progress, May 1943* (Washington, National Resources Planning Board, 1943). To gain a sense of the committee's deliberations, see ACE, 72A3173, box 15, Canadian-Alaskan Military Highway Land Planning Survey, Memorandum Report of Joint Economic Committee, 5–6 November 1943.

67. NAC, RG 85, vol. 1190, file 355-2, vol. 1, C. K. LeCapelain re: Proposed Survey of a Railroad, 7 December 1949; ibid., Memorandum to the Canadian Section, Permanent Joint Board on Defence, 16 February 1948, provides an excellent survey of official Canadian thinking on the subject. See also ibid., Keenleyside to Pearson, 13 February 1948.

68. NA, RG 59, file 842.154, Seattle Fairbanks Highway/11-749, Snow to Thompson, 7 November 1949.

Conclusion: Historiographical Reflections on the Army of Occupation

1. The major exception is the study of women which, stimulated by the intellectual currents of modern feminism, has been taking a truly international perspective. See in particular Isaksson, ed., *Women and the Military System.*

2. Gerald D. Nash, *The American West Transformed: The Impact of the Second World War* (Bloomington: University of Indiana Press, 1985).

3. Gerald Friesen, *The Canadian Prairies* (Toronto: University of Toronto Press, 1987).

4. Pierson, *They're Still Women;* Margaret Allen, "The Domestic Ideal and the Mobilization of Womanpower in World War II," *Women's Studies International Forum* 6/4 (1983); C. Gregory, *Women in Defense Work During World War II: An Analysis of the Labour Problem and Women's Rights* (New York: Exposition Press, 1974); Susan Hartmann, *The Home Front and Beyond: American Women in the 1940s* (Boston: Twayne, 1982); D'Ann Campbell, *Women at War with America: Private Lives in a Patriotic Era* (Cambridge: Harvard University Press, 1984); M. Higgonet et al., eds., *Behind the Lines: Gender and the Two World Wars* (New Haven:

Yale University Press, 1987); K. Anderson, *Wartime Women: Sex Roles, Family Relations and the Status of Women* (Westport: Greenwood, 1981); S. M. Hartmann, "Prescriptions for Penelope: Literature on Women's Obligations to Returning World War II Veterans," *Women's Studies* 5 (1978); D. Montgomerie, "The Limitations of Wartime Change: Women War Workers in New Zealand," *New Zealand Journal of History* 23, no. 1 (April 1989).

5. Sitkoff, "Racial Militancy"; Dalfiuma, *Desegregation;* Buchanan, *Black Americans;* Wynn, "War and Social Change"; Wynn, *Afro-American;* Nalty, *Strength for the Fight.*

6. Longmate, *The G.I.'s;* Smith, *Jim Crow.*

7. See in particular Rosemary Campbell, *Heroes and Lovers* (Melbourne: Melbourne University Press, 1985); Potts and Potts, *Yanks Down Under;* Moore, *Over-Sexed.*

8. For an alarmist view of this process, see D. Creighton, *The Forked Road: Canada, 1939–1967* (Toronto: McClelland and Stewart, 1976); see also R. Bothwell, I. Drummond, and J. English, *Canada, 1900 to 1945* (Toronto: University of Toronto Press, 1988).

9. Grant, *Sovereignty or Security?.*

10. A. Powell, *The Shadow's Edge: Australia's Northern War* (Melbourne: Melbourne University Press, 1988); Coates and Morrison, "Coping with the Occupation."

11. White and Lindstrom, eds., *The Pacific Theatre.* Environmental history is in its infancy, and it will be some time before an environmental history of World War II is available.

12. A. Friye, "Contemporary History as History: American Expansion into the Pacific since 1941," *Pacific Historical Review* 53 (1984); Louis, *Imperialism at Bay;* Hess, *United States' Emergence.*

13. It is significant that the lobbying group attempting to reestablish American investment in Vietnam is led by military and civilian personnel who served there in the 1960s and 1970s.

Bibliography

Archival Sources

Edmonton Municipal Archives (EMA)

Library of Congress (LC), Harold Ickes Papers

National Archives of Canada (NAC) Record Groups (RG) 10, 18, 22, 24, 36/7, 85

National Archives of the United States (NA), Washington D.C. and Suitland, Md.: Record Groups (RG) 30, 59, 92, 107,111, 112, 160, 165, 218, 253, 319, 335, 336, 338, 407

United States Army, Adjutant General's Office (AGO), Machine Records Branch (MRB)

United States Army Corps of Engineers, Office of History, Office of the Chief of Engineers, Fort Belvoir, Research Collections (ACE)

Yukon Territorial Archives (YTA), Yukon Record Group 1 (YRG), Yukon Government Records, White Pass and Yukon Route Collection, Anglican Church, Diocese of Yukon Records.

Newspapers

Calgary Albertan
Dawson Daily News
Edmonton Bulletin
Edmonton Journal
Financial Times
Fort St. John Alaska Highway News

Northern Lights
Northern Miner
North Star Magazine
Ottawa Citizen
Ottawa Journal
Prince Rupert Daily News
Regina Leader Post
Stewart News and Northern B.C. Miner
Toronto Star Weekly
Vancouver Daily Province
Vancouver News-Herald
Victoria Daily Colonist
Washington Post
Whitehorse Star

Articles

Allen, Margaret. "The Domestic Ideal and the Mobilization of Womanpower in World War II." *Women's Studies International Forum* 6/4 (1983).

Barger, Cecil. "It's a Long Road." *Alaskan Sportsman* (November 1945).

Campbell, D'Ann. "Servicewomen of World War II." *Armed Forces and Society* 6, no. 2 (Winter 1990).

Cleveland, L. "When They Send the Last Yank Home: Wartime Images of Popular Culture." *Journal of Popular Culture* 18, no. 3 (Winter 1984).

Coates, K. S. "Best Left as Indians: The Federal Government and the Indians of the Yukon, 1894–1950." *Canadian Journal of Native Studies* 4, no. 2 (Fall 1984).

Coates, K. S. "Upsetting the Rhythms: The Federal Government and Native Communities in the Yukon Territory, 1945 to 1973." In Gurston Dacks and Ken Coates, eds., *Northern Communities: The Prospects for Empowerment* (Edmonton: Boreal Institute for Northern Studies, 1988).

Coates, K. S., and W. R. Morrison. "The American Rampant: Reflections on the Impact of the U.S. Armed Forces Overseas during World War II," *Journal of World History* 2, no. 2 (fall 1991).

Coates, K. S., and W. R. Morrison. "More Than a Matter of Blood: The Churches, the Government and the Mixed Blood Populations of the Yukon and Mackenzie River Valley, 1890–1950." In F. L. Barron and J. Waldrum, eds., *1885 and After* (Regina: Canadian Plains Research Centre, 1986).

Coates, K. S., and W. R. Morrison. "War Comes to the Yukon." *The Beaver* (October/November 1989).

Coates, K.S., and Judith Powell. "Whitehorse and the Building of the Alaska Highway, 1942–1946." *Alaska History* (Spring 1989).

Cole, Terrence. "Klondike Contraptions." *The Northern Review*, no. 3/4 (Summer/Winter 1989).

de Wet, J. P. "Exploration for Oil in the Northwest Territories." *Canadian Mining Journal* (September 1944).

Diubaldo, Richard. "The Canol Project in Canadian-American Relations." Canadian Historical Association, *Historical Papers* (1977).

Fidock, Jane. "The Effect of the American 'Invasion' of Australia, 1942–1945." *Flinders Journal of History and Politics* 11 (1985).

Gagnon, Jean-Pierre. "Canadian Soldiers in Bermuda During World War One." *Histoire Sociale/Social History* 23, no. 45 (May 1990).

Guererard, Albert Jr."Novitiate." *Virginia Quarterly Review* 21, no. 1 (1945).

Hachey, T. "Jim Crow with a British Accent: Attitudes of London Government Officials Toward American Negro Soldiers in England During World War II." *Journal of Negro History* 59, no. 1 (January 1974).

Hachey, T. "Walter White and the American Negro Soldier in World War II: A Diplomatic Dilemma for Britain." *Phylon: The Atlanta University Review of Race and Culture* 39, no. 3 (Fall 1954).

Hartmann, S. M. "Prescriptions for Penelope: Literature on Women's Obligations to Returning World War II Veterans." *Women's Studies* 5 (1978).

Honigman, J. J. "On the Alaska Highway." *Dalhousie Review* (January 1944).

Honigman, John, and I. Honigman. "Drinking in an Indian-White Community." *Quarterly Journal of Studies on Alcohol* 5 (March 1945).

Iriye, Akira. "Contemporary History as History: American Expansion into the Pacific since 1941." *Pacific Historical Review* 53 (1984).

Johnston, H. "The Anglo-American Caribbean Commission and the Extension of Amrican Influence in the British Caribbean, 1942–1945." *The Journal of Commonwealth and Comparative Politics* 22, no. 2 (July 1984).

Kalisch, P. A., and M. Scobey. "Female Nurses in American Wars: Helplessness Suspended for the Duration." *Armed Forces and Society* 9, no. 2 (Winter 1983).

King, Archibald. "Further Developments Concerning Jurisdiction over Friendly Foreign Armed Forces." *American Journal of International Law* 40 (1946).

Koppes, Clayton, and G. Black. "Blacks, Loyalty and Motion Picture

Propaganda in World War II." *Journal of American History* 73, no. 2 (September 1976).

Levi, Steven. "Labor History and Alaska." *Labor History* 30, no 4 (1989).

Marchand, John. "Tribal Epidemics in the Yukon." *Journal of the American Medical Association* 123 (1943).

McCusker, Knox. "The Alaska Highway." *Canadian Surveyor* 8 (July 3).

McGuire, Philip. "Desegregation of the Armed Forces: Black Leadership, Protest and World War II." *The Journal of Negro History* 68, no. 2 (Spring 1983).

Modell, John, and Diane Steffey. "Waging War and Marriage: Military Service and Family Formation, 1940–1950." *Journal of Family History* 13, no. 2 (1988).

Montgomerie, D. "The Limitations of Wartime Change: Women War Workers in New Zealand." *New Zealand Journal of History* 23, no. 1 (April 1989).

The North Pacific Planning Project, Report of Progress, May 1943. Washington, D.C.: National Resources Planning Board, 1943.

Palmer, A. "The Politics of Race and War: Black American Soldiers in the Caribbean Theatre During the Second World War." *Military Affairs* 47, no. 2 (April 1983).

Powell, Judith. "Whitehorse and the Building of the Alaska Highway, 1942–1946." *Alaska History* (Spring 1989).

Rainey, F. "Alaskan Highway: An Engineering Epic." *National Geographic Magazine* 83, no. 2 (February–March 1943).

Renshaw, P. "Organized Labor in the United States War Economy, 1939–1945." *Journal of Contemporary History* 21 (1986).

Reynold, David. "The Churchill Government and the Black American Troops in Britain During World War II." *Royal Historical Society, Transactions* 35 (1985).

Saunders, Kay. "Conflict Between the American and Australian Governments over the Introduction of Black American Servicemen into Australia During World War Two." *Australian Journal of Politics and History* 33, no. 2 (1987).

Saunders, Kay, and Helen Taylor. "The Reception of American Servicemen in Australia During World War 2: The Resilience of 'White Australia'." *Journal of Black Studies* (June 1988).

Sitkoff, H. "Racial Militancy and Interracial Violence in the Second World War." *Journal of American History* 58 (December 1971).

Straub, Eleanor. "United States Government Policy Toward Civilian Women During World War II." *Prologue* 5 (1973).

Stuart, Richard. "The Yukon Schools Question, 1937." *Canadian Historical Review* 64, no. 1 (1983).

Sturma, M. "Loving the Alien: The Underside of Relations Between American Servicemen and Australian Women in Queensland, 1942–1945." *Journal of Australian Studies* 24 (1989).

Sturma, M. "Public Health and Sexual Morality: Venereal Disease in World War II Australia." *Signs* 13, no. 4 (1988).

Schweitzer, Mary. "World War II and Female Labor Force Participation Rates." *Journal of Economic History* 40 (1980).

Taylor, Griffith. "Arctic Survey, IV: A Yukon Domesday: 1944." *Canadian Journal of Economics and Political Science* 14, no. 3 (August 1945).

Woodman, L. "CANOL: Pipeline of Brief Glory." *The Northern Engineer* 9, no. 2 (Summer 1977).

Wynn, Neill. "War and Social Change: The Black American in Two World Wars." In B. Bond and I. Roy, eds., *War and Society*, vol. 2 (London: Crown Holm, 1977).

Books

Additional Report of the Special Committee Investigating the National Defense Program. 78th Cong., 1st sess., Report No. 10, Pt. 14. Washington, D.C.: Government Printing Office, 1944.

The Alaska Highway: Interim Report from the Committee on Roads, House of Representatives. Washington, D.C.: Government Printing Office, 1946.

Anderson, K. *Wartime Women: Sex Roles, Family Relations and the Status of Women.* Westport: Greenwood, 1981.

Banner, Lois. *Women in Modern America: A Brief History.* New York: Harcourt Brace Jovanovich, 1984.

Baptiste, F. A. *War, Cooperation, and Conflict: The European Possessions in the Caribbean, 1939–1945.* New York: Greenwood Press, 1988.

Barry, P. S. *The Canol Project: An adventure of the U.S. War Department in Canada's Northwest.* Edmonton: published by the author, 1985.

Beckles, Gordon. *Canada Comes to England.* London: Hodder and Stoughton, 1941.

Bell, Roger. *Unequal Allies: Australian-American Relations in the Pacific War.* Melbourne: Melbourne University Press, 1977.

Bennett, Gordon. *Yukon Transportation: A History.* Canadian Historic Sites Occasional Papers in Archaeology and History, No. 19. Ottawa, 1978.

Berton, Pierre. *The Mysterious North*. Toronto: McClelland and Stewart, 1956.

Bittner, Donald. *The Lion and the White Falcon: Britain and Iceland in the World War II Era*. Hamden: Archon Books, 1983.

Bond, B., and I. Roy, eds. *War and Society*, vol. 2. London: Crown Holm, 1977.

Bothwell, Robert. *Eldorado: Canada's National Uranium Company*. Toronto: University of Toronto Press, 1984.

Bothwell, R., I. Drummond, and J. English. *Canada, 1900 to 1945*. Toronto: University of Toronto Press, 1988.

British Columbia. *Report of the Commissioner of the Provincial Police . . . and Inspector of Gaols*. Victoria: King's Printer, 1941–46.

British Columbia–Yukon–Alaska Highway Commission. *Preliminary Report on Proposed Highway Through British Columbia and the Yukon Territory to Alaska*. Ottawa: Kings Printer, 1940.

Brown, Jennifer. *Strangers in Blood: Families in Fur Trade Country*. Vancouver: University of British Columbia Press, 1980.

Brownmiller, Susan. *Against Our Will: Men, Women and Rape*. New York: Simon and Schuster, 1973.

Bryant, C. *Khaki-Collar Crime*. New York: Free Press, 1979.

Buchanan, A. Russell. *Black Americans in World War II*. Santa Barbara: ABC-Clio Press, 1977.

Campbell, D'Ann. *Women at War with America: Private Lives in a Patriotic Era*. Cambridge: Harvard University Press, 1984.

Campbell, Rosemary. *Heroes and Lovers: A Question of National Identity*. Melbourne: Melbourne University Press, 1989.

Canada. *Report of the RCMP, 1940–1944*. Ottawa: King's Printer, 1941–45.

Cardoulis, John. *A Friendly Invasion*. St. Johns: Bridgewater, 1990.

Coates, K. S., ed. *The Alaska Highway: Papers of the 40th Anniversary Symposium*. Vancouver: University of British Columbia Press, 1985.

Coates, K. S. *Canada's Colonies*. Toronto: James Lorimer, 1985.

Coates, K. S., and W. R. Morrison. *Land of the Midnight Sun: A History of the Yukon*. Edmonton: Hurtig, 1988.

Coates, K. S., and W. R. Morrison. *Interpreting Canada's North: Selected Readings*. Toronto: Copp Clark, 1989.

Coates, K. S., and W. R. Morrison. *Treaty Report: Treaty 11*. Ottawa: Treaties and Historical Research Centre, 1986.

Coates, K. S., and Judith Powell. *The Modern North*. Toronto: James Lorimer, 1989.

Cohen, Stan. *The Trail of '42*. Missoula: Pictorial Histories, 1988.

Costello, John. *Love, Sex and War: Changing Values, 1939–1945.* London: Collins, 1985.

Creighton, Donald. *The Forked Road: Canada, 1939–1967.* Toronto: McClelland and Stewart, 1976.

Dalfiuma, Richard. *Desegregation of the United States Armed Forces: Fighting on Two Fronts, 1939–1953.* Columbia, Mo.: University of Missouri Press, 1989.

Diubaldo, Richard. *Stefansson and the Canadian Arctic.* Montreal: McGill-Queen's University Press, 1978.

Duffy, Quinn. *The Road to Nunavut: The Progress of the Eastern Arctic Inuit since the Second World War.* Montreal: McGill-Queen's University Press, 1988.

Dziuban, Stanley W. *Military Relations Between the United States and Canada 1939–1945.* Washington, D.C.: Department of the Army, 1959.

Eccles, William J. *The Canadian Frontier, 1534–1760.* New York: Holt, Rinehart, and Winston, 1969.

Eccles, William J. *Canada under Louis XIV, 1663–1701.* Toronto: McClelland and Stewart, 1964.

Fletcher, Marvin. *The Black Soldier and Officer in the United States Army, 1891–1917.* Columbia: University of Missouri Press, 1974.

Flynn, George Q. *The Mess in Washington: Manpower, Mobilization and World War II.* Westport: Greenwood, 1979.

Forbes-Robertson, Diana, and Roger Straus, Jr., eds. *War Letters from Britain.* New York: G. P. Putnam, 1941.

Friesen, Gerald. *The Canadian Prairies.* Toronto: University of Toronto Press, 1987.

Fumoleau, Rene. *As Long as This Land Shall Last.* Toronto: McClelland and Stewart, 1973.

Gage, S. R. *A Walk on the Canol Road.* Oakville, Ont.: Mosaic Press, 1990.

Getty, I.A.L., and A. S. Lussier, eds. *As Long as the Sun Shines and Water Flows.* Vancouver: University of British Columbia Press, 1983.

Glaberman, Martin. *Wartime Strikes: The Struggle Against the No-Strike Pledge in the UAW During World War II.* Detroit: Bewich Editions, 1980.

Government of Yukon. *Revised Population Estimates of the Yukon.* Whitehorse: Bureau of Statistics, June 1989.

Grant, Shelagh. *Sovereignty or Security?: Government Policy in the Canadian North, 1939–1950.* Vancouver: University of British Columbia Press, 1988.

Green, Lewis. *The Gold Hustlers.* Anchorage: Alaskan Northwest Publishing, 1977.

Gregory, C. *Women in Defense Work During World War II: An Analysis of the Labour Problem and Women's Rights.* New York: Exposition Press, 1974.

Hall, David. *Clifford Sifton.* 2 vols. Vancouver: University of British Columbia Press, 1982 and 1984.

Hartmann, Susan. *The Home Front and Beyond: American Women in the 1940s.* Boston: Twayne, 1982.

Hess, Gary. R. *The United States' Emergence as a Southeast Asia Power, 1940–1950.* New York: Columbia University Press, 1987.

Higgonet, M., et al., eds. *Behind the Lines: Gender and the Two World Wars.* New Haven: Yale University Press, 1987.

Isaksson, E., ed. *Women and the Military System.* New York: St. Martin's, 1988.

Kennett, Lee. *G.I.: The American Soldier in World War II.* New York: Charles Scribner's Sons, 1987.

Large, R. G. *Prince Rupert: A Gateway to Alaska and the Pacific.* Vancouver: Mitchell, 1960.

Longmate, Norman. *The G.I.'s: The Americans in Britain, 1942–1945.* London: Hutchinson, 1975.

Lotz, Jim. *People Outside: Studies of Squatters, Shack Towns, and Shanty Residents and Other Dwellings on the Fringe in Canada.* Ottawa: St. Paul's University Press, 1971.

Louis, W. Roger. *Imperialism at Bay: The United States and the Decolonization of the British Empire, 1941–1945.* New York: Oxford University Press, 1978.

Lynn, W. *From Working Girl to Working Mother: The Female Labor Force in the United States, 1820–1980.* Chapel Hill: University of North Carolina Press, 1985.

MacGregor, J. D. *The Klondike Rush Through Edmonton, 1897–98.* Toronto: McClelland and Stewart, 1970.

Mackenzie, David. *Inside the North Atlantic Triangle.* Toronto: University of Toronto Press, 1988.

Magnusson, S. A. *Northern Sphinx: Iceland and Icelanders from the Settlement to the Present.* Montreal: McGill-Queen's University Press, 1977.

McCandless, Robert. *Yukon Wildlife: A Social History.* Edmonton: University of Alberta Press, 1986.

McConachie, Grant. *Bush Pilot with a Briefcase: The Happy-go-lucky Story of Grant McConachie.* Toronto: Doubleday, 1972.

McKernan, M. *All In! Australia During the Second World War.* Melbourne: Thomas Nelson, 1983.

Michener, James. *The Journey.* Toronto: McClelland and Stewart, 1989.

Milkman, Ruth. *Gender at Work: The Dynamics of Job Segregation by Sex During World War II.* Champaign: University of Illinois Press, 1987.

Mitchell, David. *W.A.C. Bennett.* Vancouver: Douglas and McIntyre, 1983.

Minter, Roy. *White Pass: Gateway to the Klondike.* Toronto: McClelland and Stewart, 1987.

Moore, John H., ed. *The American Alliance: Australia, New Zealand and the United States, 1940–1970.* Melbourne: Cassell Australia, 1970.

Moore, John H. *Over-Sexed, Over-Paid, and Over Here.* St. Lucia: University of Queensland Press, 1981.

Morrison, W. R. *Showing the Flag: The Mounted Police and Canadian Sovereignty in the North, 1894–1925.* Vancouver: University of British Columbia Press, 1985.

Nalty, B. *Strength for the Fight: A History of Black Americans in the Military.* New York: Free Press, 1988.

Nash, Gerald D. *The American West Transformed: The Impact of the Second World War.* Bloomington: Indiana University Press, 1985.

Naske, Claus-M. *Paving Alaska's Trails: The Work of the Alaska Road Commission.* New York: University Press of America, 1986.

Neufeld, Maurice. *American Working Class History: A Representative Bibliography.* Washington, D.C.: B.P., 1983.

Palmer, Howard, and Tamara Palmer. *Alberta: A New History.* Edmonton: Hurtig, 1990.

Peet, Fred. *Miners and Moonshiners: A Personal Account of Adventure and Survival in a Difficult Era.* Victoria, B.C.: Sono Nis Press, 1983.

Pierson, Ruth. *They're Still Women after All: The Second World War and Canadian Womanhood.* Toronto: McClelland and Stewart, 1986.

Polenberg, Richard. *War and Society in the United States, 1941–1945.* New York: J. B. Lippincott, 1972.

Potts, E. D., and A. Potts. *Yanks Down Under, 1941–45.* Melbourne: Oxford University Press, 1985.

Powell, A. *The Shadow's Edge: Australia's Northern War.* Melbourne: Melbourne University Press, 1988.

Remley, David. *Crooked Road: The Story of the Alaska Highway.* New York: McGraw Hill, 1976.

Report of the Alaskan International Highway Commission. Washington, D.C.: Government Printing Office, 1940.

Schuurman, Herbert. *Canada's Eastern Neighbour: A View on Change in Greenland.* Ottawa: Supply and Services Canada, 1976.

Senior, Eleanor. *Redcoats and Patriotes: The Rebellion in Lower Canada, 1837–38.* Stittsville, Ont.: Canadian War Museum, 1985.

Smith, Graham. *When Jim Crow Met John Bull: Black American Soldiers in World War II Britain.* London, 1967.

Stacey, C. P., and Barbara Wilson. *The Half Million: The Canadians in Britain, 1939–1946.* Toronto: University of Toronto Press, 1987.

Stambuk, George. *American Military Forces Abroad: Their Impact on the Western State System.* Columbus: Ohio State University Press, 1963.

Stiehm, Judith, ed. *Women and Men's Wars.* Oxford: Pergamon Press, 1983.

Stiehm, Judith, ed. *Women's View of the Political World of Men.* New York: Transnational, 1984.

Strong, F. S., Jr. *What's It All About?: Thoughts from the Nineties.* Privately published, 1985.

Tanlons, C. L. *The State and the Unions: Labor Relations, Law and the Organized Labor Movement in America, 1880–1960.* Cambridge: Cambridge University Press, 1985.

Thompson, John H. *The Harvests of War: The Prairie West, 1914–18.* Toronto: McClelland and Stewart, 1978.

Treadwell, Mattie. *The Women's Army Corps.* Washington, D.C: Department of the Army, 1954.

Trofimenkoff, Susan Mann. *The Dream of Nation: A Social and Intellectual History of Quebec.* Toronto: Macmillan, 1982.

United States, House of Representatives. *The Alaska Highway: An Interim Report.* Washington, D.C.: Government Printing Office, 1946.

Usher, Peter. *Fur Trade Posts of the Northwest Territories, 1870–1910.* Ottawa: Department of Indian Affairs and Northern Development, 1971.

Van Kirk, Sylvia. *Many Tender Ties: Women in Fur Trade Society, 1670–1870.* Winnipeg: Watson and Dwyer, 1980; Norman: University of Oklahoma Press, 1983.

Ward, Russell. *The History of Australia: The Twentieth Century, 1901–1975.* London: Heineman, 1978.

War/Masculinity. Sydney, Australia: Intervention Press, 1985.

Watt, F. B. *Great Bear: A Journey Remembered*. Yellowknife: Outcrop Press, 1980.

White, G., and L. Lindstrom, eds. *The Pacific Theatre: Island Representation of World War II*. Melbourne: Melbourne University Press, 1990.

Winkler, Allan. *The Politics of Propaganda: The Office of War Information, 1942–1945*. New Haven: Yale University Press, 1978.

Wynn, Neil. *The Afro-American and the Second World War*. New York: Holmes and Meier, 1976.

Yukon Historical Museums Association. *Whitehorse Heritage Buildings*. Whitehorse: YHMA, 1983.

Zaslow, Morris. *The Northward Expansion of Canada*. Toronto: McClelland and Stewart, 1988.

Zaslow, Morris. *Reading the Rocks: The Story of the Geological Survey of Canada, 1842–1872*. Toronto: Macmillan, 1975.

Dissertations

Zaslow, Morris. "The Development of the Mackenzie Basin, 1922–1940." Ph.D. dissertation, University of Toronto, 1957.

Interviews

Connic Bafford. Lusk, Wyo.
Chuck Baxter. Surrey, B.C. June 1988.
Louis Cyr. Whitehorse, Yukon. June 1989.
Alex Forgie. Edmonton, Alberta, 1989.
Stacia Gallop. July 1989.
Joe Garbus.
Kitty Grant. January 1988.
Cyril Griffith. Naicam, Saskatchewan, 1989.
Daniel Johnson. January 1988.
Archie MacEachern. Vancouver, B.C.
John Mueller. Denver, Colo. April 1989 (Victoria, B.C.).
Hampton Primeaux. Indian Bayou, La., 1989.
Cale Roberts. New Westminster, B.C. June 1988.
Leslie H. (Bud) Schnurstein. May 1988.
Lake Southwick. Taylor, B.C. July 1988.
Jim and Iris Sutton. June 1988.
Charlie Taylor. Whitehorse, Yukon. January 1988.

Index

Aberhart, William, 163
Aishihik, Yukon, 41, 45, 74, 202
Alaska Highway: agreement with Canada, 35, 37; completion of pioneer road, 52–53; construction of, 40–52; early plans for, 22–24; and environment, 85–100; postwar condition, 211–216, 221–32; rebuilt by PRA, 53–60; selecting route of, 25–35
Alaska International Highway Commission, 24, 26
Alberta and Davidson Co., 204
Alcohol, control of, 118–22, 197. *See also* Native people: and alcohol
Anchorage, Alaska, 30

Barry, P. S., 66
Bear Creek, Yukon, 166
Beatton River, Yukon, 45, 62, 76, 78
Beaver Creek, Yukon, 49, 56
Bechtel-Price-Callahan consortium, 62, 160, 161, 171
Bell, James, 225
Berger Commission, 85
Berrigan, Martin, 187
Bettaney, Supt. R., 156
Big Delta, Alaska, 42
Biggar, Col. O. M., 25
Black, George, 95, 113, 116, 184, 213
Black, Martha, 26
British Columbia Provincial Police, 102, 108, 111, 112, 114, 146

Burns and Co., 194
Burwash Lake, Yukon, 52
Burwash Landing, Yukon, 34, 43, 56, 74, 75, 91, 167
Bush, Col. K., 105

Caldwell, J. B., 213
Callahan, T. H., 113–14
Camsell, Charles, 222, 231
Canadian Bank of Commerce, 195
Canadian National Railway Company, 172
Canol Pipeline, 12, 35–37, 38, 40, 56, 59, 61–67, 82, 85, 165, 168, 174,
    182, 200, 203–204, 211–12, 221, 230, 232
Carcross, Yukon, 22, 48, 73, 75, 148, 150, 202
Carswell, Elizabeth, 80
Champagne, Yukon, 22
Chilkat Pass, Alaska–B.C., 61
Chimo, P.Q., 159
Cieluch, Lester, 113
Clarke, C. H. D., 99
Clemens, W. A., 99
Clifford, Lt. Col. C. M., 165
Contact Creek, Yukon, 48, 49
Cook, Les, 34
Cornwall, J. K., 36
Cronkite, Inspector H. H., 95

Dalton, Jack, 60
Dawson City, Yukon, 18, 20, 22, 24, 26, 34, 45, 75, 83, 102, 142, 144,
    145, 151, 158, 162, 182, 191, 229; decline of, 178–79, 188, 193, 195,
    219–21, 232, 239
Dawson Creek, B.C., 19, 20, 21, 34, 40, 43, 46, 50, 52, 54, 55, 58, 72,
    111, 113, 114, 115, 119, 120, 131, 134, 139, 143–44, 146, 167, 169–71,
    198, 206, 207; explosion, 177–78
Delta, Alaska, 46
Dezdeash, Yukon, 74
Dimond, A., 33
Dowell Construction Co., 55, 59
Drake, Lawrence, 230–31
Duncan, A. C., 143–44

Edmonton, Alta., 14, 21, 27, 29, 34, 41, 66, 67, 120, 131, 132, 133, 146,
    156, 159, 160, 167, 168, 229; and Americans, 161–66, 171, 172, 179,
    202, 212
Education and schools, 174–76

Eldorado Mines, 17
Elliott, E. W., Co., 55, 56, 59

Fairbanks, Alaska, 24, 26, 29, 30, 40, 42, 48, 52, 54, 64,, 67, 131, 146,
    169, 179, 212, 221, 223
Foreign Forces Order (1941), 105–106
Fort Fitzgerald, Alta., 64, 201
Fort McMurray, Alta., 64, 140, 201
Fort McPherson, N.W.T., 65
Fort Nelson, B.C., 30, 34, 35, 42, 43, 45, 46, 54, 55, 58, 64, 74, 79, 136,
    167, 168, 201, 211, 225, 232
Fort Norman, N.W.T., 113, 155
Fort Resolution, N.W.T., 201
Fort St. James, B.C., 227
Fort St. John, B.C., 21, 30, 34, 40, 42, 45, 54, 55, 59, 131, 132, 136,
    139, 146, 158, 159, 167, 171, 175, 198, 206, 210, 223, 229
Fort Simpson, N.W.T., 64, 150, 168, 201, 202
Fort Smith, N.W.T., 64, 75, 87, 120, 140, 148, 155, 168, 201
Foster, L. G., Co., 204
Foster, Maj.-Gen. W. W., 111, 117, 202, 208–10, 221
Franks, Doctor, 116
Friesen, Gerald, 237
Frobisher Bay, N.W.T., 159

Gabrielson, Ira, 97–98
Gibben, J. E., 75, 76
Gibson, R. A., 87, 98, 188
Government of Canada: attitude to highway, 25–26, 31, 202–203; northern
    policy, 16–17, 22, 23, 37, 77, 84–86, 218–21; takeover of highway,
    211–17, 221–29; and U.S. military law, 105–13. See also Native people:
    and government
Grande Prairie, Alta., 19, 20, 21, 30, 42, 45, 229
Grimshaw Road, 64
Gruening, Gov. Ernest, 32, 53, 227–28
Gunn, J., 114

Haines Junction, Yukon, 61, 224
Haines, Alaska, 40, 60, 61, 223
Haines Road, 12, 60, 91, 202, 211, 227–29
Halvorson, Halvor L., 28, 33
Harvey, Dr. J. P., 113
Hayes, Lt. Col. T. J., 107
Hazeltine, Col. C. R., 141
Hoffmaster, P. J., 98
Hoge, Maj.-Gen. William H., 32, 34, 217

Homosexuality, 129
Hone, Leona, 133
Hone, Staff Sgt. R. C., 133
Honigman, John, 79, 82
Hudson's Bay Company, 16, 18, 149

Imperial Oil Co., 65, 204

Jackson, F. H. R., 204
Jacquot, Joe, 96
Jakes Corner, Yukon, 55, 202, 229
Janes, R. W., 133
Jeckell, George, 26, 119, 122, 149, 175, 178, 179, 188, 190, 191, 193, 197–99
Jenness, Diamond, 137
Johnston, Bessie, 78–79
Johnston, George, 22, 72
Juneau, Alaska, 24, 133

King, William Lyon Mackenzie, 24, 25
Klinck, George, 116
Klondike gold rush, 13, 14, 17, 18, 21, 22, 27, 67, 168
Kluane Lake, Yukon, 22, 56, 59, 87, 232
Kluane National Park, Yukon, 61, 91, 92, 225
Klukshu, Yukon, 74
Krug, J. A., 222

LaGuardia, Fiorello, 162
Land aquisitions, 172–73
LeCapelain, C. K., 77, 89, 91, 92, 94, 114, 117, 173, 184, 187, 198
Lend-Lease, 42
Lewis, Fulton, Jr., 160
Liard, N.W.T., 74
Lower Post, B.C., 80
Lucey, Doctor, 79
Lysyk Commission, 85
Lytle, C. F., and Green Co., 55, 56, 59

McCandless, Robert, 92
McCloud, Maj. Linwood, 42
McConachie, Grant, 21
McCrae, Yukon, 59, 186, 201
McCusker, Knox, 167
MacDougall, Don, 72
McEachern, Ronald, 186

Mackenzie, J. A., 28
Mackinnon, J. A., 27
Mackintosh, Dorothy, 166
MacLean, G. I., 23
MacNaughton, Gen. A. G. L., 217
Magnuson, Warren, 227
Marchand, J. F., M.D., 77
Martin, Inspector J. D., 153
May, "Wop," 21
Maynard, Lucien, 110, 111
Menzies, Don, 72
Moffat, Pierrepont, 25, 164, 183
Morley Bay, Yukon, 48

Nash, Gary, 159, 236
Native people: and alcohol, 81–83, 118, 150–53; and churches, 16; and dis-
    ease, 77–81; economy of, 16–17, 84; and government, 16–17, 84–85,
    100, 156–57, 219, 232; history of, 70–71; and marriage, 130; sexual re-
    lations with non-Natives, 148–57; and racism, 19, 71–73; and wage la-
    bor, 71–72, 74–76, 84, 179, 196–97
Nisutlin Bay, Yukon, 48, 55
Noble Drilling Co., 65
Norman Wells, N.W.T., 6, 16, 31, 35–36, 37, 61, 64–67, 158, 162, 167,
    201, 204, 230, 232
Northern Commercial Co., 193, 194
Northway, Alaska, 42
Northwest Staging Route, 12, 29, 31, 34, 40, 41, 42, 61, 71, 202, 211,
    217, 221

O'Connor, Brig.-Gen. J. A., 57, 216
Oakes Construction Co., 55, 56

Patterson, Eugene, 113
Pattullo, T. D., 22, 24
Permanent Joint Board on Defence, 29, 105
Phinney, L. H., 216
Pine Creek, Yukon, 43
Porsild, A. E., 99
PRA. See Public Roads Administration
Pratt, Col. Curtis, 209
Prince George, B.C., 27, 30, 45, 201, 229
Prince Rupert, B.C., 64, 67, 170, 172, 202, 216
Prostitution, 128, 145–48
Public Roads Administration, 35, 37, 53, 55, 57, 58, 131, 165, 182, 184,
    186, 200, 216. For PRA employees, see also United States Army

Rand, A. L., 99
Randolph, John, 163
Raup, Hugh, 99
Religious activity, 141, 142
Rettie, James, 231
Rocanville, Sask., 159
Rogers, Clifford, 71–72, 191
Roosevelt, Franklin D., 6, 24, 62
Roosevelt, Theodore, 7
Ross River, Yukon, 74, 79, 230
Roth, Frederick, M.D., 192
Royal Canadian Mounted Police, 17, 53, 80, 81, 83, 87, 93, 95, 102, 103,
    112, 117, 140, 145, 152, 153, 154, 156, 167

Schroeder, Peter, 207
Scott, Ruby, 145
Seddicum, Paul, 215
Service, Robert, 18
Seward, Alaska, 147–48
Sexual activity. *See under* Homosexuality; Native people; Prostitution;
    United States Army; Venereal Disease
Shortt, T. M., 99
Shrum, Gordon, 175
Sinclair, Gordon, 72
Sinclair, Major, 146–47
Skagway, Alaska, 22, 40, 50, 52, 54, 63, 120, 132, 133, 182, 228
Smarch, Virginia, 73
Smith, Ada, 132–33
Smith, R. Melville, Co., 55, 56, 59, 60, 113, 115, 139
Smithers, B.C., 30
Smith River, Yukon, 45
Snag, Yukon, 41, 45, 74
Soldier's Summit, Yukon, 52
Somervell, Lt.-Gen. B., 57
Southwick, Lake, 210
Spray, Laree, 160
Squanga Lake, Yukon, 43
Stefansson, Vilhjalmur, 13, 19, 29, 31, 36
Stephenson, Clifford, 213
Stewart, Charles, 24
Stimson, Henry, 26
Strong, Gen. F. S., 202–203, 205
Sturdevant, Brig.-Gen. C. L., 49, 215
Supreme Court of Canada, 111
Surplus goods, disposal of, 204–11

Sverdrup and Parcel Co., 132

Teslin, Yukon, 22, 45, 48, 73, 77–78, 95, 115, 148
Tok Junction, Alaska, 60, 229
Turnbull, J. Gordon, Co., 132

United Service Organizations, 136, 152
United States Army: dependents of, 131–36, 170; and environment, 10;
    Military Police, 104–106, 110, 113–17, 184; and national feelings, 9; and
    race, 8, 126, 140–42, 237; and sex, 9, 124–30, 136–57. *See also* Surplus
    goods, disposal of
United States Army Corps of Engineers, 34–36, 46, 62, 126, 133, 144,
    165, 171, 181, 182, 189, 200
United States–Canada–Alaska Prairie Highway Association, 28, 31, 227
Urquhart, Doctor, 122
Utah Construction Co., 56, 59

Valdez, Alaska, 48
Venereal disease, 127, 129, 143–47

Wahpeton Portal Highway Association, 27–28
War brides, 9
Waterways, Alberta, 64, 151, 167, 202
Watson Lake, Yukon, 30, 40, 42, 43, 44, 48, 55, 63, 74, 79, 89, 153, 168,
    176, 200, 202, 222
White Pass and Yukon Railway, 21, 24, 52, 60, 182, 192–93, 196, 203,
    214
Whitehorse, Yukon, 18, 20, 21, 22, 25, 27, 30, 34, 38, 40, 41, 43, 47, 48,
    50, 54, 58, 61, 63, 66, 67, 71, 75, 76, 78, 80, 89, 92, 98, 102, 120,
    126, 131, 133, 134, 136, 138, 142, 144, 146, 148, 149, 152, 156, 158,
    162, 167, 169, 177, 179, 181–99, 200–204, 206, 207, 216, 219, 220,
    222, 223, 224, 233, 239
Winch, Harold, 210
Wright, F. S., 27, 28
Wyman, Col. T., Jr., 140

Yellowknife, N.W.T., 17, 20
Yukon Consolidated Gold Co., 76
Yukon Fish and Game Association, 99
Yukon Territory, early history of, 18–20